Lecture Notes in Computer Science　　　　8615

Commenced Publication in 1973
Founding and Former Series Editors:
Gerhard Goos, Juris Hartmanis, and Jan van Leeuwen

Ngoc Thanh Nguyen (Ed.)

Transactions on Computational Collective Intelligence XIV

Springer

Editor-in-Chief
Ngoc Thanh Nguyen
Institute of Informatics
Wroclaw University of Technology
Wroclaw
Poland

ISSN 0302-9743   ISSN 1611-3349 (electronic)
ISBN 978-3-662-44508-2   ISBN 978-3-662-44509-9 (eBook)
DOI 10.1007/978-3-662-44509-9

Library of Congress Control Number: 2014947447

Springer Heidelberg New York Dordrecht London

Printed on acid-free paper

Springer is part of Springer Science+Business Media (www.springer.com)

Preface

It is my pleasure to present the 14th volume of LNCS Transactions on Computational Collective Intelligence. This volume includes nine interesting and original papers that have been selected via the peer-review process.

The first paper, "A Two-Armed Bandit Collective for Hierarchical Examplar Based Mining of Frequent Itemsets with Applications to Intrusion Detection" by Vegard Haugland, Marius Kjølleberg, Svein-Erik Larsen, and Ole-Christoffer Granmo, is devoted to the problem of frequent itemset mining as a collection of interrelated two-armed bandit problems. The authors propose a method to find itemsets that frequently appear as subsets in a stream of itemsets, with the frequency being constrained to support granularity requirements. A novel reinforcement scheme allows the bandit players to learn this in a decentralized and on-line manner by observing one itemset at a time.

The second paper entitled "Semantic Compression for Text Document Processing" by Dariusz Ceglarek describes the technique that allows for correct generalization of terms in some given context. Thanks to this generalization a common thought can be detected. Semantic compression can be applied in a variety of scenarios, e.g., in detection of plagiarism.

In the third paper, "On Stigmergically Controlling a Population of Heterogeneous Mobile Agents Using Cloning Resource," W. Wilfred Godfrey, Shashi Shekhar Jha, and Shivashankar B. Nair present an on-demand population control mechanism for a heterogeneous set of mobile agents along with an underlying application for their deployment as service providers in a networked robotic system. They focus on a novel concept called the cloning resource which controls the cloning behavior of agents. The results obtained in the simulation and emulation environment are described.

The fourth paper, "On the Existence and Heuristic Computation of the Solution for the *Commons Game*" by Rokhsareh Sakhravi, Masoud T. Omran, and B. John Oommen, discusses the existence of an optimal solution to *Commons Game*, and demonstrates a heuristic computation for this solution. To do this, the authors consider the cases when, with some probability, the user is aware of the approach (color) which the other players will use in the exploitation of the commons. The problem of determining the best probability value with which a specific player can play each color in order to maximize his ultimate score is investigated.

The fifth paper entitled "Method of Constructing the Cognitive State for Context-Dependent Utterances in the Form of Conditionals" by Grzegorz Skorupa proposes an exemplary method for the grounding of context-dependent utterances and a method for constructing a context-dependent model of a cognitive state. An agent's knowledge is partitioned into a few disjoint subsets. This division is the result of a classification of past environmental observations.

In the sixth paper, "Conflict Compensation, Redundancy and Similarity in Data-Bases Federation," Germano Resconi gives the algorithm to discover the weak redundant databases and also how to create the local compensation in a way to transform all the different databases in only one prototype. This is a useful method to solve conflicts among agents as databases.

The next paper, "Extended Learning Method for Designation of Co-operation" by Edyta Kucharska and Ewa Dudek-Dyduch, presents a new machine learning method for determining intelligent cooperation at project realization. The method uses local optimization task of a special form and is based on learning idea. Additionally, the information gathered during a searching process is used to prune non-perspective solutions.

In the eighth paper entitled "Methods of Prediction Improvement in Efficient MPC Algorithms Based on Fuzzy Hammerstein Models," Piotr M. Marusak proposes two methods of prediction improvement in model predictive control (MPC) algorithms utilizing fuzzy Hammerstein models. Efficiency of the MPC algorithms based on the prediction utilizing the proposed methods of improvement is demonstrated in the example control system of a nonlinear control plant with significant time delay.

In the last paper, "Visualization of Semantic Data Based on Selected Predicates," Gábor Rácz, Gergő Gombos, and Attila Kiss develop a method that aims to help to understand the structure of semantic datasets. It can reduce the size and complexity of a dataset while preserving the selected parts. The result of the method can be visualized as a labelled directed graph that is suitable to give an overview of the structure of the dataset.

June 2014   Ngoc Thanh Nguyen

Transactions on Computational Collective Intelligence

This Springer journal focuses on research on the applications of computer-based methods of computational collective intelligence (CCI) and their applications in a wide range of fields such as the Semantic Web, social networks, and multi-agent systems. It aims to provide a forum for the presentation of scientific research and technological achievements accomplished by the international community.

The topics addressed by this journal include all solutions to real-life problems, for which it is necessary to use CCI technologies to achieve effective results. The emphasis of the papers is on novel and original research and technological advancements. Special features on specific topics are welcome.

Contents

A Two-Armed Bandit Collective for Hierarchical Examplar Based Mining
of Frequent Itemsets with Applications to Intrusion Detection............ 1
  Vegard Haugland, Marius Kjølleberg, Svein-Erik Larsen,
  and Ole-Christoffer Granmo

Semantic Compression for Text Document Processing................ 20
  Dariusz Ceglarek

On Stigmergically Controlling a Population of Heterogeneous Mobile Agents
Using Cloning Resource 49
  W. Wilfred Godfrey, Shashi Shekhar Jha, and Shivashankar B. Nair

On the Existence and Heuristic Computation of the Solution
for the *Commons Game*................................... 71
  Rokhsareh Sakhravi, Masoud T. Omran, and B. John Oommen

Method of Constructing the Cognitive State for Context-Dependent Utterances
in the Form of Conditionals................................ 100
  Grzegorz Skorupa

Conflict Compensation, Redundancy and Similarity in DataBases Federation.... 120
  Germano Resconi

Extended Learning Method for Designation of Co-operation............. 136
  Edyta Kucharska and Ewa Dudek-Dyduch

Methods of Prediction Improvement in Efficient MPC Algorithms
Based on Fuzzy Hammerstein Models......................... 158
  Piotr M. Marusak

Visualization of Semantic Data Based on Selected Predicates 180
  Gábor Rácz, Gergő Gombos, and Attila Kiss

Author Index 197

A Two-Armed Bandit Collective for Hierarchical Examplar Based Mining of Frequent Itemsets with Applications to Intrusion Detection

Vegard Haugland, Marius Kjølleberg, Svein-Erik Larsen,
and Ole-Christoffer Granmo[✉]

University of Agder, Grimstad, Norway
ole.granmo@uia.no

Abstract. Over the last decades, frequent itemset mining has become a major area of research, with applications including indexing and similarity search, as well as mining of data streams, web, and software bugs. Although several efficient techniques for generating frequent itemsets with a minimum frequency have been proposed, the number of itemsets produced is in many cases too large for effective usage in real-life applications. Indeed, the problem of deriving frequent itemsets that are both compact and of high quality, remains to a large degree open.

In this paper we address the above problem by posing frequent itemset mining as a collection of interrelated two-armed bandit problems. We seek to find itemsets that frequently appear as subsets in a stream of itemsets, with the frequency being constrained to support granularity requirements. Starting from a randomly or manually selected examplar itemset, a collective of Tsetlin automata based two-armed bandit players – one automaton for each item in the examplar – learns which items should be included in the mined frequent itemset. A novel reinforcement scheme allows the bandit players to learn this in a decentralized and on-line manner by observing one itemset at a time. By invoking the latter procedure recursively, a progressively more fine granular summary of the itemset stream is produced, represented as a hierarchy of frequent itemsets.

The proposed scheme is extensively evaluated using both artificial data as well as data from a real-world network intrusion detection application. The results are conclusive, demonstrating an excellent ability to find frequent itemsets. Also, computational complexity grows merely linearly with the cardinality of the examplar itemset. Finally, the hierarchical collections of frequent itemsets produced for network intrusion detection are compact, yet accurately describe the different types of network traffic present.

1 Introduction

Over the last two decades, frequent itemset mining has become a major area of research, with applications including indexing and similarity search, as well as mining of data streams, web, and software bugs [5].

© Springer-Verlag Berlin Heidelberg 2014
N.T. Nguyen (Ed.): TCCI XIV 2014, LNCS 8615, pp. 1–19, 2014.
DOI: 10.1007/978-3-662-44509-9_1

The problem of finding frequent itemsets can be formulated as follows. Consider a set I of n items, $I = \{i_1, i_2, \ldots, i_n\}$. A *transaction* T_i, $1 \leq i \leq m$, is defined as a subset of I, $T_i \subseteq I$, collectively referred to as a transaction set: $\mathcal{T} = \{T_1, T_2, \ldots, T_m\}$. When an arbitrary set X is a subset of a transaction T_i, $X \subseteq T_i$, one says that T_i supports X. The *support* of X is then simply the number of transactions T_i in $\mathcal{T}$ that supports X, $support(X) = |\{T_i \in \mathcal{T} | X \subseteq T_i\}|$, with $|\cdot|$ denoting set cardinality. The notion of interest in this paper – the *frequency* of an itemset – can then be defined as follows:

Definition 1 (Itemset Frequency). *The frequency of itemset X, freq(X), is defined as the fraction of transactions T_i in $\mathcal{T}$ that supports X:*

$$freq(X) = \frac{|\{T_i \in \mathcal{T} | X \subseteq T_i\}|}{|\mathcal{T}|}.$$

In all brevity, the goal of frequent itemset mining is to produce the itemsets, X_j, that commonly appear in the transactions, T_i, of a transaction set, $\mathcal{T}$. By exploring all of the possible item subsets, X_j, of each transaction $T_i \in \mathcal{T}$, the candidate frequent itemsets are identified and organized in a search space, so that the frequent ones can be efficiently extracted. The frequent itemsets, in turn, form the basis for building associations between itemsets in the form of rules, $A \Rightarrow B$, meaning that whenever itemset A is contained in a transaction, itemset B appears too (with a certain frequency).

The pioneering work of R. Agrawal et al. [2], introduced a framework for finding all of the itemsets surpassing a minimum frequency, and for building association rules that relates the frequent itemsets. It was here the concepts of *support* and *confidence* (the frequency by which the precedent of a rule follows the antecedent of the rule) were introduced. This work triggered a cascade of new results expanding the foundation laid, as briefly sampled here. For a full treatment of current status and future directions, the reader is referred to one of the many surveys on frequent pattern mining, for instance a recent one by Han et al. [5].

One avenue of research involves different kinds of measures besides *support* and *confidence*, such as *lift* [4], *itemset share* [3] and *collective strength* [1]. Furthermore, different approaches to mining with adaptively set minimum *support* thresholds have been investigated. This includes using the Chi-square test for correlation [4] to measure statistical significance of a rule, which allows rules with arbitrarily small *support* to be extracted, as long as sufficient statistical significance is ensured. Another direction of research concerns mining with *constraints* on the itemsets involved, for instance in the form of rule templates [6] or in the form of a wide range of operators such as absence or presence of items [10], extended with *support* constraints [16]. Other work further involves mining of sequential rules to find sequential patterns, including remarkably efficient algorithms such as SPADE [17]. Recently, a number of closely related problems have been addressed, such as mining of structural patterns, high-dimensional datasets, and closed and maximal frequent itemsets, further explored in [5].

Although several efficient techniques for generating frequent itemsets with a minimum frequency have been proposed, as exposed above, the number of itemsets produced is in many cases too large for effective usage in real-life applications. Indeed, the problem of deriving frequent itemsets that are both compact and of high quality, so that they are tailored to perform well in specific real-life applications, remains to a large degree open [5].

1.1   Paper Contributions

The approach introduced in the present paper is quite distinct from the above families of techniques, as briefly explained here and further clarified in the following. A characteristic and typical property of algorithms for frequent itemset mining is that they perform an exhaustive search of the space of candidate frequent itemsets, ranking the found itemsets according to some measure, like *support*. Research advances through the development of better ways of organizing and pruning the candidate itemset spaces, to deal with larger itemset spaces or to produce the frequent itemsets with less computations. Although itemset spaces often can be intelligently organized to support efficient searches, managing the search requires memory consuming data structures and/or time consuming computations, leading to scalability problems. After all, the number of possible itemsets grows exponentially with the number of unique items in the transaction set.

In this paper we introduce a completely different approach to frequent itemset mining that possesses several unique properties:

- In contrast to being based on extensive and dynamically built data structures, the memory footprint of the approach introduced here is both constant and small in size — at most, the scheme only requires one bit per unique item, $i_j \in I = \{i_1, i_2, \ldots, i_n\}$, to organize the search for frequent itemsets. Additionally, each of the n unique items are associated with a dedicated deterministic Learning Automata [13], which is a finite state machine whose state is represented merely by a single integer.
- Furthermore, instead of enumerating itemsets explicitly through exhaustive search, our scheme is light-weighted when it comes to computation. The Learning Automata simply performs a guided random walk in the space of frequent itemset candidates, with each computational step involving an increment or a decrement of the integers associated with the Learning Automata. Yet, the Learning Automata, as a collective, converge rather rapidly and accurately towards producing itemsets that possess a user specified frequency.
- Relying on the above convergence property, the scheme is invoked recursively, with each recursion step producing a new collection of frequent itemset, thus forming a hierarchy of frequent itemsets. In this manner, a progressively larger part of the transaction set is described.
- Also, as a consequence of the latter properties, our scheme operates online, allowing it to process a single transaction at a time, arbitrarily ordered, and with history remembered as part of the Learning Automata states. This is

ideal for instance for network intrusion detection (one of our application domains), where network packets arrive sequentially, in an endless stream.
- Finally, since our scheme is based on Learning Automata, it also handles itemsets with stochastic items, that is, itemsets whose items are randomly included or excluded from the itemset based on some unknown distribution. Again, this is ideal for network intrusion detection since network packets usually contain some fields that for all practical purposes appear as random from the perspective of a single network packet.

We achieve the above properties by posing frequent itemset mining as a collective intelligence problem, modelled as a collection of interrelated *two-armed bandit* problems. The two-armed bandit problem [11] is a classical optimization problem where a player sequentially pulls one of multiple arms attached to a gambling machine, with each pull resulting in a random reward. The reward distributions are unknown, and thus, one must balance between exploiting existing knowledge about the arms, and obtaining new information.

Our proposed scheme can be summarized as follows. Starting from a randomly or manually selected examplar transaction, a collective of so-called Tsetlin automata [13] based bandit players – one automaton for each item in the examplar – aims to learn which items should be included in the mined frequent itemset, and which items should be excluded. A novel reinforcement scheme allows the bandit players to learn this in a decentralized and on-line manner, by observing transactions one at a time, as they appear in the transaction stream. The above procedure is invoked recursively, with each recursion step producing a new collection of frequent itemset, thus forming a hierarchy of frequent itemsets. In this manner, a progressively larger part of the itemset stream is described. Since each bandit player learns simply by updating the state of a finite automaton, and since the reinforcement feedback is calculated purely from the present transaction and the corresponding decisions of the bandit players, the resulting memory footprint is minimal. Furthermore, computational complexity grows merely linearly with the cardinality of the examplar transaction.

The above hierarchical Tsetlin automata based formulation of frequent itemset mining provides us with four distinct advantages:

1. Any desired target itemset frequency can be obtained without spending any more memory than what is required by the Tsetlin automata in the collective (one integer per automaton).
2. Itemsets are found by the means of on-line collective learning, supporting processing of on-line data streams, such as streams of network packets.
3. An examplar transaction is used to focus the search towards frequent itemsets that are both compact and of high quality, tailored to perform well in real-life applications.
4. Our hierarchical organization of the frequent itemsets supports a progressively more fine-granular summary of the transaction set at hand, as the depth of the hierarchy is increased. This opens up for frequent itemset based network anomaly detection, as will be discussed later in this paper.

1.2   Example Application — Network Anomaly Detection

Network intrusion detection has been a particularly promising application area for frequent itemset mining [14,15]. In so-called network anomaly detection, huge amounts of network packet data needs to be mined so that the patterns of normal traffic can be found, and so that anomalous traffic can be distilled as deviations from the identified patterns. Although not based on frequent itemset mining, the packet byte based anomaly detection approach of Mahoney [8] is particularly fascinating in this perspective because it achieves state-of-the-art anomaly detection performance simply by inspecting 48 bytes from the header of network packets.

In order to investigate to what degree the properties of our bandit problem based approach to frequent itemset mining can be taken advantage of in network anomaly detection, we also introduce a novel packet byte based anomaly detection scheme in this paper. Formulated as a frequent itemset mining problem, each network packet i is seen as a transaction T_i and each byte value from the network packet is seen as an item belonging to the transaction. In other words, in this application we are looking for frequent itemsets consisting of byte-value pairs, such as $\{dstaddr1 : 24, dstaddr2 : 34, tcpflag : 12\}$, which is an itemset that identifies network packets with destination $24.34. * .*$ and with the tcp-flag set to 12.

1.3   Paper Organization

The paper is organized as follows. First, in Sect. 2 we present our decentralized Tsetlin automata based solution to frequent itemset mining, as well as a novel reinforcement scheme that guides the collective of Tsetlin automata towards a given target itemset frequency. The recursive approach to building a hierarchy of frequent itemsets is introduced in Sect. 3. Then, in Sect. 4 we demonstrate the performance advantages of the introduced scheme, including its ability to robustly identify compact itemsets that are useful for summarizing both artificial as well as real-life data. Finally, in Sect. 5 we offer conclusions as well as pointers to further work.

2   A Collective of Two-Armed Bandit Players for Examplar Based Frequent Itemset Mining

We here target the problem of finding frequent itemsets with a given support by *on-line* processing of transactions, taking advantage of so-called transaction *examplars*. To achieve this, we design a collective of Learning Automata (LA) that builds upon the work of Tsetlin and the linear two-action automaton [9,13]. Generally stated, an LA performs a sequence of actions on an *Environment*. The Environment can be seen as a generic *unknown* medium that responds to each action with some sort of reward or penalty, generated *stochastically*. Based on the responses from the Environment, the aim of the LA is to find the action

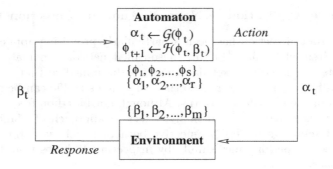

Fig. 1. A Learning Automaton interacting with an Environment

that minimizes the expected number of penalties received. Figure 1 shows the interaction between a LA and the Environment.

As illustrated in the figure, an LA can be defined in terms of a quintuple [9]:

$$\{\underline{\Phi}, \underline{\alpha}, \underline{\beta}, \mathcal{F}(\cdot, \cdot), \mathcal{G}(\cdot, \cdot)\}.$$

$\underline{\Phi} = \{\phi_1, \phi_2, \ldots, \phi_s\}$ is the set of internal automaton states, $\underline{\alpha} = \{\alpha_1, \alpha_2, \ldots, \alpha_r\}$ is the set of automaton actions, and, $\underline{\beta} = \{\beta_1, \beta_2, \ldots, \beta_m\}$ is the set of inputs that can be given to the automaton. An output function $\alpha_t = \mathcal{G}[\phi_t]$ determines the next action performed by the automaton given the current automaton state. Finally, a transition function $\phi_{t+1} = \mathcal{F}[\phi_t, \beta_t]$ determines the new automaton state from the current automaton state as well as the response of the Environment to the action performed by the automaton.

Based on the above generic framework, the crucial issue is to design automata that can learn the optimal action when interacting with the Environment. Several designs have been proposed in the literature, and the reader is referred to [9,12] for an extensive treatment.

2.1   The Item Selector Automaton (ISA)

Our LA based scheme for solving frequent itemset problems is centered around the concept of an *examplar* transaction $T_E \subset I$. With the examplar transaction T_E as a basis, the goal of our scheme is to identify an itemset $X \subseteq T_E$ whose frequency, *freq(X)*, is equal to a specific target frequency γ.

At the heart of our scheme we find an Item Selector Automaton (ISA). In brief, for each item i_j in T_E, a dedicated ISA, based on the Tsetlin automaton [13], is constructed, having:

- States: $\underline{\Phi} = \{-N-1, -N, \ldots, -1, 0, \ldots, N-2, N\}$.
- Actions: $\underline{\alpha} = \{\textit{Include}, \textit{Exclude}\}$.
- Inputs: $\underline{\beta} = \{\textit{Reward}, \textit{Penalty}\}$.

Figure 2 specifies the $\mathcal{G}$ and $\mathcal{F}$ matrices.

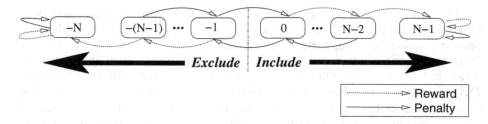

Fig. 2. An ISA choosing between including or excluding an item from candidate frequent itemsets

The $\mathcal{G}$ matrix can be summarized as follows. If the automaton state is positive, then action *Include* will be chosen by the automaton. If on the other hand the state is negative, then action *Exclude* will be chosen. Note that since we initially do not know which action is optimal, we set the initial state of the ISA randomly to either '-1' or '0'.

The state transition matrix $\mathcal{F}$ determines how learning proceeds. As seen in the graph representation of $\mathcal{F}$ found in the figure, providing a *reward* input to the automaton *strengthens* the currently chosen action, essentially by making it less likely that the other action will be chosen in the future. Correspondingly, a *penalty* input *weakens* the currently selected action by making it more likely that the other action will be chosen later on. In other words, the automaton attempts to incorporate past responses when deciding on a sequence of actions.

Note that our ISA described above deviates from the traditional Tsetlin automaton in one important manner: State $-N$ and state $N - 1$ are absorbing. This allows the ISA to converge to a single state, rather than to a distribution over states, thus artificially introducing an unambiguous convergence criterion.

2.2   Reinforcement Scheme

Since each item i_j in the transaction examplar T_E is assigned a dedicated ISA, ISA_j, we obtain a collective of ISA. The reinforcement scheme presented here is incremental, processing one transaction at a time at discrete time steps. At each time step s, a transaction $T_i \in \mathcal{T}$ is presented to the collective of ISA, whose responsibility is to propose a candidate itemset $X(s)$ for that time step. By on-line processing of the transactions, the goal of the ISA is to converge to proposing an itemset X^* that is supported with frequency, $freq(X^*) = \gamma$, with probability arbitrarily close to 1.

To elaborate, each automaton, ISA_j, chooses between two options at every time step s: shall its own item i_j be included in $X(s)$ or shall it be excluded? Based on the decisions of the ISAs as a collective, a candidate itemset $X(s)$ for time step s is produced. A response from the Environment is then incurred as follows. First it is checked whether the present transaction T_i supports $X(s)$, and based on the presence or absence of support, each ISA_j is rewarded/penalized according to the following novel reinforcement scheme.

The novel reinforcement scheme that we propose rewards an automaton ISA_j based on the decision of the automaton at time step s and based on whether the present transaction T_i supports the resulting candidate itemset $X(s)$. In brief, if ISA_j decides to include item i_j in $X(s)$, we have two possibilities. If T_i supports $X(s)$, ISA_j is rewarded. On the other hand, if T_i does not support $X(s)$, then ISA_j is randomly penalized with probability $r = \frac{\gamma}{1-\gamma}$ (assuming $\gamma < 0.5$). The other decision ISA_j can make is to exclude item i_j from $X(s)$. For that decision, ISA_j is randomly rewarded with probability $r = \frac{\gamma}{1-\gamma}$ if T_i does not support $X(s) \cup \{i_j\}$. On the other hand, if T_i supports $X(s) \cup \{i_j\}$, then the ISA is penalized.

The above reinforcement scheme is designed to guide the collective of learning automata as a whole towards converging to including/excluding items in $X(s)$ so that the frequency of $freq(X(s))$ converges to γ, with probability arbitrarily close to 1.

Note that because multiple variables, and thereby multiple ISA, may be involved when constructing the frequent itemset, we are dealing with a game of LA [9]. That is, multiple ISA interact with the same Environment, and the response of the Environment depends on the actions of several ISA. In fact, because there may be conflicting goals among the ISA involved, the resulting game is competitive. The convergence properties of general competitive games of LA have not yet been successfully analyzed, however, results exist for certain classes of games, such as the Prisoner's Dilemma game [9].

In order to maximize speed of learning, we initialize each ISA randomly to either the state '-1' or '0'. In this initial configuration, the actions will be switched relatively quickly because only a single state transition is necessary for a switch. Accordingly, the joint state space of the ISA is quickly explored in this configuration. However, as learning proceeds and the ISA move towards their boundary states, i.e., states '$-N$' and '$N-1$', the exploration calms down. Accordingly, the search for a solution to the frequent itemset problem at hand becomes increasingly focused.

Furthermore, note that we keep a time step counter for each ISA. When a certain cut off threshold has been achieved, we force one of the ISA to converge if it has not yet done so. This enforcement resets the counters of the other ISA, allowing them to adapt to the new configuration. The purpose of this mechanism is to increase convergence speed in ambiguous decision making cases where two different actions provide more or less the same feedback.

3   A Hierarchical Collective of Two-Armed Bandit Players

The two-armed bandit problem based scheme proposed in the previous section seeks to produce an itemset X that is supported by a fraction γ of the transactions T_i contained in a transaction set $\mathcal{T}$. In this section, we take advantage of the latter scheme in order to produce a compact summary of the *complete* transaction set T. The summary is formulated as a hierarchy of frequent item-sets. At each "level" in the hierarchy, every transaction in T is supported by at least one frequent itemset, and with each level descended, the granularity of the frequent itemsets increases. In this manner, multiple degrees of granularity, from coarse grained to fine grained, are concurrently maintained in the hierarchy. We achieve this by the means of a recursive algorithm, presented below. We explore the expressive power of this hierarchical approach in the next section, using the frequent itemset hierarchy as the basis for a network anomaly detection system.

Algorithm 1. Hierarchy Construction

Input: Transactions T; Maximal coarseness $\gamma_{\max}$
Output: Hierarchy H of frequent itemsets
1: Queue Q; # *Queue for organizing breadth first construction of hierarchy*
2: Hierarchy H; # *Hierarchy of frequent itemsets*
3: # *Empty frequent itemset {} as root, supporting all transactions in T*
4: Q.enqueue($[\{\}, T, \gamma_{\max}]$);
5: H.root($\{\}$);
6: # *Breadth first expansion of hierarchy nodes, starting from root*
7: **while not** Q.empty() **do**
8:     $[X_P, T_P, \gamma_P] \leftarrow$ Q.dequeue();
9:     # *Identifies candidate children nodes of parent P*
10:    $C \leftarrow$ Frequent_Itemset_Generation($[X_P, T_P, \gamma_P]$);
11:    # *Expands parent P with children nodes who has coarseness greater than or equal to the minimum coarseness sought:*
12:    **for** $[X_C, T_C, \gamma_C] \in C$ **do**
13:        **if** $\gamma_C \geq \gamma_{\min}$ **then**
14:            Q.enque($[X_C, T_C, \gamma_C]$);
15:            H.addChild(X_P, X_C);
16:        **end if**
17:    **end for**
18: **end while**
19: **return** H;

As seen in Algorithm 1, the input to the hierarchy construction algorithm is the transaction set T to be summarized, as well as the maximum, $\gamma_{\max}$, and the minimum, $\gamma_{\min}$, coarseness sought. Each node P in the hierarchy built is associated with a frequent itemset X_P, a transaction set T_P, and a coarseness γ_P, organized as a triple $[X_P, T_P, \gamma_P]$. As initialization, the root node is assigned an empty itemset, the complete transaction set T, and the maximum coarseness $\gamma_{\max}$. The hierarchy is then built breadth first, based on a queue of hierarchy nodes, initialized to contain the root node. Each node $[X_P, T_P, \gamma_P]$ dequeued is expanded producing a collection of candidate children $[X_C, T_C, \gamma_C] \in C$. If the coarseness γ_C of a triple is greater than or equal to $\gamma_{\min}$, the triple is enqueued and the frequent itemset X_C is added to the hierarchy H as a child of X_P.

The scheme for expanding a node P to produce candidate children $C \in C$ is shown in Algorithm 2. As seen, the candidate children are built one by one,

---

Algorithm 2. Frequent Itemset Generation

Input: Parent itemset X_P; Parent transactions $\mathcal{T}_P$; Parent coarseness γ_P
Output: Collection $\mathcal{C}_P$ of itemset-transactions-coarseness triples $[X_i, \mathcal{T}_i, \gamma_i], i \in \{1, \dots, n\}$,
    such that $\mathcal{T}_P = \bigcup_{i=1}^n \mathcal{T}_i$ and for $i \neq j : \mathcal{T}_i \cap \mathcal{T}_j = \emptyset$

1: $\mathcal{C}_P \leftarrow \{\}$; # *Collection of child triples empty initially*
2: $\mathcal{T}_R \leftarrow \mathcal{T}_P$; # $\mathcal{T}_R$ *keeps track of remaining unsupported transactions*
3: $\gamma_C \leftarrow \gamma_P$; # γ_C *keeps track of current level of coarseness*
4: # *Keeps producing child triples until all transactions in* $\mathcal{T}_P$ *are supported* $(\mathcal{T}_R \neq \emptyset)$
5: **while** $\mathcal{T}_R \neq \emptyset$ **do**
6:     # *Generates itemsets until one more fine-grained than the parent itemset is found*
7:     $X_C = \text{ISA\_Collective}(\mathcal{T}_R, \gamma_C)$; # *Invokes ISA collective on remaining transactions*
8:     **if** $X_C \subseteq X_P$ **then**
9:         $\gamma_C \leftarrow 0.999 \cdot \gamma_C$; # *Reduces target coarseness*
10:     **else**
11:         $\mathcal{C}_P \leftarrow \mathcal{C}_P \cup [X_C, \{T_i \in \mathcal{T}_R | X_C \subseteq T_i\}, \gamma_C]$; # *Adds new triple to child set*
12:         $\mathcal{T}_R \leftarrow \{T_i \in \mathcal{T}_R | X_C \nsubseteq T_i\}$; # *Removes transactions supporting* X_C
13:     **end if**
14: **end while**
15: **return** $\mathcal{C}_P$;

---

using the ISA collective proposed in the previous section. The ISA collective is repeatedly invoked on the part of the parent transaction set $\mathcal{T}_P$ that is still unsupported by the current collection of generated children. Since the children itemsets are to offer a finer granularity than the parent itemset, a child itemset that is a superset of the parent itemset is rejected, triggering a reduction in coarseness γ_C sought. If the child itemset is a superset of the parent itemset, on the other hand, it is added to the collection of candidate children.

In combination, the above two algorithms ensure that the coarseness, γ_C, of a child C always is less than or equal to the coarseness, γ_P, of its parent, P. Furthermore, all the transactions $T_i \in \mathcal{T}_P$ of a parent is supported by at least one of the frequent itemsets of its children $\mathcal{C}_P$, $\forall T_i \in \mathcal{T}_P, \exists [X_C, \mathcal{T}_C, \gamma_C] \in \mathcal{C}_P : X_C \subseteq T_i$. Note that the children transaction sets $\mathcal{T}_C$ jointly contain all of the transactions in the parent transaction set $\mathcal{T}_P$. These properties are taken advantage of in the next section to build a rule based network packet anomaly detection system.

4   Empirical Results

In this section we evaluate our proposed scheme using both artificial data as well as data from a real-world network intrusion detection application. We first evaluate the ISA collective separately, before we evaluate the hierarchical invocation of ISA collectives, as presented in the previous section.

4.1   Artificial Data

For the evaluation on artificial data we constructed a collection of transactions in a manner that by selecting the correct itemset X, one can achieve a frequency, $freq(X)$, of either $0.0, 0.125, 0.25, \ldots, 0.75, 0.875, 1.0$. The purpose is to challenge the scheme by providing a large number of frequency levels to choose among, with only one of these being the target frequency γ that our scheme must converge to. By varying the target frequency γ in the latter range, we also investigate the robustness of our scheme towards low, medium, and high frequency itemsets.

We here report an ensemble average after conducting 100 runs of our scheme. Given a target frequency γ, each run produces an itemset X^*, with X^* being supported by an actual frequency $freq(X^*)$. By comparing the sought target frequency γ with the achieved frequency $freq(X^*)$, the convergence accuracy of our scheme is revealed.

We first study convergence accuracy when any subset $X \subset T_E$ of the examplar transaction T_E either have a support frequency, $freq(X)$, equal to the target frequency γ, 1, or 0. Then the goal of the ISA collective is to identify the subset $X \subset T_E$ with frequency γ. As seen in Fig. 3, our scheme achieves this goal with remarkable accuracy.

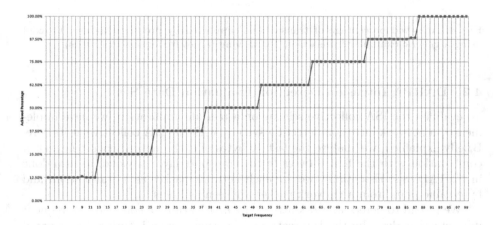

Fig. 3. Achieved percentage of transactions supported by produced itemset (y-axis) using a specific examplar transaction, for varying target frequencies γ (x-axis)

We observe that for any of the target frequencies γ listed in the figure, on average our ISA collective identifies itemsets X^* with frequencies $freq(X^*) \in \{0.0, 0.125, 0.25, \ldots, 0.75, 0.875, 1.0\}$ that either equals γ or surpasses γ with the least possible amount: $freq(X^*) \geq \gamma \wedge freq(X^*) - 0.125 < \gamma$.

When using a generic transaction examplar T_E instead — one that contains item subsets $X \subseteq T_E$ of any arbitrary frequency level $freq(X) \in \{0.0, 0.125, 0.25, \ldots, 0.75, 0.875, 1.0\}$, the challenge increases. The ISA collective then also have the option to produce frequencies in close vicinity of the target frequency γ. Figure 4 reports the resulting convergence accuracy, and as seen, it is now more difficult for the collective of ISA to always produce an itemset X with a transaction support frequency exactly equal to γ. Still, the itemsets produced are always close to a nearby neighbor of γ in $\{0.0, 0.125, 0.25, \ldots, 0.75, 0.875, 1.0\}$.

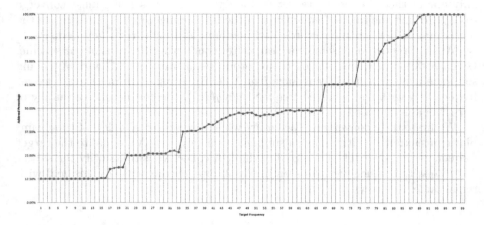

Fig. 4. Achieved percentage of transactions supported by produced itemset (y-axis) using a generic examplar transaction, for varying target frequencies γ (x-axis)

4.2   DARPA Intrusion Detection Evaluation Data Set

To evaluate the ISA collective scheme on a real life application, we have implemented a network intrusion detection system, with the ISA collective at its core. Briefly explained, we analyze the last 40 bytes of each network packet header in combination with the first 8 bytes of the transport layer payload, as also done in NETAD [8].[1] Essentially, we see each network packet as a transaction, and byte-value pairs from a network packet are seen as items.

We intend to detect network attacks by first learning a collection of frequent itemsets that describe the key features of normal network traffic – and based on these frequent itemsets, reporting network packets as anomalous when they do not support any of the learned frequent itemsets. We use the 1999 DARPA Intrusion Detection Evaluation data set [7] for training and testing our system. This data set simulates network traffic occurring in a small US Air Force base that is connected to the Internet. The internal network is connected to the Internet by a CISCO router, and network traffic is captured on both sides of this router. The captured traffic is made available in separate files based on the origin of the network traffic — outside, from the Internet, or inside, from the internal network.

---

[1] Note that in contrast to NETAD, we analyze both ingoing and outgoing network packets, for greater accuracy.

During training, we use one week of normal traffic data, learning one frequent itemset at a time by randomly picking examplar transactions (network packets) from the normal traffic data. Each time the collective of ISA converges to a new frequent itemset, all network packets that support this itemset are removed from the normal traffic data, and the procedure is repeated on the network packets remaining, to learn each kind of traffic being present. This step produces the first level of children nodes in the hierarchy, the children of the root. Each of the produced children are now associated with a disjoint subset of the network packets, and by recursively invoking the ISA collective on these subsets, a more fine granular representation of the network packets are found. Again, coarseness is controlled by gradually reducing γ from γ_{max} to γ_{min}.

As an example, a frequent itemset hierarchy generated from the network packets of Week 1 of the DARPA data set is shown in Fig. 5. In brief, multiple children are needed to support the parent transactions (network packets). Furthermore, node expansion stops when the transaction set of a node contains less than 5 % of the total population of network packets. Notice the hierarchy compactness achieved despite the huge amount of network packets present in the DARPA data set and despite the fine grained target granularity ($\gamma_{min} = 0.05$) sought.

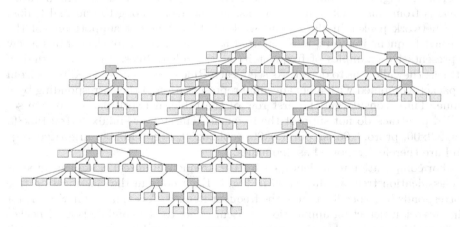

Fig. 5. Example of a frequent itemset hierarchy that was generated based on one week of training data from the 1999 DARPA IDS Evaluation Set. Each node in the hierarchy corresponds to a single frequent itemset

To gain further insight into the hierarchy generation process, Fig. 6 reports the total number of iterations spent by each ISA, grouped by network packet byte position. The figure shows that certain packet bytes and their values are "easier" to learn than others. Basically, we observe that the greater the diversity of values associated with a network packet byte (high entropy), the more iterations are needed to decide upon whether to include the corresponding item in the frequent itemset being constructed by the ISA collective. For instance, the values contained in the content bytes (byte 40 to 48) of a packet are by nature highly diverse, and thus require more time for learning an appropriate decision.

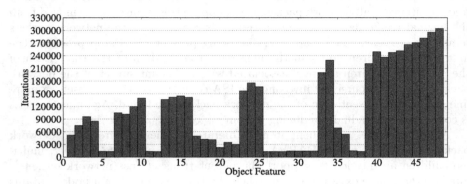

Fig. 6. Total number of iterations performed by ISAs to generate complete hierarchy, grouped by network packet byte position

For testing, the second week of the DARPA data set is used. The network packets from this week contain attacks, interspersed among the normal traffic. If a network packet in the second week of data does not support any of the learned frequent itemsets, it is reported as an anomaly. Table 1 contains a few representative examples of frequent itemsets, called Rules, and which kind of attacks they allow us to detect. As seen, each Rule consists of selected bytes from a packet, combined with a hexadecimal representation of the corresponding byte value. Thus, considering the first row of the table, network packets of the so-called ps-attack do not support the frequent itemset {ver+ihl:0x45, frag1:0x40, frag2:0x00, proto:0x06, srcport1:0x00, tcphl:0x50, urgptr1:0x00, urgptr2:0x00}, and are therefore reported as anomalies.

For computational efficiency, each Rule (frequent itemset) is implemented as a classification tree, as illustrated in Fig. 7. Each node in the classification tree corresponds to a specific item of the frequent itemset. As explained in Sect. 1, for the intrusion detection application an item refers to the combination of packet byte position and packet byte value, represented as a bit string. A non-match marks that the transaction being analyzed is unsupported, and accordingly, can be "blocked" by the network anomaly detection system unless another matching itemset can be found. For the frequent itemset reported in the figure, the target coarseness γ was set to 0.5, and as can be seen, the resulting Rule matches a percentage of 49.9 % of the network packets, i.e., very close to the target.

To further demonstrate the effect minimum coarseness γ_{min} has on anomaly detection sensitivity, Fig. 8 plots the *anomaly scores* for three unique frequent itemset hierarchies, each with different granularity constraints. An anomaly score was introduced to differentiate between different levels of the hierarchy — a packet not being supported by the more coarse frequent itemsets closer to the root is more aggravating than minor deviations closer to the leaf nodes. In order to capture such effects, we trace a path through the hierarchy, starting from the root, and continuing, level-by-level, with the child that supports the current transaction. When the path reaches a node P whose children do not support the current transaction, the transaction is assigned the anomaly score:

$$48 - 2 \cdot |X_P|.$$

In other words, the smaller the frequent itemset the larger the anomaly score. For instance, a transactions that stops being supported immediately after the root, will have the maximum anomaly score possible, which is 48. The plots in Fig. 8 highlights particularly anomalous packets as spikes, while packets recognized as normal possessing anomaly score less than or equal to zero. Notice that as the hierarchy coarseness increases, from top to bottom in the figure, the number of spikes decreases. Although the number of detected anomalies is at its highest with low coarseness, all of these anomalies are not necessarily *true attacks* (finer granularity may lead to *false* alarms). Thus, to quantify the anomaly detection capability of our scheme, Table 2 provides the estimated detection probability for attacks (detection rate), as well as the average number of false alarms produced for a whole week of network traffic. The table shows that the best detection rates were achieved by the hierarchies that were trained on Week 1 data, and which "leaves" possessed a minimum granularity $\gamma_{min} = 0.05$.

Table 1. Transaction examplars

Rule	Attacks
ver+ihl:0x45, frag1:0x40, frag2:0x00, proto:0x06, srcport1:0x00, tcphl:0x50, urgptr1:0x00, urgptr2:0x00	ps
ver+ihl:0x45, dscp:0x00, frag1:0x00, frag2:0x00, proto:0x06, tcphl:0x50, urgptr1:0x00, urgptr2:0x00	ps
ver+ihl:0x45, dscp:0x00, len:0x00, frag1:0x40, frag2:0x00, ttl:0x40, proto:0x06, dstaddr1:0xac, dstaddr2:0x10, dstport1:0x00, dstport2:0x17, tcphl:0x50, recwd1:0x7d, recwd2:0x78, urgptr1:0x00, urgptr2:0x00, pld1:0x00, pld5:0x00, pld7:0x00, pld8:0x00, pld9:0x00	ps, guesstelnet, sendmail

To conclude this investigation, Table 3 provides an overview of the attack types that remain undetected by the hierarchies that we produced. Note that only network packets originating from outside the firewall were used in these tests. In other words, the attacks that take place purely on the inside of the firewall were left undetectable as a consequence of the experimental setup. Also undetectable are the locally executed attacks that do not generate any network traffic. This leaves us with only two attacks that could have been detected, but were not: one instance of *guesspop* and one instance of *land* (the other instance is on the inside), which reveals a remarkable detection rate/false positive ratio.

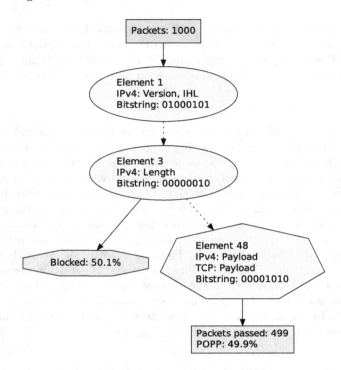

Fig. 7. Classification tree based implementation of frequent itemset transaction support determination

As a final note, observe that since each bandit player learns simply by updating the state of a finite automaton, and since the reinforcement feedback is calculated purely from the present itemset and the corresponding decisions of

Table 2. Results from IDS evaluation using the DARPA set

Parameters		Rate			False positives		
Training data	Granularity	avg	min	max	avg	min	max
Week 1 outside	1 %	0.56	0.55	0.57	412.67	392	453
	5 %	0.73	0.72	0.74	123	120	129
	10 %	0.43	0.42	0.44	61.67	52	69
Week 3 outside	1 %	0.54	0.50	0.58	427	426	429
	5 %	0.63	0.57	0.66	88.33	81	96
	10 %	0.54	0.53	0.55	59.67	58	61
Week 1 + 3 outside	1 %	0.54	0.52	0.56	418	404	436
	5 %	0.61	0.57	0.66	82	68	94
	10 %	0.46	0.43	0.53	47.33	40	61

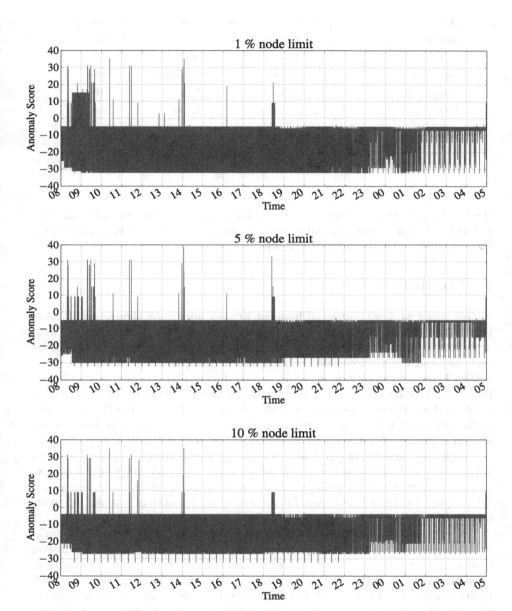

Fig. 8. Comparison of anomaly distribution between three frequent itemset hierarchies of different granularity.

Table 3. Undetected DARPA attack types

Alias	Instances	Console/remote	Inside/outside	Stealthy
anypw	2	Console	–	No
dict	6	Remote	Inside	No
guesspop	1	Remote	Outside	No
illegalsniffer	14	Remote	Inside	Mix
land	2	Remote	Both	No
ntfsdos	3	Console	–	No
resetscan	1	Remote	Inside	Yes
sshprocesstable	12	Remote	Inside	No

the bandit players, the resulting memory footprint is minimal (usually one byte per ISA). Furthermore, computational complexity grows merely linearly with the cardinality of the examplar itemset.

5   Conclusion

In this paper we have addressed frequent itemset mining by the means of a collective of so-called Item Selector Automata (ISA). By on-line interaction with a stream of transactions, the collective of ISA decides which items should be excluded and which should be included in a frequent itemset, with items being chosen from a randomly or manually selected examplar itemset. A novel reinforcement scheme guides the ISA towards finding a candidate itemsets that is supported by transactions with a specified frequency. By invoking the latter procedure recursively, a progressively more fine granular summary of the itemset stream is produced, represented as a hierarchy of frequent itemsets.

Since each bandit player learns simply by updating the state of a finite automaton, and since the reinforcement feedback is calculated purely from the present itemset and the corresponding decisions of the bandit players, the resulting memory footprint is minimal. Furthermore, computational complexity grows merely linearly with the cardinality of the examplar itemset.

In extensive evaluation using both artificial data and data from a real-world network intrusion detection application, we find the results quite conclusive, demonstrating that the ISA collective possesses an excellent ability to find frequent itemsets at various levels of support. Furthermore, the sets of frequent itemsets produced for network intrusion detection are compact, yet accurately describe the different types of network traffic present, allowing us to detect attacks in the form of anomalies.

In our further work, we intend to develop formal convergence proofs for the ISA collective. We are also presently investigating a hierarchical scheme for organizing ISA collectives, with the purpose of increased scalability.

References

1. Aggarwal, C.C., Yu, P.S.: A new framework for itemset generation. In: PODS 98, Symposium on Principles of Database Systems, Seattle, WA, USA, pp. 18–24 (1998)
2. Agrawal, R., Imielinski, T., Swami, A.: Mining association rules between sets of items in large databases. In: Proceedings of the ACM SIGMOD International Conference on Management of Data, Washington D.C., May 1993, pp. 207–216 (1993)
3. Barber, B., Hamilton, H.J.: Extracting share frequent itemsets with infrequent subsets. Data Min. Knowl. Disc. **7**, 153–185 (2003)
4. Brin, S., Motwani, R., Ullman, J.D., Tsur, S.: Dynamic itemset counting and implication rules for market basket data. In: SIGMOD 1997, Proceedings ACM SIGMOD International Conference on Management of Data, Tucson, Arizona, USA, May 1997, pp. 255–264 (1997)
5. Han, J., Chen, H., Xin, D., Yan, X.: Frequent pattern mining: current status and future directions. Data Min. Knowl. Disc. **15**(1), 55–86 (2007)
6. Klemettinen, M., Mannila, H., Ronkainen, P., Toivonen, H., Verkamo, A.I.: Finding interesting rules from large sets of discovered association rules. In: Adam, N.R., Bhargava, B.K., Yesha, Y. (eds.) Third International Conference on Information and Knowledge Management (CIKM'94), pp. 401–407. ACM Press (1994)
7. Lippmann, R., Haines, J., Fried, D., Korba, J., Das, K.: The 1999 DARPA off-line intrusion detection evaluation. Comput. Netw. **34**(4), 579–595 (2000)
8. Mahoney, M.V.: Network traffic anomaly detection based on packet bytes. In: Proceedings of ACM-SAC 2003, pp. 346–350. ACM (2003)
9. Narendra, K.S., Thathachar, M.A.L.: Learning Automata: An Introduction. Prentice Hall, Englewood Cliffs (1989)
10. Srikant, R., Vu, Q., Agrawal, R.: Mining association rules with item constraints. In: Heckerman, D., Mannila, H., Pregibon, D., Uthurusamy, R. (eds.) Proceedings of the 3rd International Conference Knowledge Discovery and Data Mining (KDD-97), pp. 67–73. AAAI Press (1997)
11. Sutton, R.S., Barto, A.G.: Reinforcement Learning: An Introduction. MIT Press, Cambridge (1998)
12. Thathachar, M.A.L., Sastry, P.S.: Networks of Learning Automata: Techniques for Online Stochastic Optimization. Kluwer Academic Publishers, Dordrecht (2004)
13. Tsetlin, M.L.: Automaton Theory and Modeling of Biological Systems. Academic Press, New York (1973)
14. Vaarandi, R., Podins, K.: Network IDS alert classification with frequent itemset mining and data clustering. In: Proceedings of the 2010 IEEE Conference on Network and Service Management. IEEE (2010)
15. Wang, H., Li, Q.-H., Xiong, H., Jiang, S.-Y.: Mining maximal frequent itemsets for intrusion detection. In: Jin, H., Pan, Y., Xiao, N., Sun, J. (eds.) GCC 2004 Workshops. LNCS, vol. 3252, pp. 422–429. Springer, Heidelberg (2004)
16. Wang, K., He, Y., Cheung, D.W.: Mining confident rules without support requirement. In: Proceedings of the Tenth International Conference on Information and Knowledge Management, pp. 89–96. ACM Press, New York (2001)
17. Zaki, M.: Spade: an efficient algorithm for mining frequent sequences. Mach. Learn. **42**(1–2), 31–60 (2001)

Semantic Compression for Text Document Processing

Dariusz Ceglarek[(✉)]

Poznan School of Banking, Poznan, Poland
dariusz.ceglarek@wsb.poznan.pl

Abstract. Ongoing research on novel methods and tools that can be applied in Natural Language Processing tasks has resulted in the design of a semantic compression mechanism. Semantic compression is a technique that allows for correct generalization of terms in some given context. Thanks to this generalization a common thought can be detected. The rules governing the generalization process are based on a data structure which is referred to as a domain frequency dictionary. Having established the domain for a given text fragment the disambiguation of possibly many hypernyms becomes a feasible task. Semantic compression, thus an informed generalization, is possible through the use of semantic networks as a knowledge representation structure. In the given overview, it is worth noting that the semantic compression allows for a number of improvements in comparison to already established Natural Language Processing techniques. These improvements, along with a detailed discussion of the various elements of algorithms and data structures that are necessary to make semantic compression a viable solution, are the core of this work. Semantic compression can be applied in a variety of scenarios, e.g. in detection of plagiarism. With increasing effort being spent on developing semantic compression, new domains of application have been discovered. What is more, semantic compression itself has evolved and has been refined by the introduction of new solutions that boost the level of disambiguation efficiency. Thanks to the remodeling of already existing data sources to suit algorithms enabling semantic compression, it has become possible to use semantic compression as a base for automata that, thanks to the exploration of hypernym-hyponym and synonym relations, new concepts that may be included in the knowledge representation structures can now be discovered.

Keywords: Semantic compression · Text clustering · Semantic network · Natural language processing · Information retrieval · Plagiarism detection · Knowledge acquisition

1 Introduction

Intellectual activities related to the gaining of knowledge by people or organizations and the creativity involved in establishing valuable and unique relations are factors that stimulate the formation of intellectual capital. As part of

© Springer-Verlag Berlin Heidelberg 2014
N.T. Nguyen (Ed.): TCCI XIV 2014, LNCS 8615, pp. 20–48, 2014.
DOI: 10.1007/978-3-662-44509-9_2

knowledge management it has been proposed that knowledge resources be publicly available. However, among an organizations information resources there is also sensitive information as well as information that must be protected from falling into the wrong hands. Therefore, knowledge resources are subjected to the rigors of the appropriate security policy, which should prevent information leaks or other forms of infringement of an intellectual property rights. Due to widespread electronic storage, processing and transfer of information, IT systems which are specially designed for this purpose are being more frequently used to protect information resources.

The quality of the functioning of existing mechanisms for protecting such resources depends on many factors. However, it is noticeable that there is a growing tendency for using artificial intelligence algorithms or computational linguistics methods as part of such mechanisms, and that these mechanisms employ increasingly more complex knowledge representation structures (e.g. semantic networks or domain-specific ontologies). The occurrence of intellectual property infringement is constantly on the rise, with corporate and academic resources being particularly under threat. A significant part of corporate information resources is non-confidential and expressed in the form of text and, hence, it cannot be secured by using fingerprinting technologies, as information content itself has intellectual value. In a world that is entirely based on knowledge, intellectual property is contained in various scientific, expert and legal papers. The growing number of incidents connected with the unlawful use of intellectual property is related to increasing access to information. Factors that reinforce the occurrence of such incidents are: constantly easier access to information technologies, free access to information resources stored in an electronic form, especially on the Internet, as well as mechanisms enabling rapid search for information. This is a global phenomenon and it also applies to the academic community with regard to the most sensitive issue appropriation of scientific achievements in all kinds of scientific publications. The existing solutions and systems protecting intellectual property are usually limited to searching for borrowings or plagiarisms in specified (suspicious) documents in relation to documents stored in internal repositories of text documents and, thus, their effectiveness is greatly limited by the size of their repositories.

Detection of borrowings comprises local similarity analysis [25, 26], text similarity analysis and global similarity analysis [24, 27]. Global similarity analysis uses methods based on citation similarity as well as stylometry, that is, a method of analyzing works of art in order to establish the statistical characteristics of an authors style which helps to determine a works authorship. Text similarity analysis is carried out by checking documents for verbatim text overlaps or by establishing similarity through measuring the co-occurrence of sets of identical words/concepts (based on similarity measures characteristic of retrieval systems). Systems used to detect borrowings differ in terms of the range of sources they search through. These might be public Internet resources or corporate or internal databases; such systems may even use the retrieval systems database indexes. An important attribute of the existing systems is their ability to properly determine borrowings/plagiarisms in relation to the real number and rate of borrowings. A high level of system precision here means a small number of false positives, whereas a high level of system recall means that it detects the majority of borrowings/plagiarisms in an analyzed set of documents. The most popular existing systems use knowledge representation structures and methods that are characteristic of information retrieval systems processing information for classification purposes at the level of words or strings, without extracting concepts. Moreover, these systems use, as similarity indicators, criteria such as the fact that a coefficient of similarity between documents understood as a set of words appearing in compared documents exceeds several tens of percent and/or the system has detected long identical text passages in a given work. A negative answer from systems of this kind indicating the lack of borrowings in a given document from documents stored in the above-mentioned repositories does not mean that it does not contain borrowings from, for example, documents located at a different Internet address.

The SeiPro2S (Semantically Enhanced Intellectual Property Protection System - SEIPro2S) [22] system was created by the author meets the above-mentioned requirements. Obtained system has been designed to protect resources from the unauthorized use of intellectual property, including its appropriations. The most commonly known example of such treatment is plagiarism, which, as is well known, infringes intellectual property and is based on misappropriation of another person's work or a portion thereof (other people's creative elements) by hiding the origins of that work. In the SeiPro2S system the author used a semantic network as a knowledge representation structure because of its ability to accumulate all the knowledge about the semantics of concepts, which makes it usable in systems that process natural language. It was inspired by works such as [3,13,17]. The most important principle of this system is that it will carry out a variety of tasks aimed at protecting intellectual property. The resulting system is not closed and uses both a local repository and all publicly available Internet resources. This mechanism is shown in Fig. 3, whereas the systems architecture and functioning is described in detail in [22]. This system uses a semantic network and follows the so-called text-refinement procedure which is characteristic of the processing of text documents. As part of this procedure it also uses mechanisms such as: text segmentation, morphological analysis, eliminating words that do not carry information, identifying multi-word concepts, disambiguating polysemic concepts. The SeiPro2S system basic task is to determine whether a given text document contains borrowings from other documents (both those stored in a local text document repository and on the Internet).

Furthermore, a suspicious document which is analyzed for borrowings might have undergone various stylistic transformations, which cause it to be regarded by such systems as largely or completely different from other documents as far as long and seemingly unique sentences are concerned. This stylistic transformations include such operation as shuffling, removing, inserting, or replacing words or short phrases or even semantic word variation created by replacing words by one of its synonyms, hyponyms, hypernyms, or even antonyms.

For the above-mentioned reasons there is a need to construct such a mechanism protecting intellectual property contained in text information documents which are expressed in a different way but which have the same information value in semantic terms to be understood as identical or at least very similar.

Semantic compression was designed to handle certain situations, e.g. plagiarism detection in large corpora of documents. Soon afterwards the potential was noticed to enhance the idea of semantic compression and to apply the tools crafted for it to other tasks.

Thus, it became apparent that semantic compression can be a valuable tool in tasks that are in the domain of Information Technology per se, where the chief objective of any technology that can be defined as such, is to present a user with a number of results that fit his or her personal search requirements.

Such a possibility is not straightforward when it comes to pure semantic compression, which can be summarized as **an effective technique for an informed generalization of terms in a given context under additional requirement of minimizing information loss.**

The above summary underlines the need for the recognition of a correct context of any given term. This is a difficult task that probably cannot be completed in 100 % correctly without a sentient mind that would serves as a discriminator equipped with knowledge on not only many of the possible term denotations, but also on the cultural connotations that would allow to draw decisive conclusions.

Nevertheless, the author demonstrated that semantic compression achieves good results when a number of prerequisites is met. The mechanism of semantic compression was implemented in the Semantically Enhanced Intellectual Property Protection System - SEIPro2S [22]. The most important features of semantic compression mechanisms are:

- semantic compression was defined and presented as a technology that can find its place in Natural Language Processing tasks
- the definition and implementation of frequency dictionaries that make semantic compression possible in presence of ambiguity (defined as in [12] along with algorithms supporting the proper choice of a hypernym in a given context [20] (more information available in [5]))
- lossless refactoring of WordNet [15] into WiSENet so that experiments on the quality of semantic compression are possible both in Polish and English documents (introduced in [4])
- highly specialized Finite State Automaton that allows for the automation of building rules allowing for the extraction of data that was not previously defined in the semantic network [11]
- a collaborative approach using local semantic compression which is a specialization of its general case by taking into account frequencies of concepts not in the global case but in the domain that a given document represents (introduced in [6]).

As this work aims to summarize already invested effort and to introduce a number of previously, unpublished results, its structure has to reflect the already available artifacts. Thus, the introductory section is followed by a section concerning semantic compression and its domain-based variety. The following is a section covering the details of a semantic network that is a base structure for operations of semantic compression itself and its additional applications. Following this is a section devoted to the application of the semantic compression to a semi-automated augmentation of itself through the selection of plausible terms fitting pre-defined patterns. Later, further scenarios in which semantic compression can be used are described along with its advantages as compared to other solutions. The article is concluded with a summary section discussing the obtained results and their quality.

2   Semantic Compression

As was explicitly rendered in the introduction, semantic compression is a technique that has to provide a more general term for the technique in question, i.e. where a term exists in some context that decides on its meaning as seen by a sentient mind. Therefore, when an algorithm has to compute a generalization of a given term it has to carefully choose the degree of generalization. If the generalization is too broad there is considerable information loss. There are cases when this can be a positive feature (as in clustering tasks [16]), but when semantic compression is used to prepare a document for a human user (in a human-readable form) this is not acceptable at all.

Historically, semantic compression was conceived in its global form and later, due to the change in its application domain, it had to be adjusted by further refinement of the generalization strategies. This section presents both varieties along with data obtained from the experiments, thus demonstrating their efficiency and effectiveness.

2.1   Global Semantic Compression

The idea of global semantic compression was introduced by the author in 2010 [5] as a method of improving text document matching techniques both in terms of effectiveness and efficiency. Compression of text is achieved by employing a semantic network and data on term frequencies (in the form of a frequency dictionary). The least frequent terms are treated as unnecessary and are replaced by more general terms (their hypernyms are stored in a semantic network). As a result, the reduced number of terms can be used to represent a text document without significant information loss, which is important from the perspective of processing resources (especially in tasks that require the use of a vector space model [1,8]).

Furthermore, a reduction in the number of terms helps in dealing with linguistic phenomena, which are problematic in Natural Language Processing [19]. The most commonly referenced phenomena of this type are polysemy and synonymy [12]. When multiple terms used to describe the same or very similar concept occur relatively rarely, they can be replaced by one common, more general, concept. Due to the employment of statistical analysis in the domain context, already mentioned frequency dictionaries are prepared and let the system deal with polysemic concepts with less effort and a lower error rate than solutions which do not employing such a technique.

As was stated earlier, the procedure of replacing more specific concepts with more general concepts cannot cause significant loss of information. To exemplify this, let us consider a document that is devoted to some biological study. A number of species is mentioned in Latin. Automatic categorization will cause the Latin concepts to extend the vector describing the document, thus they will complicate the whole process. The logical conclusion is that every Latin name of some particular fish can be replaced by a fish concept. As a result, the whole task is carried out with fewer resources and with no significant information loss. Of course, this can only be applied to a specific corpus of documents where these Latin names are rare, thus omissible. The choice of concepts for the generalization is domain-dependent. The data steering this process are in the above mentioned domain frequency dictionaries.

In general, semantic compression enables Natural Language Processing tasks, such as text matching, to operate on a concept level, rather than on a level of individual terms. This can be achieved not only by gathering terms around their common meanings (known from the synset based approach [15]), but also by replacing longer phrases with their more compact forms.

The emphasized concept level allows to capture a **common meaning expressed with a different set of terms**.

Let us demonstrate the idea by introducing some sentences that shall be processed by semantic compression, so that they can be marked as vehicles for the same message. Please note that this is not the result of an actual implementation as it is heavily dependent on the structure and size of the employed semantic network. Actual examples will be given later.

Sentence A. The life span of a cell depends upon the wear and tear on that cell.

Sentence B. Cell's lifetime reposes on accumulated damage.

Sentence A generalized. The period of time of a cell relies on damage on that cell.

Sentence B generalized. Cell's period of time relies on accumulated damage.

The generalizations demonstrated here artificially prepared, yet close to the outputs provided by the SHAPD2 algorithm [23] that was designed by the author. Apart from the fact that the generalization of concepts is not capable of analyzing concept interdependencies and is not able to exchange some phrases according to grammatical rules, they still allow us to make an informed guess that these two differently worded sentences convey some common meaning.

It is worth recalling that semantic compression is a lossy type of compression; yet the loss of information is minimal if the least frequent concepts are selected and are replaced by more general concepts, so their meaning remains as similar to the original meaning as possible. The compression ratio can be tuned easily by setting the number of concepts to be used to describe the text documents. Experiments that were conducted to measure the quality of the method in Natural Language Processing tasks showed, that the number of words can be reduced to about 4,000 without a significant deterioration of the classification results. The idea of a frequency-driven concept choice is shown in Fig. 1. The goal here is to demonstrate how less general concepts (terms captured in a semantic network) can be replaced by more general concepts. The actual algorithm is given in the following subsection.

2.2   Algorithm for Semantic Compression

Let us assume that, initially, we are given a list k_i of M key concepts, used to create M-dimensional vectors representing the documents, and a target condition: the desired number of key concepts is N (where $N < M$).

First of all, the total frequency of each concept $f(k_i)$ has to be computed for all documents in the documents corpus. This is achieved by computing the cumulated term frequency, i.e. by adding the sum of hyponyms frequencies to the frequency of the hypernym. In the second step, incorporation of information from the synonymy relation is carried out in which the synonym with the largest cumulated frequency is chosen. Finally, the terms with the largest cumulative frequency are selected. Moving upwards in the hierarchy, the cumulative concept frequency is calculated by adding the sum of hyponyms' frequencies to the frequency of the hypernym: $cumf(k_i) = f(k_i) + \sum_j cumf(k_j)$, where k_i is a hypernym of k_j - in pseudocode Algorithm 1. The cumulated frequencies are to be sorted and the N concepts with top values are selected as target key concepts (descriptor list) - see Algorithms 2 and 3.

Finally, the algorithm defines the *compression mapping rules* for the remaining $(M - N)$ words in order to handle every occurrence of k_j as its hypernym k_i in further processing. If necessary (when a hypernym has not been selected as a descriptor), the mapping rules can be nested.

This is essential as it allows to shorten individual vectors by replacing terms with lower information capacity by their descriptors (refer to Fig. 1). The described method of semantic compression results in a reduction of vector space dimensions by $(M - N)$. As a result, a part of the specific information, which is proportional to the information capacity of concepts not selected as descriptors, is lost.

2.3   Global Semantic Compression Evaluation

It is now time to carefully describe a situation in which semantic compression can be applied. Let us imagine that a document is an artifact to be matched against a corpus of other documents. This can take place in a variety of occasions; one of them is the intellectual property system (such as SEIPro2S). In order to apply semantic compression it is postulated that the system is equipped in various domain-specific corpora. These corpora let the system come up with a set of word frequencies that is specific to some area of interest (medicine, computer science, mathematics, astronomy, biology, etc.). To illustrate this, let us consider the following scenario. When the system processes a document that is a piece of news concerning recent advances in antibiotics research which has been

Algorithm 1. Selection of a concept used to represent those generalized concepts, followed by calculation of the cumulated concept instance frequency in document corpus C

$S(v)$ - set of synonyms for a concept v
$V-$ vector of concepts stored in the semantic network
$V'-$ topologically sorted vector V
$V''-$ reversed vector V'
l_v- number of occurrences of a concept v in corpus C
H_v- set of hypernyms for a concept v
//*choosing representing synonym*
$max = 0$
$n = 0$
$sum = 0$
for $s \in S(v)$ **do**
   $sum = sum + l_s$
   if $l_s > max$ **then**
      $max = l_s$
      $n = s$
   end if
end for
$l_n = sum$
//*calculating cumulated frequency for hypernymy*
for $v \in V''$ **do**
   $p = card(H_v)$
   for $h \in H_v$ **do**
      $l_h = l_h + \frac{l_v}{p}$
   end for
end for

---

posted in some popular magazine, we can take advantage of the domain corpora. Establishing a document domain is a simple task, that takes into account the variety of tools provided by the NLP; yet it will allow us to undertake additional steps.

When both the potential reader and the system are aware of the document type we can use the semantic network to compress concepts. When we come back to the scenario with the news concerning advances in antibiotics we can safely assume that this is not a highly specialized article. Thus, any reference to penicillin or ampicillin is a possible point where semantic compression can be applied. The semantic network stores data on concepts and their mutual relationships - a good semantic network will store data that will reflect the fact that penicillin is a type of antibiotic, as is ampicillin.

The result of applying semantic compression is visible in shortening the global vector by 3 elements (see Fig. 1). Instead of entries for an antibiotic, penicillin and ampicillin, we can store just the first entry. Analogical actions should be performed for concepts that are too specific in the context of the processed document.

Algorithm 2. Choosing N concepts in a domain-compressed semantic network

L - vector storing number of concept occurrences in document corpus C
$L-$ vector L sorted in a descending order
$f-$ number of occurrences of m-th concept in vector L'
for $v \in L$ **do**
  if $l_v \geq f$ **then**
    $d_v = v$
  else
    $d_v = FMax(v)$
  end if
end for

Algorithm 3. FMax procedure - finding a descriptor for a hypernym with the highest frequency

FMax(v):

$max = 0$
$x = \emptyset$
for $h \in H_v$ **do**
  if $d_h \neq \emptyset$ **then**
    if $l_d h > max$ **then**
      $max = l_d h$
      $x = d_h$
    end if
  end if
end for
return x

The author devised an experiment to verify whether semantic compression does indeed yield better results when applied to specific text-processing tasks there was devised an experiment. The evaluation experiment was performed by making a comparison of the clustering results for texts that were not semantically compressed with those that were [10]. For the experiment was used a document corpus consisting of documents coming from the following domains: *business, crime, culture, health, politics, sport, biology and astronomy.*

In order to verify the results, all of the documents were initially labeled manually with a category. All of the documents were written in English.

The clustering procedure was performed 8 times. The first run was done without the semantic compression mechanism: all of the identified concepts (about 25000 - this is only about a fifth of all the concepts in the research material) were included. Then the semantic compression algorithm was used to gradually reduce the number of concepts; it started with 12000 and preceded with 10000, 8000, 6000, 4000, 2000 and 1000 concepts.

The classification results were evaluated by being compared with the labels specified by the document editors: the ratio of correct classifications was calculated [1,9]. The outcome is presented in Tables 1 and 4. The loss of classification

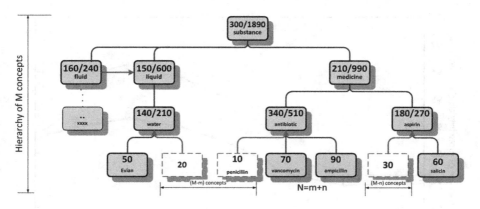

Fig. 1. Selection of N concepts with top cumulative frequencies

Table 1. Classification quality for two runs, the upper line denotes the results when semantic compression was enabled

Clustering features	1000	900	800	700	600	Average
All concepts	94.78 %	92.50 %	93.22 %	91.78 %	91.44 %	92.11 %
12000 concepts	93.39 %	93.00 %	92.22 %	92.44 %	91.28 %	91.81 %
10000 concepts	93.78 %	93.50 %	93.17 %	92.56 %	91.28 %	92.23 %
8000 concepts	94.06 %	94.61 %	94.11 %	93.50 %	92.72 %	93.26 %
6000 concepts	95.39 %	94.67 %	94.17 %	94.28 %	93.67 %	93.95 %
4000 concepts	95.28 %	94.72 %	95.11 %	94.56 %	94.06 %	94.29 %
2000 concepts	95.56 %	95.11 %	94.61 %	93.89 %	93.06 %	93.96 %
1000 concepts	95.44 %	94.67 %	93.67 %	94.28 %	92.89 %	93.68 %

quality is virtually insignificant for a semantic compression strength which reduces the number of concepts to 4000.

As was briefly remarked in an earlier section the conducted experiment indicates that the semantic compression algorithm can be employed in classification tasks to significantly reduce the number of concepts and the corresponding vector dimensions. As a result, tasks with extensive computational complexity are performed more quickly.

A set of examples of semantically compressed text fragments (for 4000 chosen concepts) is now given. Each compressed fragment is presented after the original fragment.

1a The information from AgCam will provide useful data to agricultural producers in North Dakota and neighboring states, benefiting farmers and ranchers and providing ways for them to protect the environment

1b information will provide adjective data adjective producer American state adjective state benefit creator provide structure protect environment.

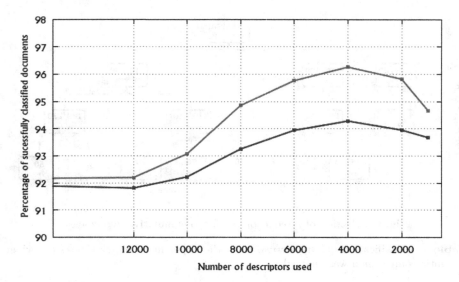

Fig. 2. Classification quality for two runs, upper line denotes results when the semantic compression was enabled

2a Researchers trying to restore vision damaged by disease have found promise in a tiny implant that sows seeds of new cells in the eye. The diseases macular degeneration and retinitis pigmentosa lay waste to photoreceptors, the cells in the retina that turn light into electrical signals carried to the brain

2b researcher adjective restore vision damaged by-bid disease have found predict tiny implant even-toed ungulate seed new cell eye disease macular degeneration retinitis pigmentosa destroy photoreceptor cell retina change state light electrical signal carry brain.

3a Together the two groups make up nearly 70 % of all flowering plants and are part of a larger clade known as Pentapetalae, which means five petals. Understanding how these plants are related is a large undertaking that could help ecologists better understand which species are more vulnerable to environmental factors such as climate change

3b together two group constitute percent group flowering plant part flowering plant known means five leafage understanding plant related large undertaking can help biologist better understand species more adjective environmental factor such climate change (Fig. 2).

Figure 3 presents the average evaluation results from two classification tasks. The loss of classification quality is virtually insignificant for a semantic compression strength which reduces the number of concepts to 6000. Stronger semantic compression and further reduction of the concept number entails a deterioration of the classification quality (which can, however, be still acceptable).

The conducted experiment indicates that the semantic compression algorithm can be employed in classification tasks in order to significantly reduce the

Table 2. Evaluation of a classification with semantic compression task 1 (780 documents) results.

Clustering features	1000	900	800	700	600	Average
Without SC	93.46%	90.90%	91.92%	92.69%	89.49%	91.69%
12000 concepts	91.92%	90.38%	90.77%	88.59%	87.95%	89.92%
10000 concepts	93.08%	89.62%	91.67%	90.51%	90.90%	91.15%
8000 concepts	92.05%	92.69%	90.51%	91.03%	89.23%	91.10%
6000 concepts	91.79%	90.77%	90.90%	89.74%	91.03%	90.85%
4000 concepts	88.33%	89.62%	87.69%	86.79%	86.92%	87.87%
2000 concepts	86.54%	87.18%	85.77%	85.13%	84.74%	85.87%
1000 concepts	83.85%	84.10%	81.92%	81.28%	80.51%	82.33%

Table 3. Evaluation of a classification with semantic compression task 2 (900 documents) results.

Clustering features	1000	900	800	700	600	Average
Without SC	93.78%	93.89%	93.11%	92.56%	92.11%	92.03%
12000 concepts	93.00%	94.00%	94.00%	91.33%	90.78%	91.49%
10000 concepts	93.33%	94.22%	93.56%	93.44%	92.22%	92.33%
8000 concepts	92.78%	93.22%	94.22%	93.33%	90.89%	91.79%
6000 concepts	92.56%	93.44%	92.22%	92.89%	91.00%	91.26%
4000 concepts	92.00%	92.44%	91.22%	90.89%	90.22%	90.03%
2000 concepts	92.33%	91.78%	89.89%	90.56%	89.67%	89.44%
1000 concepts	92.00%	92.00%	88.33%	87.11%	83.78%	86.90%

number of concepts and the corresponding vector dimensions. As a result, tasks with extensive computational complexity are performed faster (with linearithmic complexity).

To summarize, semantic compression is more effective when a text domain is identified and an appropriate domain frequency dictionary is used to perform the process. It should be emphasized that the more compact the context frame is, the better. Ideally, the context frame that decides about which frequency dictionary should be used, should be coverage on a one-to-one basis with a single sentence. Unfortunately, due to the previous observations, this is not possible.

2.4   Domain Based Semantic Compression

Global semantic compression combines data from two sources: the term frequencies from the frequency dictionary and the concept hierarchy from the semantic network. Usually one extensive semantic network is used for a given language

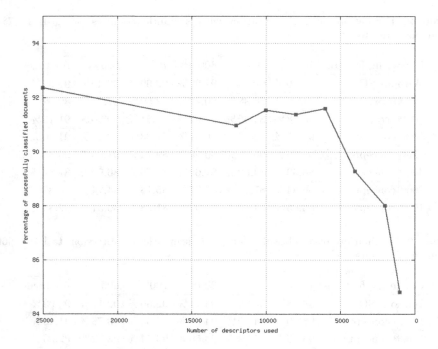

Fig. 3. Experiments' results of classification quality

(e.g. WiSENet [7] for English based on WordNet [15], SenecaNet for Polish [22]) and thus it is able to include linguistic knowledge covering multiple domains.

The varying characteristics based on the term frequency in some domain have a crucial impact on functioning of the semantic compression's algorithm, as term frequencies are a decisive factor in identifying the least frequent terms to be replaced by their hypernyms in a given domain.

In order to give an illustrative example we will consider a document originating from nature studies where the life of common rodents is discussed. On the other hand, let us consider a document from Information Technology which is focused on Human Computer Interfaces. Both documents have passages where the concept *mouse* is to be found. Domain-based semantic compression allow to generalize the concept *mouse* into two different less specific concepts, i.e. different concepts for every domain. In nature studies the concept *mouse* can be generalized as a rodent while when dealing with the term in Information Technology it can be regarded as an electronic device. Global semantic compression with a low number of final output concepts, thus a high level of compression, would choose the hypernym according to the overall frequency which might introduce unnecessary chaos.

Further experiments conducted by the author confirmed, that natural language tasks employing domain-based semantic compression yield better results

Table 4. Classification quality using semantic compression with an enabled proper names dictionary enabled

Clustering features	1000	900	800	700	600	Average
All concepts	94.78 %	92.50 %	93.22 %	91.78 %	91.44 %	92.11 %
12000 concepts	93.56 %	93.39 %	93.89 %	91.50 %	91.78 %	92.20 %
10000 concepts	95.72 %	94.78 %	93.89 %	91.61 %	92.17 %	93.08 %
8000 concepts	95.89 %	95.83 %	94.61 %	95.28 %	94.72 %	94.86 %
6000 concepts	96.94 %	96.11 %	96.28 %	96.17 %	95.06 %	95.77 %
4000 concepts	96.83 %	96.33 %	96.89 %	96.06 %	96.72 %	96.27 %
2000 concepts	97.06 %	96.28 %	95.83 %	96.11 %	95.56 %	95.83 %
1000 concepts	96.22 %	95.56 %	94.78 %	94.89 %	94.00 %	94.66 %

when its general form is used. As was exemplified, this is because domain frequency dictionaries better reflect language characteristics.

Domain-based semantic compression is easily implementable with already crafted artifacts as long as a certain procedure is applied to the processed text. When the domain is established for a text fragment, a specific domain frequency dictionary can be applied to perform local generalization by avoiding extreme cases and touching concepts that are too general in the context of a given domain. This differentiates domain-based semantic compression from global compression, as the latter maximizes savings in terms of a possibly shortest length of a vector that represents the processed documents. Yet, in the envisioned test application, avoiding the introduction of unfamiliar (from the domain point of view) concepts is an important advantage that is readily exploited for the benefit of the interested users.

Thus, the proposed procedure was tested on a group of users in order to verify applicability of Domain-Based Semantic Compression. This was done to measure whether it increased the level of text comprehension. This measurement cannot be done without a human user, due to the elusive nature of evaluating the explored problem. As an outcome the author gathered feedback from users participating in the experiment.

To summarize the results, it should be emphasized that the applying a locally adjusted domain frequency dictionary improves readability and allows for exclusion of generalized concepts that do not fit into the context. Additional comments offered by the surveyed users contain the following remarks:

- domain-based semantic compression can better fit the text context and allow for less misunderstandings
- it uses concepts that are less ambiguous, thus it allows for better understanding of the text
- in many cases global semantic compression causes a generalized concept to have a different meaning

- O godzinie 19:42:06 Księżyc dotknie cienia Ziemi. Stopniowo od wschodniej strony nasz satelita będzie "pożerany" przez cień naszej planety. O godzinie 20:49:34 cień całkowicie pochłonie Księżyc. Jego barwa powinna stać się krwisto czerwona na skutek oświetlenia promieniami słonecznymi zagiętymi w ziemskiej atmosferze. Maksimum zaćmienia wypadnie o godzinie 21:20:36.

- O godzinie 19:42:06 Księżyc dotknie cienia Ziemi. Stopniowo od wschodniej strony nasz satelita będzie konsumowany przez cień naszej planety. O godzinie 20:49:34 cień całkowicie przyłączy Księżyc. Jego barwa powinna stać się kolorowo czerwona na skutek działania promieniami słonecznymi nierównymi w ziemskiej atmosferze. Maksimum zaćmienia usunie o godzinie 21:20:36.

Fig. 4. Sample question from the user survey: the Polish version was used throughout the experiments

- global semantic compression produces a text that is perceived as being unrelated and whose meaning is unclear
- global semantic compression introduces concepts there are outside of the domain.

The performed experiment consisted of a set of four samples presented to the participants. There were 32 participants in the experiment. The participants that were surveyed had not received any training in the domains that were in the samples presented to them. Every sample comprised 3 text fragments. The first fragment was an unmodified text fragment taken from a corpus at random. The only constraint that every fragment had to follow was that its domain should be as unambiguous as possible. The chosen fragment was then transformed first by domain-based semantic compression and second, it was transformed by global semantic compression. The participant had to make a choice of whether he or she preferred the first transformation or the second transformation. He or she had to make a choice three more times and at the end share his or her opinions on his or her decisions and the motivation behind them. The sample for Polish is given in Fig. 4 and for English in Fig. 5. Please note that the experiment was in Polish and these were solutions that were discussed in their initial form.

The whole experiment was conducted using the SenecaNet semantic network and extensions derived from the project Morfologik [14] project. Inclusion of the Morfologik dictionary allowed for automatic changes of declination and conjugation of the word forms. This is a difficult task for languages such as Polish due to the large number of forms that are possible for every word (including gender, person and grammatical aspect). Effort was made to achieve over 95.5 % of correct transformations where every transformation was a two-phase process. It is worth noting that for an error the author understands an error to be a change from verb or adjective to noun. First, a concept was identified, then it was checked whether it could be a candidate for generalization. Secondly, when a

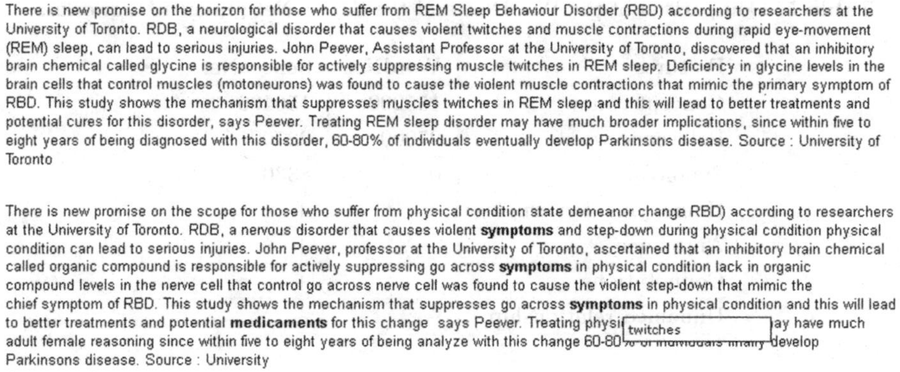

There is new promise on the horizon for those who suffer from REM Sleep Behaviour Disorder (RBD) according to researchers at the University of Toronto. RDB, a neurological disorder that causes violent twitches and muscle contractions during rapid eye-movement (REM) sleep, can lead to serious injuries. John Peever, Assistant Professor at the University of Toronto, discovered that an inhibitory brain chemical called glycine is responsible for actively suppressing muscle twitches in REM sleep. Deficiency in glycine levels in the brain cells that control muscles (motoneurons) was found to cause the violent muscle contractions that mimic the primary symptom of RBD. This study shows the mechanism that suppresses muscles twitches in REM sleep and this will lead to better treatments and potential cures for this disorder, says Peever. Treating REM sleep disorder may have much broader implications, since within five to eight years of being diagnosed with this disorder, 60-80% of individuals eventually develop Parkinsons disease. Source : University of Toronto

There is new promise on the scope for those who suffer from physical condition state demeanor change RBD) according to researchers at the University of Toronto. RDB, a nervous disorder that causes violent **symptoms** and step-down during physical condition physical condition can lead to serious injuries. John Peever, professor at the University of Toronto, ascertained that an inhibitory brain chemical called organic compound is responsible for actively suppressing go across **symptoms** in physical condition lack in organic compound levels in the nerve cell that control go across nerve cell was found to cause the violent step-down that mimic the chief symptom of RBD. This study shows the mechanism that suppresses go across **symptoms** in physical condition and this will lead to better treatments and potential **medicaments** for this change says Peever. Treating physi twitches ay have much adult female reasoning since within five to eight years of being analyze with this change 60-80% of individuals finally develop Parkinsons disease. Source : University

Fig. 5. Sample text from applying domain-based semantic compression on an English corpus

concept was generalized, a proper form had to be applied in order to present user performing an evaluation with a maximally uncluttered text fragment. Excerpts from the survey and the transformed text are given for Polish and English.

3 Semantic Network as a Key Data Structure for Semantic Compression

As was earlier emphasized, any reasonable text transformation that promises informed choices when substituting one term for another one of a more general nature that fits into the text's domain must be based on a structure capable of storing a variety of semantic relations.

A number of structures ranging from simple dictionaries through thesauruses to ontologies were applied in these types of categories [21]. Out these the semantic network was proven to be the best solution due to its outstanding features coupled with a lack of unnecessary complexity.

The WiSENet is a semantic network that captures data from the WordNet but these data are structured in a manner following that of the SenecaNet. The features of the SenecaNet, WiSENet and the transformation procedure along with a detailed discussion on various implementation details are given below.

3.1 SenecaNet Features and Structure

The SenecaNet is a semantic network that stores relations among concepts for Polish. It stores over 156400 concepts, other features are listed in Table 5. This was the first semantic network to be used in Semantic Compression.

It meets the requirements of a semantic network in every aspect. The concepts are represented as a list. There is a specific format that allows for fast traversal and a number of check-up optimizations that the SenecaNet implements. Each

Table 5. Comparison of the WordNet and the SenecaNet semantic networks

Features	WordNet	SenecaNet
Concept count	155200	156400
Polysemic words	27000	22700
Synonyms	0	8330
Homonyms, hypernyms	+	+
Antonyms	−	+
Connotations	+	+
Unnamed relationship	−	+

entry is stored in a way that allows to reference connected concepts in an efficient manner. Every entry from this list conveys information on the actual descriptor to be found in the text as well as the hypernyms, synonyms, antonyms and descriptors that are in an unnamed relation to the given descriptor.

There is an additional rule that every descriptor can occur exactly one time on the leftmost part of the entry when the whole semantic network is considered. This restriction introduces an extremely important feature, i.e. there can be no cycles in a structure devised in this manner.

Each descriptor can have one or more hypernyms (a heterarchy as in [21]). Each descriptor can have one or more synonyms. The synonyms are listed only once on the right side of the entry, they do not occur on the leftmost part of entry, as this is an additional anti-cycle guard.

An excerpt from the WiSENet format is given below in Table 6 to illustrate the described content.

Table 6. Example of the SenecaNet notation

Barack Obama $\leftarrow$ $politician, \#president(USA), \#citizen_of(USA), \epsilon Noun$
car $\leftarrow$ $vehicle, \&engine, \epsilon Noun$
gigabyte $\leftarrow$ $computer memory unit, \&byte, \epsilon Noun$
Real Madrid $\leftarrow$ $football team, @Madrid, \epsilon Noun$
volume unit $\leftarrow$ $unit of measurement, @volume, \epsilon Noun$
Jerusalem $\leftarrow$ $city, : Palestine Authority, \epsilon Noun$
Anoushka Shankar $\leftarrow$ $musician, \#sitarist, \#daughter(Ravi Shankar), \epsilon Noun$
Hillary Clinton $\leftarrow$ $politician, \#secretary of state(USA), \#citizen_of(USA), \epsilon Noun$

For many applications the structure of semantic network is transparent, i.e. it does not affect the tasks the net is applied to. Nevertheless, semantic compression is much easier when the descriptors are represented by actual terms and when their variants are stored as synonyms.

Algorithm 4. Algorithm for the WordNet to the SenecaNet format (WiSENet) transformation

---

WN - WordNet, as a list of synsets identified by descriptors d
S - synset, containing multiple lemmas l
$F[l]$ - number of synsets containing lemma l
SN - output WiSENet structure
for all $(d, S) \in WN$ **do**
  for all $l \in S$ **do**
    $F[l] + +$
  end for
end for
for all $(d, S) \in WN$ **do**
  parse lemma from synset descriptor
  $l = split(d, ".")[0]$
  if $F[l] = 1$ **then**
    lemma can be used as synset descriptor
    $d = l$
  else
    for all $l \in S$ **do**
      if $F[l] = 1$ **then**
        $d = l$
        exit
      end if
    end for
  end if
  $SN[d] = S$
end for

3.2 WordNet to SenecaNet Conversion

When faced with the implementation of semantic compression for English one has to use a solution that has similar capabilities as those on SenecaNet. Building up a new semantic network for English is a great task that would surpass the author's capabilities, thus he turned to existing solutions. The WordNet proved to be an excellent resource, as it was applied by numerous research teams to a great number of tasks which yielded good results.

The author had to confront the challenge of converting a synset-oriented structure into new semantic network without cycles operating on the descriptors in order to be recognized as actual concepts in the processed text fragments. An algorithm to accomplish this has been devised. It operates on sets by taking into account data on every lemma stored in a given synset and synsets (therefore their lemmas) that are hypernyms to the processed synset.

The synset is understood as a group of concepts that have similar meaning. Under close scrutiny many concepts gathered in one synset fail to be perfect synonyms to each other. They share a common sense, yet the degree to which they do varies. A lemma is any member of the synset; it can be a single concept or a group of concepts representing some phrase [15].

Before the algorithm is given, an example of a naive approach to the problem is demonstrated. This shall enable the reader to follow the process of a semantic network transformation in greater detail and with less effort.

In order to avoid graph cycles in the target structure, the author needed to modify the way one chooses terms to describe a synset. The best situation is when a lemma contained in a synset descriptor belongs only to that synset, i.e. the lemma itself is a unique synset descriptor. In other situations the author tried to find another lemma from the same synset which would satisfies the condition. The experiments proved that this produces the desired networks, but cannot satisfy the criterion for a lack of losses during the transformation. The obtained semantic network consisted of only 25000 terms serving as concepts, where a total of 86000 noun synsets were processed. Eventually, a "synthetic" synset descriptor was developed. The introduction of synthetic descriptors is not contrary to the author's ambitions to convert the WordNet into WiSENet in a lossless manner along with using actual concepts as concept descriptors. Synthetic descriptors are always the result of untangling of some cycle, thus, they can always be outputted as actual concepts to be found in the processed text.

Please refer to Figs. 6 and 7 to see a visualization of this process. Please notice that the term "approximation" is contained in several synsets: thus, it fails as a concept descriptor (see Fig. 6). One can easily observe that the term "bringing close together" occurs exactly once, thus it can replace the synthetic descriptor "approximation.n.04".

All of this is gathered in Tables 7 and 8.

Table 7. Companion table for Fig. 6

Synset	Terms	Parent synset
change of integrity	change of integrity	change.n.03
joining.n.01	joining, connection, connection	change of integrity
approximation.n.04	approximation, bringing close together	joining.n.01
approximation.n.03	approximation	version.n.01
approximation.n.02	approximation	similarity.n.01
estimate.n.01	estimate, estimation, approximation, idea	calculation.n.02

In order to remedy the issues as detailed above, the procedure to transform the WordNet structure efficiently is given below. For a pseudocode description please refer to the listing in Algorithm 4.

The first step of the procedure is to build a frequency dictionary (F) for lemmas by counting the synsets containing a given lemma. The algorithm loops through all of the synsets in WordNet (WN), and all the lemmas in the synsets (S) and counts every lemma occurrence. In the second step it picks a descriptor (possibly a lemma) for every synset. Next, it begins checking whether a synset descriptor (d) contains a satisfactory lemma. After splitting the descriptor (the

Table 8. Companion table for Fig. 7

Term	Parents
change of integrity	change.n.03
approximation	bringing close together,
	approximation.n.02, estimate.n.01, approximation.n.03
approximation.n.02	similarity.n.01
approximation.n.03	version.n.01
bringing close together	joining
joining	change of integrity
estimate.n.01	calculation.n.02
estimate	estimate.n.02, estimate.n.01, estimate.n.05,
	appraisal.n.02, estimate.n.04, compute, count on

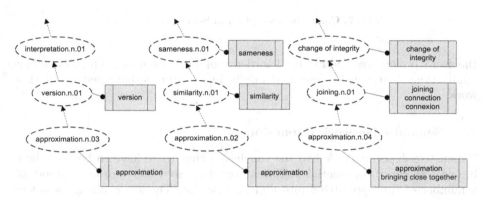

Fig. 6. WordNet synset description

partition point is the first dot in the synset description) and taking the first element of the resulting list the algorithm examines, whether such a lemma occurs exactly once throughout all of the synsets - if the answer is positive then it can be used as a new synset descriptor. If it is not, it loops through the lemmas from the examined synset and checks if there is any unique lemma which can be utilized as a descriptor. In case no unique lemma is found, a genuine WordNet descriptor is used.

4 Applications

One of the most important applications where Semantic Compression can be used is the semi-automated expansion of itself. Another preparation, presented as a viability test of Domain-Based Semantic Compression are generalized documents presented in a human-readable form and in a way that correlates with

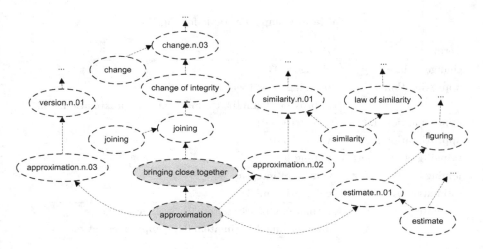

Fig. 7. Concepts description in SenecaNet format

the user's preferences and his/her knowledge of a given domain. There are other applications that will be discussed briefly in the summarizing section of this work.

4.1   Semantic Network Expansion

Exhaustive experiments led to the conclusion that there have to be seed data in order to capture potential unknown concepts. Seed data are understood as a number of concepts fitting into a given rule slot. The key challenge was the bootstrapping nature of all the experiments. One wants a more exhaustive model, and there is no easy way to sidestep the investment of time and effort into this task. Ideally, one could use a fairly large body of skilled specialists that would extended WiSENet by including data stored in various resources. Unfortunately, the author could not afford to do this, thus the methods that have been devised strive for maximum output with minimum input. This can be true even if the minimum input in some cases can be as much as 40000 of specific proper name concepts used as seed data.

4.2   Algorithm for Matching Rules

All of the operations are performed with WiSENet as the structure containing the necessary concepts. The first important step in the algorithm is a procedure that unwinds the rule into all of the hyponyms stored inside the network. This operation can be a considerable cost in terms of execution as it has to traverse all possible routes from a chosen concept to the terminal nodes in the network. After completion a list of rules is obtained, listing every possible permutation of the concepts from the semantic network. To shorten the processing time, one can specify the number of levels that procedure shall descend in during its course of execution.

The next phase of the algorithm is to step through the textual data in order to find matches on the computed rules. The stepping through is done by employing a bag of concepts algorithm. The bag of concepts was implemented as a Finite State Automaton with advanced methods for triggering desired actions (automaton working as a transducer). The transducer allows the SenecaNet network to become of a comparable size and performance quality as the WordNet which carries out NLP tasks. In addition, through the use of an unnamed relationship in SenecaNet, the quality of the mechanism finding the proper meaning of ambiguous terms increased. The tasks being carried out by the SeiPro2S system for English are made possible through the adoption of WordNet and by having it adjusted to already existing tools crafted for SEIPro2S. At any state it checks whether any of the rules to be matched is completed. The automated method of expansion of new concepts and new lexical relationships in the SenecaNet network uses a specially constructed transducer. A discussion covering the details of transducer implementation is beyond the scope of this article. Nevertheless, it can be visualized as a frame passing through the textual data. With every shift towards the end of text fragment, concepts inside the frame are used to check whether they trigger any of the rules obtained in the first phase. The size of the bag is chosen by the researcher, yet the performed experiments show that the best results are obtained for a bag sized 8–12 when the rules are 2–5 concepts long.

The bag of concepts algorithm is a good idea, as it tolerates mixins and concept order permutations. All matchings are performed after the initial text processing phase has been performed. The text processing phase (also called the *text refinement procedure*) consists of well-known procedures such as applying a stop list and term normalization.

A mixin is in this case a passage of text that serves some purpose to original text, yet it separates two or more concepts that exist in one of the computed rules.

Consider the following examples:

```
Rule - disease (all hyponyms), therapy (all hyponyms)
```

```
Match in: chemotherapy drug finish off remaining cancer
Matched concepts: therapy -> chemotherapy, disease -> cancer
Mixin: drug finish off remaining
```

```
Match in: gene therapy development lymphoma say woods
Matched concepts: therapy -> gene therapy, disease -> lymphoma
Mixin: development
```

```
Match in: cancer by-bid using surgery chemotherapy
Matched concepts: therapy -> chemotherapy, disease -> cancer
Mixin: by-bid using surgery
```

The examples are taken from one of the experiments performed with a biology corpus. It can be observed that the bag of concepts performs well in various cases, as it handles long mixins and concept permutation. An additional observation should be made that concepts which were hyponyms to those in the original example rule were matched (as was referenced earlier).

All the experiments that were performed took into account the possibility of matching more than a single rule. Thus, a mechanism for triggering a set of rules was devised and was signaled earlier along with the bag of concepts.

The procedure of matching rules holds internal registers which store rules that are actively valid with a given bag of concepts. To give an example, please consider a set of three rules:

rule 1: university, city (all hyponyms)
rule 2: university, city (all hyponyms), country (all hyponyms)
rule 3: person (all hyponyms), academic.

A given exemplary text fragment: *A team of chemists led by chemistry professor David Giedroc from Indiana University (in Bloomington, USA) described a previously unknown function of a protein they now know is responsible for protecting a major bacterial pathogen from toxic levels of copper. Co-author with Giedroc on the paper is professor Michael J. Maroney of the University of Massachusetts. The results were published Jan. 27 in Nature Chemical Biology.*

The procedure will match and matches previously defined rules:

rule number 1 with university → university, Bloomington → city, *newconcept*: *Indiana University in Bloomington*
rule number 2 with university → university, Bloomington → city, USA → country, *newconcept*: *Indiana University in Bloomington*
rule number 3 with David → first name, professor → academic, *newconcept*: *David Giedroc = professor(Indiana University, University in Bloomington)*
rule number 3 with Michael → first name, professor → academic, *newconcept*: *Michael J. Maroney = professor(University of Massachusetts).*

When a complete rule or its part is mapped, it is presented to the user to accept the match or reject it. The user can decide whether he or she is interested in total matches all partial matches. When the bag of concepts drops earlier concepts and is filled with new concepts, the rules that were not matched are dropped from the register of valid rules. The whole process of matching rules is presented in Fig. 8.

The algorithm in pseudocode is presented in listing 5.

4.3   Experiment with Semantic Compression Based Pattern Matching

The devised algorithm was used to perform an experiment on biology-related data. The test corpus consisted of 2589 documents. The total number of words in the documents was over 9 million. The essential purpose of the experiment

---

Algorithm 5. Algorithm for matching rules using WiSENet and bag of concepts

---

SN − Semantic Network
R − semantic relation pattern
BAG − currently active bag of concepts
Rule − set of processed rules

//attach rule triggers to concepts in semantic network
mapRulesToSemNet(SN, R[])
for all *Rule* ∈ *R* **do**
  for all *Word, Relations* ∈ *Rule* **do**
    N = getNeighbourhood(SN, Word, Relations)
    for all *Word* ∈ *N* **do**
      createRuleTrigger(SN, Word, Rule)
    end for
  end for
end for
 //text processing: tokenization, phrases, stop list
T = analyzeText(Input)
for all *Word* ∈ *T* **do**
  if *count(BAG) = size(BAG)* **then**
    //first, deactivate rules hits for a word
    //that drops out from bag of words
    oldWordpop(Bag)
  end if
  for all *Rule* ∈ *getTriggers(SN, oldWord)* **do**
    unhit(Rule, Word)
    push(Bag, Word)
    for all *Rule* ∈ *getTriggers(SN, Word)* **do**
      //take all relevant rules and activate word hit
      hit(Rule, Word)
      if *hitCount(Rule) = hitRequired(Rule)* **then**
        //report bag of words when hits reaches required number
        report(Rule, Bag)
      end if
    end for
  end for
end for

---

was to find specialists and their affiliations. This converges with the motivating scenario, as WiSENet was enriched by specialists (and their fields of interest), universities, institutes and research centers. The experiment used the following rules:

rule 1 first name (all hyponyms), professor (all hyponyms), university (all hyponyms)

rule 2 first name (all hyponyms), professor (all hyponyms), institute (all hyponyms)

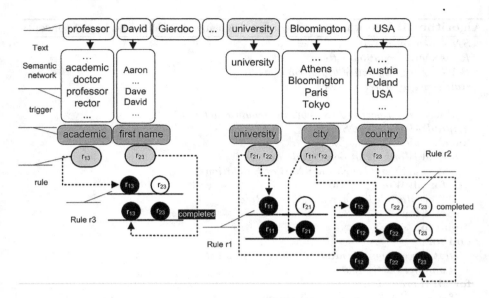

Fig. 8. Process of matching rules from the example.

rule 3 first name (all hyponyms), professor (all hyponyms), research center (all hyponyms)

rule 4 first name (all hyponyms), professor (all hyponyms), department (all hyponyms)

rule 5 first name (all hyponyms), professor (all hyponyms), college (all hyponyms).

The size of the bag of concepts was set at 8 elements. Additionally, all rules were to match exactly all of the concepts.

Out of 1326 documents where a concept "professor" was found, the prepared rules matched 445 text fragments. This gives a recall rate of 33.56 %. Precision of results was 84.56 %. This level was found to be very satisfactory, especially when taking into account that, due to the algorithm, there can be duplicates of matched text fragments (due to the multiple triggering of rules inside the current bag of concepts).

In addition, the experiment resulted in 471 concepts that were previously unknown to WiSENet. The context and type of rules that matched the text fragments led to extremely efficient updates of the semantic network.

Table 9 demonstrates the sample results from the experiment. Please note that a match on its own does not discover new concepts. The rules present potential fragments that with high likelihood, contain new concepts that can be included into the semantic network.

Table 9. Sample results of experiments with rules based on the WiSENet on a corpus of biology-related documents. The discovered concepts are written under the matches. Multiple activated rules were omitted.

Text fragment	Match/discovered concept	Rule
Explain senior author Douglas Smith Md professor department neurosurgery director **Douglas Smith**	Douglas professor department	5
Feb proceedings national academy of sciences researcher University of Illinois entomology professor Charles Whitfield postdoctoral **Charles Whitfield**	University of Illinois professor Charles	1
Design function biological network she-bop visiting professor Harvard University Robert Dicke fellow visiting **Robert Dicke**	Professor Harvard University Robert	1
Modify bacteria Thomas Wood professor –Artie– –McFerrin– department chemical engineering have **Thomas Wood**	Thomas professor department	5
Matthew –Meyerson– professor pathology Dana –Farber– cancer institute senior associate **Matthew Meyerson**	Matthew professor institute	2
An assistant professor medical oncology Dana –Farber– cancer institute researcher broad assistant **Dana Farber**	Professor Dana institute	2
Vacuole David Russell professor molecular microbiology –Cornell's– college veterinary medicine colleague **David Russell**	David professor college	4

5   Conclusions

Research efforts on developing and extending semantic compression and its applications can be considered as valuable. What is more, the article presents a variety of new research artifacts such as:

- formulation of the notion of semantic compression
- rules for the preparation of frequency dictionaries
- the bag of concepts algorithm
- the system for domain-based semantic compression
- transforming the English semantic network WordNet into a SenecaNet format (WiSENet)
- the algorithm for pattern matching with semantic compression
- the automaton of pattern matching.

All of the above achievements were used in a number of experiments that tested various characteristics. It was proven that the clustering of documents that underwent semantic compression was more efficient than the same procedure on a corpus of uncompressed data. The increase on efficiency for already good results (the average was 92.11 %) amounted to an additional 4.16 %).

What is more, domain-based semantic compression tested as a live system with active participants demonstrated that semantic compression aided by resources such as Morfologik proved to satisfactory with its results to users.

Semantic compression-based patterns are an interesting option for the retrieval of concepts that were previously unknown to a semantic network. What is more, the syntax of the patterns is straightforward, and possibly anyone understanding the idea of a less or more general concept can use it to design, own patterns that can be fed into the pattern matching system.

References

1. Baeza-Yates, R.A., Ribeiro-Neto, B.: Modern Information Retrieval. Addison-Wesley Longman Publishing Co. Inc., Boston (1999)
2. Boyd-Graber, J., Blei, D.M., Zhu, X.: A topic model for word sense disambiguation. In: EMNLP (2007)
3. Burrows, S., Tahaghoghi, S.M.M., Zobel, J.: Efficient plagiarism detection for large code repositories. Softw.: Pract. Exper. **37**(2), 151–175 (2007)
4. Ceglarek, D., Haniewicz, K., Rutkowski, W.: Quality of semantic compression in classification. In: Pan, J.-S., Chen, S.-M., Nguyen, N.T. (eds.) ICCCI 2010, Part I. LNCS, vol. 6421, pp. 162–171. Springer, Heidelberg (2010)
5. Ceglarek, D., Haniewicz, K., Rutkowski, W.: Semantic compression for specialised information retrieval systems. In: Nguyen, N.T., Katarzyniak, R., Chen, S.-M. (eds.) Advances in Intelligent Information and Database Systems. SCI, vol. 283, pp. 111–121. Springer, Heidelberg (2010)
6. Ceglarek, D., Haniewicz, K., Rutkowski, W.: Domain based semantic compression for automatic text comprehension augmentation and recommendation. In: Jędrzejowicz, P., Nguyen, N.T., Hoang, K. (eds.) ICCCI 2011, Part II. LNCS, vol. 6923, pp. 40–49. Springer, Heidelberg (2011)
7. Ceglarek, D., Haniewicz, K., Rutkowski, W.: Towards knowledge acquisition with WiSENet. In: Nguyen, N.T., Trawiński, B., Jung, J.J. (eds.) New Challenges for Intelligent Information and Database Systems. SCI, vol. 351, pp. 75–84. Springer, Heidelberg (2011)
8. Erk, K., Padó, S.: A structured vector space model for word meaning in context. In: EMNLP, pp. 897–906. ACL (2008)

9. Frakes, W.B., Baeza-Yates, R.A. (eds.): Information Retrieval: Data Structures & Algorithms. Prentice-Hall, Upper Saddle River (1992)
10. Hotho, A., Staab, S., Stumme, G.: Explaining text clustering results using semantic structures. In: Lavrač, N., Gamberger, D., Todorovski, L., Blockeel, H. (eds.) PKDD 2003. LNCS (LNAI), vol. 2838, pp. 217–228. Springer, Heidelberg (2003)
11. Khan, L., McLeod, D., Hovy, E.: Retrieval effectiveness of an ontology-based model for information selection. VLDB J. **13**, 71–85 (2004)
12. Krovetz, R., Croft, W.B.: Lexical ambiguity and information retrieval. ACM Trans. Inf. Syst. **10**, 115–141 (1992)
13. Lukashenko, R., Graudina, V., Grundspenkis, J.: Computer-based plagiarism detection methods and tools: an overview. In: Proceedings of the 2007 International Conference on Computer Systems and Technologies, CompSysTech '07, New York, NY, USA, pp. 40:1–40:6. ACM (2007)
14. Mikowski, M.: Automated building of error corpora of polish. In: Lewandowska-Tomaszczyk, B. (ed.) Corpus Linguistics, Computer Tools, and Applications State of the Art, PALC 2007, pp. 631–639. Peter Lang, Frankfurt am Main, Berlin, Bern, Bruxelles, New York, Oxford, Wien, (2008)
15. Miller, G.A.: WordNet: a lexical database for english. Commun. ACM **38**, 39–41 (1995)
16. Nock, R., Nielsen, F.: On weighting clustering. IEEE Trans. Pattern Anal. Mach. Intell. **28**(8), 1223–1235 (2006)
17. Ota, T., Masuyama, S.: Automatic plagiarism detection among term papers. In: Proceedings of the 3rd International Universal Communication Symposium, IUCS '09, pp. 395–399, New York, NY, USA. ACM (2009)
18. Sanderson, M.: Word sense disambiguation and information retrieval. In: Croft, W.B., van Rijsbergen, C.J. (eds.) SIGIR '94, pp. 142–151. ACM/Springer, London (1994)
19. Sinha, R., Mihalcea, R.: Unsupervised graph-based word sense disambiguation using measures of word semantic similarity. In: ICSC, pp. 363–369. IEEE Computer Society (2007)
20. Snow, R., Jurafsky, D., Ng, A.Y.: Learning syntactic patterns for automatic hypernym discovery. In: Advances in Neural Information Processing Systems (NIPS 2004), November 2004. This is a draft version from the NIPS preproceedings; the final version will be published by April 2005
21. Staab, S., Hotho, A.: Ontology-based text document clustering. In: Klopotek, M.A., Wierzchon, S.T., Trojanowski, K. (eds.) Intelligent Information Processing and Web Mining. Advances in Soft Computing, vol. 22, pp. 451–452. Springer, Heidelberg (2003)
22. Ceglarek, D.: Architecture of the semantically enhanced intellectual property protection system. In: Burduk, R., Jackowski, K., Kurzynski, M., Wozniak, M., Zolnierek, A. (eds.) CORES 2013. AISC, vol. 226, pp. 711–720. Springer, Heidelberg (2013)
23. Ceglarek, D.: Single-pass corpus to corpus comparison by sentence hashing. In: Badica, A., Trawinski, B., Nguyen, N.T. (eds.) Recent Developments in Computational Collective Intelligence - Concepts. Applications and Systems, volume 7092 of Studies in Computational Intelligence, pp. 167–177. Springer, Heidelberg (2013)
24. Hoad, T.C., Zobel, J.: Methods for identifying versioned and plagiarized documents. J. Am. Soc. Inf. Sci. Technol. **54**(3), 203–215 (2003)
25. Charikar, M.S.: Similarity estimation techniques from rounding algorithms. In: Proceedings of the Thirty-Fourth Annual ACM Symposium on Theory of Computing, STOC '02, pp. 380–388. ACM (2002)

26. Manber, U.: Finding similar files in a large file system. In: Proceedings of the USENIX Winter 1994 Technical Conference on USENIX Winter 1994 Technical Conference, WTEC'94, Berkeley, CA, USA, p. 2. USENIX Association (1994)
27. Stein, B., Lipka, N., Prettenhoferr, P.: Intrinsic plagiarism analysis. Lang. Resour. Eval. **45**(1), 63–82 (2010). Springer, Netherlands

On Stigmergically Controlling a Population of Heterogeneous Mobile Agents Using Cloning Resource

W. Wilfred Godfrey[1], Shashi Shekhar Jha[2(✉)], and Shivashankar B. Nair[2]

[1] Department of Information and Communication Technology,
ABV-Indian Institute of Information Technology and Management Gwalior,
Gwalior, M.P., India
godfrey@iiitm.ac.in
[2] Department of Computer Science and Engineering,
Indian Institute of Technology Guwahati, Guwahati, Assam, India
{j.shashi,sbnair}@iitg.ernet.in

Abstract. Cloning can greatly enhance the performance of networked systems that make use of mobile agents to patrol or service the nodes within. Uncontrolled cloning can however lead to generation of a large number of such agents which may affect the network performance adversely. Several attempts to control a population of homogeneous agents and their clones have been made. This paper describes an on-demand population control mechanism for a heterogeneous set of mobile agents along with an underlying application for their deployment as service providers in a networked robotic system. The mobile agents stigmergically sense and estimate the network conditions from within a node and control their own cloning rates. These agents also use a novel concept called the Cloning Resource which controls their cloning behaviour. The results, obtained from both simulation and emulation presented herein, portray the effectiveness of deploying this mechanism in both static and dynamic networks.

Keywords: Mobile agents · Cloning · Population control · Cloning resource · Typhon

1 Introduction

Mobile agents are programs that can act autonomously and also carry their execution state and data as they migrate. This makes them ideal candidates for transferring and also embedding intelligence in distributed systems. These agents have been used in network management, monitoring, routing and load balancing [1–6] and also in variety of other applications including information retrieval, robotics, etc. [7–10].

Mobile agents have been used for patrolling [11,12] the nodes of a network. These agents attempt to visit the nodes at some regular intervals and provide the service they carry. With all agents carrying the same service (homogeneous), the kind of patrolling addressed by most researchers is merely a mechanism to

© Springer-Verlag Berlin Heidelberg 2014
N.T. Nguyen (Ed.): TCCI XIV 2014, LNCS 8615, pp. 49–70, 2014.
DOI: 10.1007/978-3-662-44509-9_3

ensure that any one of the agents visits each of the nodes at uniform intervals. The mechanisms cited by Chu *et al.* [11] assume that a node once visited will never require nor regenerate a request for the service of an agent for a specific period of time till its turn to be visited again. Nodes get serviced by the agents in a round-robin like manner. Thus if a node which has just been visited, generates a request for a service once again, it will have to wait for its turn which will occur only when all other nodes have been serviced. The patrolling mechanisms suggested in [11] and by Sempé and Drogoul [12] do not seem to take care of on-demand servicing. Active patrolling would mean satisfying requests generated by nodes within a network as quickly as possible, irrespective of whether they were serviced in the recent past. Patrolling in the real-world means moving around in a manner so as to provide attention to both, recently visited and not-recently visited locations within an area alike based on the urgency of the situation at that location. Godfrey and Nair [13] have proposed an architecture for a multi-robot networked system which uses mobile agents to provide services to robots in a round robin manner. The robotic nodes communicate with each other over a wireless communication link. Each robotic node provides a software framework for hosting and enabling mobile agents to arrive from or migrate to another such node. The mobile agents carry a service as their payload and provide them to a robotic node whenever they reach a node that has requested for the same. The term service is used to generically denote what the agent carries as payload. This could be for instance the source code for a robotic task, rules or information.

In order to support active patrolling, Godfrey and Nair [14] have described a mechanism termed *PherCon*, which combines both the Pheromone and Conscientious strategies to achieve agent migration towards the requesting nodes. All robotic nodes forming the network are capable of diffusing virtual pheromones [15] as and when a service is required. These pheromones tend to attract the relevant mobile agents within the network towards the *Robotic node Requesting a Service* (RRS). The RRS pro-actively diffuses pheromones to its neighbouring nodes which in their turn diffuse them at lower concentrations to their neighbours thus generating a pheromone concentration gradient network across the RRS [14]. The mobile agents each carrying different services (or code for the tasks) patrol the network in a conscientious [16] manner avoiding visits to recently visited nodes. When they hit upon a pheromone trail at a node, they switch to pheromone tracking and follow the shortest path along the pheromone concentration gradient to eventually reach and service the RRS. Such an active form of patrolling serves to avoid longer waiting times on part of those nodes which have been visited recently but have generated their request immediately after a visit by the relevant mobile agent. The model is well suited for applications that make use of heterogeneous mobile agents wherein every agent carries a different set of services as its payload. Figure 1 depicts the structure of the pheromone. The first field contains the RRS ID that initially generates the pheromone. The second field contains the requested service type. The concentration and life-time occupy the third and fourth fields while the last one points to the previous node. Godfrey and Nair [17] have also shown how localized cloning within the pheromone

Fig. 1. Structure of the virtual pheromone [14]

gradient can decrease RRS service times. Localized cloning however yields only marginal effects. In order to effectively patrol and provide on-demand services in a networked scenario using heterogeneous mobile agents, cloning needs to be performed by every agent based on its demand. Agents whose services (payloads) are more often requested should clone proportionately so as to provide a quicker service. With the build-up of more clones within a network, the service times are bound to fall but not for long. A large number of clones can clutter the network increasing migration times and thus deteriorating the performance of the system.

In scenarios as in [14] where the nodes (RRSs) asynchronously generate requests for a service, the waiting times can be further decreased if the mobile agents populating the network are made to clone proportionate to their demand within the network. Cloning a mobile agent carrying a certain task as its payload, in large numbers based on its utility may theoretically decrease waiting times of those nodes that request this specific task. However in practice, this may not be a viable alternative since the network may have several nodes requesting different tasks. If all the pertinent agents were to clone in large numbers at the same time, they would quickly clutter and choke up the system. Cloning thus needs to be carried out judiciously based on the network conditions and also demand (number of nodes requesting a service or RRSs). Mobile agents need to also back-off and die in case of choke-ups. Decisions on whether to or not to clone or to back-off have to be made autonomously by the agent and not in consultation with others. Mobile agents in real-world application scenarios such as the robotic network described in [13] will need to make a decision on whether to or not to clone by sensing the active medium they migrate through, in a stigmergic manner [18]. In this paper we describe a method by which the mobile agents, populating and migrating within the robotic network as in [14,17], unilaterally approximate the status of the network and judiciously decide the extent to which they need to clone. This paper extends our previous work [19] and describes an attempt to design an adaptive, on-demand cloning controller for controlling a population of a heterogeneous set of mobile agents in both static and dynamic networks.

2   Motivation and Related Work

Mobile agents share all characteristics of their static counterparts but stand apart in their capability to migrate and clone autonomously. The concept of cloning featured in mobile agents helps increase their population and indirectly allows for parallel operation and information transfer across a network. It can also aid in the upward scalability of a distributed system. Cloning can thus make a large impact in the performance of mobile agent based applications. Glitho et al. [20] discuss a mobile agent based approach that outperforms traditional client-server based architectures in a multi-party event scheduling problem. The authors argue that if the number of agents is increased it would reduce the response time and enhance performance. Such an increase in number of agents could be made inherent to the system by using the concept of cloning. In grid computing scenarios too, mobile agents could increase their numbers by cloning to find the requested resource at a faster pace. Jin et al. [21] have proposed a routing model for grid computing using mobile agents. They have used two types of agents to collect and update the dynamic changes in the routing information coupled with a naive form of cloning to boost performance. Hamza et al. [22] describe the use of mobile agents in the domain of cloud computing for discovery of web services. Cloning, if used in their model, could expand the search area leading to faster discovery of services. Various other application domains such as agent based data-mining [23], distributed information management [2], Internet based e-commerce [6], monitoring and routing the networks [3] can greatly benefit if cloning of mobile agents is used.

Having multiple copies of an agent can not only enable parallel execution but can also provide fault-tolerance, thus increasing both robustness and efficiency of the system. The down side is that an increased population of mobile agents may result in higher network resource utilization which in turn may deteriorate the performance of the system. While on one side increasing the population of agents using cloning increases its performance, uncontrolled cloning can flip the same and cause the network to become overcrowded. To substantiate such a claim, we performed experiments using a 200-node connected network. The network capacity or the maximum number of agents that the network could accommodate was varied from 0 to 1200. As a performance measure, we recorded the number of Step-Counts required to service 100 RRSs. The agents were allowed to clone to maximize their performance.

Figure 2 shows the graph depicting the nature by which the number of Step-Counts (time) required to service 100 RRSs decreases initially with increasing number of agents (including their clones) and then increases due to cluttering within the network. It can be observed that when the dots, that indicate the Step-Counts, are connected the resulting curve seems to be parabolic in nature. Ideally, the value of the number of agents in the network should coincide with that at the vertex of the parabola for the fastest possible service. Thus it can be inferred that in practice one should ensure that the number of agents (including clones) should always lie to the left of the axis of this parabola. The graph therefore endorses the imperative need for controlled cloning so as to ensure that the total number of agents including clones populating the network remains high while also providing minimal service times. In scenarios where heterogeneous mobile agents populate the network, it is essential that the total number of such agents remain optimal so as to provide low RRSs service times and also that the agents clone proportionate to their demand. The mechanism should therefore facilitate the depletion of agents that are no more in demand thereby giving

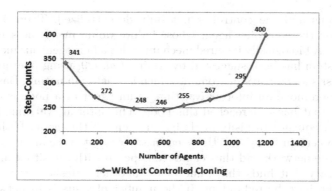

Fig. 2. Graph depicting the Step-Counts required to service 100 RRSs without any control on cloning

way to other in-demand agents while also maintaining the net population at an optimal value that does not cause cluttering or severe network contention. Hence, a controlled, adaptive and demand based cloning can ensure that the performance remains well near the achievable optimum. The work described in this paper augments the *PherCon* [14] migration strategy to achieve lower waiting times to service a node in a network populated by heterogeneous agents.

Suzuki *et al.* [24,25] have addressed the control of a population of mobile agents in dynamic networks. Their mechanism is based on the popular ecological model which assumes that the population of a single species converges to a number in proportion to the amount of *food* available in its environment. Every node in their network generates *food* at regular intervals in proportion to the number of its links to other nodes. An agent migrates to a node, consumes the *food* within the node and clones in proportion to the excess *food* it cannot consume. An agent which does not get *food* starves and thus is eliminated. Two algorithms have been cited - one in which an agent is provided with the actual number of links in a vertex and the other wherein the agent makes an estimate of the link density. The latter algorithm proves to be a useful aid in calculating the *food* to be generated in case of dynamic networks where the nodes are mobile causing a change in topology and hence the links. Ma *et al.* [26] and Golebiewski *et al.* [27] describe algorithms that use a mobile agent population control protocol wherein each node keeps at most one copy of an agent. If there is a single agent in a node then a new agent is born with a certain probability p, computed based on the fraction of target nodes. In this case, the agents make use of a random migration policy. Another mechanism for population control of agents within the Internet described in [28] uses three types of entities - a node, an executor agent and a controller agent. Each of these agents has some energy which gets consumed as it performs its respective tasks. When the energy level falls below a certain threshold, the agent requests for more energy from its controller. If the latter does not respond immediately, the agent becomes an *orphan* and is thus removed from the network. This protocol is complex in terms of inter-entity communications and the control is not fully decentralized. There is a heavy dependency on the controller agent whose failure would mean the same for the entire system. A biologically inspired mechanism for a homogeneous mobile agent patrolling system has been suggested by Amin *et al.* [29] using pheromones. An agent that visits a node lays pheromone which is volatile in nature. Based on the amount of pheromone an inter-arrival time of an agent at a node is calculated by the agent that has just reached this node. This inter-arrival time is used to estimate the frequency of visits made by an agent to this node. If this time is higher than a certain threshold, the agent assumes that there are lesser number of agents in the network and thus clones to cope up with the situation at hand. On the contrary if it finds this value below another threshold the agent kills itself assuming it to be redundant. If the number of visits is in between these two thresholds the agent merely migrates to a neighbouring node. Bakhouya and Gaber [30] focus on the dynamic regulation of the mobile agent population in a distributed system inspired by concepts from the biological immune system. They embed three basic behaviors onto the mobile agents viz. cloning, moving and killing and attribute them to three different antibodies, each suppressing or stimulating the other. The behaviour to be chosen depends on the inter-arrival time of the agents at a particular node, similar to what has been suggested by Amin *et al.* [29], which in turn controls the agent population.

All the mechanisms cited so far support population control of a homogeneous set of mobile agents and are inherently suited for a regular patrolling problem where the inter-arrival times between visits made by the same type of agent are to be kept a constant or a minimum. Further in all these mechanisms the maximum number of agents is a factor of the total number of nodes in the network which needs to be known *a priori*. These mechanisms are thus neither scalable for different types of agents nor adaptive in terms of their manner of controlling the agent population. Instead they merely try to ensure that the existence of a certain number of agents of the same type (homogeneous) will not clutter the network and thus avoid network contention. For instance, if each agent were to take an opinion (such as stimulations or suppressions as mentioned in [30]) from other agent peers, this additional communication would cause further overheads on the network. With a large number of such agents communicating and transacting stimulations and suppressions to one another, as suggested by Farmer *et al.* [31], progress of their movement towards the respective RRSs would be greatly retarded.

In the next section, we discuss the architecture of the proposed cloning controller and the inherent mechanism to regulate a heterogenous population of mobile agents and their clones.

3   The Proposed Cloning Controller

We describe herein, a cloning control mechanism suited for active patrolling which is both scalable and adaptive in nature. Cloning is controlled egocentrically by each mobile agent without imposing any overheads for communicating with other mobile agents across the network, thus making the mechanism well suited for distributed systems. There is no centralized mechanism to serve information of any kind to these agents.

3.1 Architecture of Cloning Controller

Figure 3(a) depicts the composition of the cloning controller residing within each node. Each node in the network has a queue into which all the mobile agents hosted by it are lined up before migrating to another node. Thus mobile agents migrate from the intra-node queue of one node to that of a neighbour. If the node is an RRS, and the incoming agent has the requested service then the same is downloaded onto the node before the agent enters the queue for onward migration to a neighbouring node. Apart from the service or code for a task, the mobile agents carry within themselves a record of their current life-time, cloning resource and the number of rewards received. These concepts have been dealt within subsequent sections.

A *Queue-Manager* controls the intra-node queue. The *De-queue* (DQ) Controller within this manager performs the job of handshaking with a node in its immediate neighbourhood by sending a request for the migration of an agent within its associated intra-node queue to the next node via REQ_{DQ}. It receives the acknowledgement from its peer in the other node via ACK_{DQ}. The *En-queue* (NQ) Controller performs the task complementary to the *De-queue* Controller and caters to requests for migration of an agent residing in another node into its intra-node queue using REQ_{NQ} and ACK_{NQ} in a similar fashion. Migrations are performed only if the queue in the next node has a vacant slot. The *Life-time Monitor cum Queue-Compactor* unit ensures that the life-times of each of the agents within the queue are decremented in each step and the queue is compacted as and when an agent dies within the queue. The agent reads the *Cloning Pressure*, ρ, from the *Cloning Pressure Register* resident within the *Queue-Manager*. The cloning pressure is calculated based on the number of agents populating the intra-node queue and has been dealt with in a subsequent section on the dynamics of the controller.

3.2 Stigmergic Sensing

Stigmergy is a form of indirect communication wherein the entities of a system communicate amongst each other through their environment [18]. This type of communication is prevalent in social insects such as ants, wasps, honey bees, etc. [32]. In this work, the mobile agents form the entities while the nodes in the network makes up the environment. Whenever an agent lands on a node, it provides its services to the node if the latter has generated a request for the same. The agent is then queued in the intra-node queue present at this node and made to wait for its turn to migrate to the next robotic node. A higher number of agents in this queue essentially means more waiting times within it and also that node to node migrations have been taking more time. Such increased migration times convey a cluttered network condition. Likewise, a lesser number

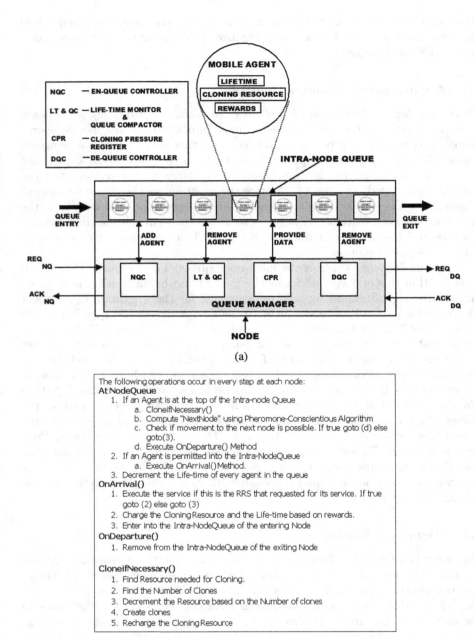

Fig. 3. (a) Architecture of the Cloning Controller (b) The Cloning Control Mechanism

of agents within the queue means less number of the agents populating the network. The intra-node queue form part of the environment of the agent and indirectly conveys the current status of the network. By examining this queue, a mobile agent thus stigmergically senses the current network condition based on the number of agents, and clones proportionately.

Figure 3(b) shows the mechanism behind the stigmergic cloning control. A queue threshold (Q_{Th}) determines the maximum number of agents allowed in the intra-node queue. The basic objective is to ensure that this queue is moderately filled so as to achieve quicker migrations and hence faster service for all the RRSs. Agent migrations can be realized only if there is a vacancy in the intra-node queue of the destination node; else the agent needs to wait within the queue of the current node while also expending its life-time. If we assume that cloning by agents causes their numbers to increase to a level that there are no empty slots within any of the intra-node queues in the network, then no agent will be in a position to migrate. This will mean that the network is choked-up. Only when some of the mobile agents within the intra-node queues die out due to their decreasing life-times, will other agents with higher-life times be able to migrate to vacancies created by their dead counterparts in other intra-node queues. Thus, the agents need to clone in such a contained manner so as to increase their numbers to result in a faster service of the RRSs but at the same time ensure that such a choke-up of the network is never reached.

3.3 Cloning Resource - The Underlying Rationale and Functions

The concept of a resource [33, 34] can greatly alter an otherwise linear cloning mechanism. We argue that biological glands [35] cannot secrete in large amounts continuously and are limited by an inherent *resource*. This is much like squeezing a completely wet piece of sponge to extract a certain amount of water. The squeezing force required to extract a certain quantity of water initially is far less than the force required to extract the same amount of water a second time. Water, in this case, is the *resource* being extracted. In biological systems, the resource is recharged by various factors which include the nutrients supplied to the gland over periods of time.

We embed a similar mechanism to emulate a *cloning resource* which is replenished by rewards that a mobile agent gains after servicing an RRS. With the cloning resource charged using such rewards, its chances of generating more clones also increases. Apart from rewards, the cloning resource of a mobile agent is also boosted periodically based on its current value and certain ambient conditions. The dynamics of cloning and the manner of resource charging have been discussed in later sections.

The cloning controller works based on a reactive mechanism to maintain the population of mobile agents within the networked system. This mechanism, embedded within each agent, senses the number of existing mobile agents in the intra-node queue waiting for their turn to migrate to the next node. The number of agents within this queue potentially gives a feeling of the network conditions based on which the agent decides whether or not to clone. The extent of cloning depends on the following parameters:

1. The *Cloning Resource* available within the agent,
2. The *Rewards* it has gained by servicing the RRSs and
3. The *Cloning Pressure* which is proportional to the number of vacant slots in the queue.

Cloning resource is charged partly by rewards and partly by an inherent charging mechanism embedded within the agent. Apart from a cloning resource, agents also have a life-time stamped on them which increases with the rewards they acquire as they service the RRSs.

3.4   Dynamics of Mobile Agent Cloning

Initially at time $t = 0$, the system consists of only parent agents –at least one per type of agent which always exists and never dies. These agents continue to populate the network all through ensuring that at least one copy of their service (payload) exists within the network. In subsequent discussions we will use the term *agent* to refer to either the parent agent or the clone unless otherwise specified. An agent makes the decision to clone based on several factors and the total number of clones generated affects the overall performance of the system in terms of both the utilization of the network resources and also RRS servicing times. The decision as to whether or not an agent, resident in node N at time t, should clone is made based on the *Cloning Pressure*, $\rho_c(t)$ given by Eq. (1).

$$\rho_c^N(t) = \begin{cases} Q_{Th} - Q_N(t) \text{ for } \rho_c(t) > 0 \\ 0 \qquad\qquad\qquad \text{otherwise} \end{cases} \tag{1}$$

where Q_{Th} is the *Queue Threshold* and $Q_N(t)$ is the number of mobile agents populating the queue at time t in node N. A mobile agent M residing at node N, generates C number of clones at time t based on Eq. (2).

$$C^M(t) = \rho_c^N(t)\{R_{av}^M(t)/R_{max}\} \tag{2}$$

where R_{av}^M is the available cloning resource within the agent M and R_{max} is the maximum cloning resource an agent can possess. C is rounded off to the next lowest integer. Initially all parent agents have the maximum cloning resource to their credit i.e. $R_{av} = R_{max}$. The cloning resource is depleted from an agent M for every cloning session based on Eq. (3).

$$R_{av}^M(t+1) = R_{av}^M(t) - C^M(t)R_{min} \tag{3}$$

where R_{min} is the minimum cloning resource required to generate a clone. Each of the clones needs to be conferred this minimum value of resource. This value is extracted from the personal cloning resource of the agent that created the clones.

If this agent cannot afford to confer this minimum amount of resource then its cloning is inhibited. The cloning resource is charged based on the Eq. (4).

$$R_{av}^M(t+1) = \begin{cases} R_{av}^M(t) + \tau_c e^{-1/R_{av}(t)} + \tau_r Rew(t) & \text{for } R_{av}^M(t) \geq 1, \rho_c^N(t) \leq 1 \\ R_{av}^M(t) + \tau_c + \tau_r Rew(t) & \text{for } R_{av}^M(t) < 1, \rho_c^N(t) < 1 \\ R_{av}^M(t) + \tau_c e^{(1-1/x)} + \tau_r Rew(t) & \text{for } \rho_c^N(t) > 1 \text{ where } x = \rho_c^N(t) \\ R_{max} & \text{if } R_{av}^M(t+1) > R_{max} \end{cases}$$

(4)

where $Rew(t)$ is taken to be 1 if the agent is able to service an RRS; else it is zero at time t. τ_c and τ_r are non-zero positive constants. Care is taken to ensure that the cloning resource, R_{av}, never exceeds its maximum value R_{max} and if so it is brought down to the latter. Every mobile agent or clone has, in addition to the cloning resource, a life-time conferred on it at the time it is created. The life-time $L(t)$ is decremented in every time step according to Eq. (5).

$$L(t+1) = L(t) - 1 \tag{5}$$

Life-times of the agents are increased by a factor as and when these agents earn rewards as given by Eq. (6).

$$L(t+1) = L(t) + \sigma Rew(t) \tag{6}$$

where L(t) is the life-time of an agent at time t and σ is a non-zero positive integer constant.

4   Results and Discussions

The mechanism of cloning controller was simulated together with the mobile robotic nodes hosting mobile agents which migrate using the Pheromone-Conscientious (*PherCon*) [14] mechanism. A stand-alone simulator for the above setup was coded in Java^{TM} as a discrete event system simulator together with a rendering engine.

Two pertinent terms with respect to the simulator are: (i) *Run*: It signifies one complete simulation cycle. (ii) *Step*: A run comprises several discrete steps. Many operations may be executed during each such step by both the robotic nodes and the mobile agents comprising the network. The count of the steps is referred to as the *Step-count*.

Simultaneous multiple mobile agent migrations do not occur in the same step-count. This ensures that the simulation closely matches the real world wherein when two entities transact with one another, a third entity desirous of a transaction with any of the former two, needs to wait for the transaction to end. Hence at any given step-count while an agent is migrating from the queue in node A to that in node B, no other agents are allowed to migrate to either of these nodes. Further, in such a state no other agents from A or B can migrate to other nodes.

The simulation was carried out using 200 nodes with an initial population of 8 parent agents designated *Agent-0* through *Agent-7* where *Agent-0* carries code for *Service-0* and *Agent-1* carries code for *Service-1* and so on. One run

of the simulation was carried out for 1000 step-counts. The values of the parameters used in the simulations are $R_{max} = 100$, $R_{min} = 10$, $R_{av} = R_{max}$ for
the initial population of agents and $R_{av} = R_{min}$ for the clones when they are
created, $L = 30$, $Q_{Th} = 4$, $\tau_c = 0.1$, $\tau_r = 100$ and $\sigma = 7$. A set of 194 RRSs
requesting for *Service-0* through *Service-7*, were generated at discrete simulation
steps in a random manner. The RRSs then diffuse pheromones for the requested
service across their neighbours. One simulation run, each comprising 1000 step-
counts was carried out separately in the absence and presence of the cloning
resource. Results were obtained by observing the maximum number of mobile
agents generated and the total number of step-counts required to satisfy 194
RRSs.

The graph in Fig. 4(a) shows a plot of the variation of the total number of
agents and the number of RRSs serviced with the simulation step-counts when
the cloning resource feature was disabled. This was done by assuming that all
agents and their clones are free to always clone repeatedly irrespective of their
cloning resource value. Disabling the feature was achieved by considering the
factor (R_{av}/R_{max}) in Eq. (2) to be unity always. It can be observed from this
graph that only 191 out of 194 RRSs were satisfied in 1000 step-counts using a
total agent population of around 700 in the network. The population of mobile
agents seems to continue to hover around 700 even though no more RRSs were
generated and a few were still waiting to be serviced, thus needlessly consuming
precious bandwidth and resources.

The graph in Fig. 4(b) depicts the performance of the cloning controller using
the concept of the cloning resource. Using just 101 agents, all 194 RRSs were
satisfied in 743 step-counts. This graph also shows a sharp increase in the number agents proportional to the RRSs generated within the network followed by
its decrease to a very low value after most of the RRSs are serviced. The increase
and decrease conforms to the rate at which the RRSs are generated and serviced
thus exhibiting an adaptive behaviour on part of the cloning controller. Further
the number of agents populating the network when almost no RRSs exist, is

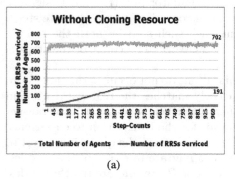

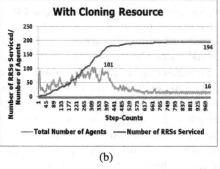

(a)   (b)

Fig. 4. Graph depicting the variation of the total number of agents and the RRS service
times for (a) Without Cloning Resource and (b) With Cloning Resource

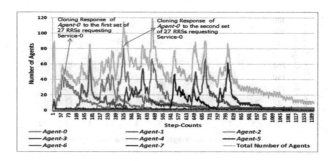

Fig. 5. Graph showing the increase and decrease in the number of each type of agent—
Agent-0 through *Agent-7*

just about 15 in contrast to 700 in the previous case saving the precious computational resource which could be utilized for other purposes or entities within the network. The heterogeneous mobile agents thus clone based on their own decision but also ensure that they do not grow too large in number so as to curb the migrations of the other types of agents.

Simulations were also conducted with a total of 292 RRSs generated over 1000 step-counts. On an average around 30 RRSs requested for the same type of service. RRSs requesting a certain type of service were generated in an interleaved fashion every 100 step-counts. In addition 27 RRSs once again requesting *Service-0* carried by *Agent-0* were generated starting from step-count 250 onwards. Figure 5 shows the nature by which the number of agents of each type increase to a maximum and then go down to a minimum after the corresponding RRSs are satisfied. It can also be seen that the rate of generation of the clones of *Agent-0* in the second phase after the 250th step-count is much faster than that in the initial stage. As an agent services more RRSs it gains both cloning resource and life-time due to the rewards it accrues in doing so.

Increased life-times make some of these agents to live longer. When the second burst of RRSs occurred, the population of *Agent-0* and its clones had not died down to the minimum. This facilitated the generation of a larger number of clones in a short period of time causing the steep peak. The graph also shows how the overall population of heterogeneous agents varies. It can be seen that this value is contained below 120 and goes down rapidly when no RRSs populate the network indicating clearly that the heterogeneous mobile agent population controls itself selectively and on-demand. All unnecessary clones are automatically flushed once all the RRSs have been serviced. The existing parent agents (*Agent-0* through *Agent-7*) then continue to patrol the network in a conscientious manner thereby allowing other network related activity.

Figure 6 shows the effect of the variation of the intra-node queue length, Q_{Th}, on the number of agents and clones generated and the step-counts taken to service a constant number of RRSs (100 in this case) using the cloning resource. It can be observed from the graph that at low Q_{Th} values the total number of agents and clones generated is also low thereby taking more steps to service

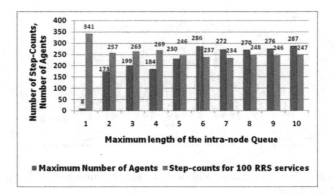

Fig. 6. Variation in the number of Mobile Agents and Clones and Step-counts to service 100 RRSs for different values of Q_{Th}

all the 100 RRSs. As the Q_{Th} value increases the performance increases due to an increase in number of agents and clones generated. However further increase in Q_{Th} beyond 4, does not portray any drastic change in performance. Both the number of agents and clones and the number of step-counts consumed vary within a narrow band between 240 and 250. Thus even though with higher values of Q_{Th} the agents or their clones find more empty spaces in the queue they refrain from needless over-cloning. Such a judicious cloning coupled with minimal service times of the RRSs, can provide more space to other entities that populate the network. In real networks, inter-node communications and message passing will also use network resources such as the bandwidth. Since the cloning controller consumes only a part of these resources and that too only on-demand it ensures that a fair amount of networking resources is always available for the other communications. Thus choke-ups will rarely occur in such networks.

4.1   Performance in Dynamic Networks

Since the underlying application was aimed towards controlling mobile agent cloning in multi mobile robot networked systems as cited in [14], it is important to evaluate the performance of the same when the robotic nodes hosting mobile agents move relative to one another. In order to compare the performance of the cloning controller in both static and dynamic networks, simulations similar to that described in Sect. 2 were carried out using a 200 node network. The agents however used the proposed cloning control mechanism.

Figure 7 shows the variation in the performances for servicing 100 RRSs for both the static and dynamic cases. With cloning controller mechanism active within the agents, the maximum number agents to satisfy 100 RRSs oscillate in between 150 to 300 for both the static and dynamic networks. For lower number of agents and clones, the Step-Counts required for the service to be completed is high. As the number of these agents and clones increases the Step-Counts

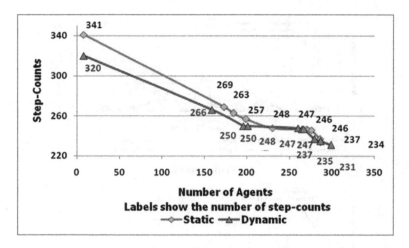

Fig. 7. A comparison of the performance of the Cloning Controller when used in Static and Dynamic Networks

decrease and hover around 230–260, for both the static and dynamic cases. The graphs clearly indicate that the cloning controller works almost the same way in both the scenarios and contains the mobile agent population to the left of the axis of the parabola as discussed in Sect. 2.

4.2   Emulation on Real Networks

To validate the efficacy of the proposed cloning control mechanism on real networks, the same was emulated over a LAN using the Typhon [36] mobile agent framework. Typhon facilitates various mobile agent functionalities such as mobility, code-carrying ability, cloning of mobile agents, etc. Each instantiation of Typhon within a computer emulates a robotic node. The Typhon framework allows several such instantiations or nodes to co-exist in a single computer (localhost).

50 Typhon based nodes (instantiations) were distributed amongst seven PCs connected within a LAN to emulate a robotic network. Each node was capable of running its own cloning controller. Experiments were performed on both static and dynamic networks. In the dynamic case, nodes were made to freely connect to any other node in the network and also drop connections to any of their neighbours thus emulating mobility of robotic nodes. The dynamic network was generated using the Erdős-Rényi $G(n, p)$ model [37] where n is the nodes in the network and p is the probability of making or breaking a connection. We have chosen $p = 0.5$. The emulation was performed with an initial population of 5 different types of parent agents designated as *Agent-0* through *Agent-4*. The Pheromone-Conscientious (*PherCon*) [14] mechanism was embedded in the agents for migration within the network. Except for the value of L which was

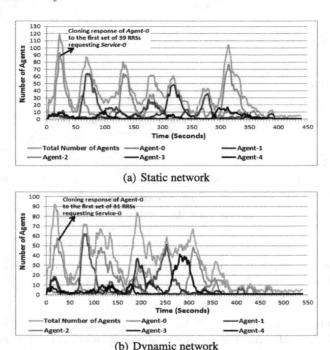

(a) Static network

(b) Dynamic network

Fig. 8. Graph showing the change in population of agents viz. *Agent-0* through *Agent-4* in the emulation - (a) In a Static Network and (b) In a Dynamic network

taken to be 10 s, all other parameter values used were same as those used in the simulation.

Figures 8(a) and (b) depict the variations in the populations of the different types of agents (including clones) in the static and dynamic networks respectively. The RRSs requesting different types of services (*Service-0* through *Service-4*) were randomly generated in both the networks. In order to test the efficacy of the cloning controller, a relatively high demand for a particular service was created within the network by increasing the probability of generating RRSs that requested this service. It was found from the log that in the static case 237 RRSs were generated while that in the dynamic was 252. It can be noted that the results obtained from the emulation conform to those obtained from simulation (see Fig. 5). In Fig. 8(a) since a high demand for *Service-0* was generated in the first 50 s (37 RRSs), the population of *Agent-0* increased drastically while those of the others were found to be low. After the 50th second the demand for *Service-1* increased causing a rapid increase in the population of *Agent-1*. Subsequently, the graph shows similar responses for agents viz. *Agent-2*, *Agent-0*, *Agent-3*, *Agent-1* followed by *Agent-2*, indicating their greater demands. A similar trend can be observed for the dynamic network, response of which is shown

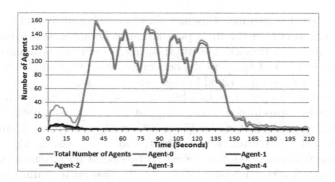

Fig. 9. Variation in the population of *Agent-0* when all nodes were forced to become RRSs requesting *Service-0* repeatedly

in Fig. 8(b). Further, it can be observed that the populations of all agents (or clones) die rapidly as soon as the respective RRSs are serviced.

In order to find the approximate upper bound of the number of agents that could actually populate the 50-node network we forced all nodes to become RRSs repeatedly. Figure 9 shows the variation in the number of agents when all nodes were made to request *Service-0* repeatedly. As can be seen the maximum number of clones (including the parent agent) that populate the network during this run is 160 which is less than 200 (queue length at each node × total number of nodes in the network). If 200 agents were to populate this 50-node network there would be no space for their movement to other nodes since the intra-node queues within all the nodes are full. This would thus result in a cluttering and eventually a choke-up. The graph indicates clearly that even if we load the network by generating the largest number of RRSs (in this case 50) repeatedly, the total number of agents remains well below 200 thus providing vacancies in the intra-node queues and facilitating proper mobility of agents within the network.

In Figs. 8(a) and (b), the total population of the agents (including clones) within the network always remains below 120 in case of static and 92 in case of the dynamic network indicating clearly that mobility of agents within the network is facilitated all through. The total population is well below the empirically found upper limit of 160. Thus the cloning control mechanism is able to stigmergically curtail the agent population well within limits thus avoiding choke-ups and also ensuring effective service to all RRSs.

5   Comparison with Other Approaches

Earlier approaches [24, 25, 27, 28, 30] to mobile agent population control endeavour to ensure that their total number never exceeds a fraction of the number of nodes of the network they populate. The agents are assumed to be homogeneous. They do not mention how a heterogeneous set of agents can be handled or whether demand-based selective rise and fall of different agent populations can be controlled. For instance Golebiewski *et al.* [27] and Suzuki *et al.* [24,25] describe mechanisms to maintain a population of homogeneous agents both in static and dynamic networks. The total agent population is maintained to a fraction of the number of nodes in the network. Their target application domain is different from the one described in this paper, though.

The mechanism proposed by Golebiewski *et al.* [27] preserves a parameter p (referred to as the reproduction probability) at each node and maintains at least one copy of an agent at each node. Though their algorithm may seem intuitive, the calculation of this parameter p is non-trivial. They assume the network to be fully connected and node and agents to be operating synchronously. Their results were obtained through simulations which allow such assumptions. In real networks these assumptions do not hold, making such workable implementations impossible unless some global parameters such as the total number of nodes and the desired number of agents are known a priori. Heterogeneity of agents and the selective control, of their respective populations, is never considered.

Marina Flores-Badillo *et al.* [28] have discussed an algorithm to manage the agent population in work flow automation. Their system uses three types of agents viz. controller agents, executer agents and blackboard agents. The protocol uses the concept of energy as the time-to-live (ttl) for the controller and executor agents for their functioning in the network. These ttls are controlled by the application. This protocol is complex and has tightly coupled entities as there is a large amount of communication and dependency among all the three types of agents. Further, the control is not distributed and involves a large amount of book-keeping to keep track of the locations of the agents and their respective energies. Though their protocol may be suitable for the domain of work-flow automation, communication complexities and non-localized decisions render it to be unsuitable for use in real dynamic and distributed environments.

Suzuki *et al.* [24,25] proposed an agent population mechanism in dynamic networks using the single species (homogeneous) population model. They estimate the link densities of each node in a dynamic network and then generate food required to be consumed by agents so as to live and clone. Though, their simulation results portray that it is possible to maintain the agent population up to a given fraction of the nodes in a network (within 20 % of error), they do not account for the overhead generated due to the communication complexity $(O(|Nbk| * N)$, Nbk = Set of nodes at k distance; N = Number of nodes in the network) of their approximation. If we extend their mechanism to cater to the control of the populations of a heterogeneous set of agents, this complexity further increases per node and the food stored and maintained within the node would also be heterogeneous in nature. Further an *a priori* knowledge of the actual number of different types of (heterogeneous) agents in the system needs to be known. An approximation on the frequency of visits made by these agents also needs to be reformulated.

Bakhouya and Gaber [30] have proposed an algorithm inspired by the immune network theory [31]. Their algorithm caters to the need of a dynamic distributed system wherein they have used the inter-arrival-times of different agents as cues to tune the agent population. They have modeled three behaviours for the mobile agents viz. Migration, Cloning and Termination and just like B-Cells in the immune system, their relative concentration decides which of these is triggered. Their method does not require the number of agents and nodes in the network to be known *a priori* and uses agent's inter-arrival times to sense the agent population.

However, heterogeneity of the agents is not taken into account. Since the number of agents to be populated in the network (N) is optimized independent of number of different types of agents (α) available in the system, their algorithm could choke the system by generating αN agents (N number of agents for each type). In real networks populated with a heterogeneous set of agents, delays could occur due to large queues at the bottle-neck links. If these network delays are to be taken into account, they may inadvertently cause the respective nodes to process based on larger inter-arrival times to eventually destabilize the agent population. If one were to extend their model to support a heterogeneous set of mobile agents it would mean that each node maintain the inter-arrival times of every type of agent. Every time a new type of agent is introduced into the system the nodes may require be either reprogramming or embedding with a mechanism to identify such new agents. The knowledge of the number of the types of agents (α) would need to be known *a priori* thus affecting scalability of the system. All this naturally would increase the computational and space overheads within each node in the network.

The population control mechanism proposed in this paper remedies the problems with these earlier approaches by allowing a heterogeneous set of agents to co-exist in a dynamic distributed network without compromising the upper bound on the total agent population. Since the per node computations do not require any specific information on the type of an agent, new agents may be introduced into the network on-the-fly without hindering performance. The control mechanism described herein focuses on a demand based system that is capable of selectively controlling the rise and fall of different types of mobile agents based on their requirement at the nodes in the network. If the need for certain types of agents is high, their population grows proportionately based on their demand in the network while those of the others wane, ensuring that the network does not get choked up. One may intuitively infer that the inherent demand based policy frees up network resources by lowering the number of agents and allowing for quicker movement of high demand agents within the network. Further, the proposed mechanism uses minimal node-to-node communications (for migrating an agent from one queue to another) which greatly reduces communication overheads within the network and hence saves on bandwidth.

6   Conclusions

Most of the state of the art population control mechanisms are directed towards controlling the cloning of a homogenous set of agents. Controlling a clone population in heterogeneous mobile agent based scenarios is non-trivial. We described a novel demand based adaptive mechanism for controlling the population of a heterogeneous set of mobile agents using stigmergic sensing of the condition of the network. Stigmergic sensing becomes essential in the real world since it is not possible for each mobile agent to communicate with all the others to compute the true global information on its population. This sensing, based on the number of mobile agents queued up for migration, coupled with a cloning resource charged by rewards accrued by servicing RRSs, facilitates a more effective utilization of the available network resources. Clonal resource and life-time also facilitate a faster response when the same type of service is requested very frequently by the nodes. The mechanism provides for a faster service of numerous RRSs and at the same time judiciously consumes network resources allowing other entities that may populate the network to use the same. The mechanism described herein, uses a stigmergic technique to allow both mobile agents and other information to flow efficiently within the network. The results obtained from the emulation reveals the practical viability of the mechanism of cloning control. The paper also explains the adaptive nature of the mechanism and its robustness even in dynamic scenarios.

The mechanism can be further enhanced using concepts from the Natural Immune Systems so that a highly rewarded agent could become an Immune memory with life-time comparable with that of its original parent. This will ensure that further responses to the generation of RRSs will be much faster. In future we envisage using mobile agents coupled with such a clonal controller in the domain of wireless mobile networks so as to improve their quality of service.

Acknowledgements. The authors wish to thank the Department of Science and Technology, Government of India, for the funding provided under the FIST scheme to set up the Robotics Lab. (www.iitg.ernet.in/cse/robotics) at the Department of Computer Science and Engineering, Indian Institute of Technology Guwahati, where the entire reported work was carried out.

The second author would like to acknowledge Tata Consultancy Services for their support under TCS-RSP.

References

1. Chess, D., Harrison, C., Kershenbaum, A.: Mobile agents: Are they a good idea? In: Tschudin, C.F., Vitek, J. (eds.) MOS 1996. LNCS, vol. 1222, pp. 25–45. Springer, Heidelberg (1997)
2. Dale, J.: A mobile agent architecture to support distributed resource information management. Master's thesis, January 1996
3. Manvi, S.S., Venkataram, P.: Mobile agent based approach for QoS routing. IET Commun. 1(3), 430–439 (2007)
4. Van Thanh, D.: Using mobile agents in telecommunications. In: Proceedings of 12th International Workshop on Database and Expert Systems Applications, 2001, pp. 685–688. IEEE (2001)
5. Wei, C., Yi, Z.: A multi-constrained routing algorithm based on mobile agent for MANET networks. In: Proceedings of International Joint Conference on Artificial Intelligence, 2009. JCAI'09, pp. 16–19. IEEE (2009)

6. Pathak, H., Nipur, Garg, K.: A fault tolerant comparison internet shopping system: best deal by using mobile agent. In: Proceedings of International Conference on Information Management and Engineering, 2009. ICIME '09, pp. 541–545 (2009)
7. Yamaya, T., Shintani, T., Ozono, T., Hiraoka, Y., Hattori, H., Ito, T., Fukuta, N., Umemura, K.: MiNet: building ad-hoc peer-to-peer networks for information sharing based on mobile agents. In: Karagiannis, D., Reimer, U. (eds.) PAKM 2004. LNCS (LNAI), vol. 3336, pp. 59–70. Springer, Heidelberg (2004)
8. Cragg, L., Hu, H.: Application of mobile agents to robust teleoperation of internet robots in nuclear decommissioning. In: Proceedings of IEEE International Conference on Industrial Technology, 2003, vol. 2, pp. 1214–1219. IEEE (2003)
9. Cragg, L., Hu, H.: A multi-agent system for distributed control of networked mobile robots. Meas. Control 38(10), 314–319 (2005)
10. Cragg, L., Hu, H.: Mobile agent approach to networked robots. Int. J. Adv. Manuf. Technol. 30(9–10), 979–987 (2006)
11. Chu, H.N., Glad, A., Simonin, O., Sempe, F., Drogoul, A., Charpillet, F.: Swarm approaches for the patrolling problem, information propagation vs. pheromone evaporation. In: Proceedings of 19th IEEE International Conference on Tools with Artificial Intelligence, 2007. ICTAI 2007, vol. 1, pp. 442–449. IEEE (2007)
12. Sempé, F., Drogoul, A.: Adaptive patrol for a group of robots. In: Proceedings of IEEE/RSJ International Conference on Intelligent Robots and Systems, 2003. IROS 2003, vol. 3, pp. 2865–2869. IEEE (2003)
13. Godfrey, W.W., Nair, S.B.: An immune system based multi-robot mobile agent network. In: Bentley, P.J., Lee, D., Jung, S. (eds.) ICARIS 2008. LNCS, vol. 5132, pp. 424–433. Springer, Heidelberg (2008)
14. Godfrey, W.W., Nair, S.B.: A pheromone based mobile agent migration strategy for servicing networked robots. In: Suzuki, J., Nakano, T. (eds.) BIONETICS 2010. LNICST, vol. 87, pp. 533–541. Springer, Heidelberg (2012)
15. De Castro, L.N.: Fundamentals of Natural Computing: Basic Concepts, Algorithms, and Applications, vol. 11. CRC Press, New York (2006)
16. Minar, N., Kramer, K.H., Maes, P.: Cooperating mobile agents for dynamic network routing. In: Hayzelden, A.L.G., Bigham, J. (eds.) Software Agents for Future Communication Systems, pp. 287–304. Springer, Heidelberg (1999)
17. Godfrey, W.W., Nair, S.B.: Mobile agent cloning for servicing networked robots. In: Desai, N., Liu, A., Winikoff, M. (eds.) PRIMA 2010. LNCS (LNAI), vol. 7057, pp. 336–339. Springer, Heidelberg (2012)
18. Bonabeau, E.: Editor's introduction: stigmergy. Artif. Life 5(2), 95–96 (1999)
19. Godfrey, W.W., Nair, S.B.: A mobile agent cloning controller for servicing networked robots. In: Proceedings of 2011 International Conference on Future Information Technology. IPCSIT 2011, pp. 81–85. IACSIT Press (2011)
20. Glitho, R., Olougouna, E., Pierre, S.: Mobile agents and their use for information retrieval: a brief overview and an elaborate case study. IEEE Network 16(1), 34–41 (2002)
21. Jin, Y., Qu, W., Zhang, Y., Wang, Y.: A mobile agent-based routing model for grid computing. J. Supercomput. 63(2), 431–442 (2013)
22. Hamza, S., Okba, K., Aïcha-Nabila, B., Youssef, A.: A Cloud computing approach based on mobile agents for Web services discovery. In: 2012 Second International Conference on Innovative Computing Technology (INTECH), pp. 297–304 (2012)
23. Stahl, F., Gaber, M., Bramer, M., Yu, P.: Pocket data mining: towards collaborative data mining in mobile computing environments. In: 2010 22nd IEEE International Conference on Tools with Artificial Intelligence (ICTAI), vol. 2, pp. 323–330 (2010)

24. Suzuki, T., Izumi, T., Ooshita, F., Masuzawa, T.: Biologically inspired self-adaptation of mobile agent population. In: Proceedings of Sixteenth International Workshop on Database and Expert Systems Applications, 2005, pp. 170–174. IEEE (2005)
25. Suzuki, T., Izumi, T., Ooshita, F., Masuzawa, T.: Self-adaptive mobile agent population control in dynamic networks based on the single species population model. IEICE Trans. Inf. Syst. **90**(1), 314–324 (2007)
26. Ma, J., Voelker, G.M., Savage, S.: Self-stopping worms. In: Proceedings of the 2005 ACM Workshop on Rapid Malcode, pp. 12–21. ACM (2005)
27. Golebiewski, Z., Kutylowski, M., Luczak, T., Zagórski, F.: Self-stabilizing population of mobile agents. In: Proceedings of IEEE International Symposium on Parallel and Distributed Processing, 2008. IPDPS 2008, pp. 1–8. IEEE (2008)
28. Flores-Badillo, M., Padilla-Duarte, A., López-Mellado, E.: A population control protocol for mobile agent based workflow automation. In: Proceedings of IEEE International Conference on Systems, Man and Cybernetics, 2009. SMC 2009, pp. 4059–4064. IEEE (2009)
29. Amin, K.A., Mikler, A.R., Prasanna, V.I.: Dynamic agent population in agent-based distance vector routing. Neural Parallel Sci. Comput. **11**(1 & 2), 127–142 (2003)
30. Bakhouya, M., Gaber, J.: Adaptive approach for the regulation of a mobile agent population in a distributed network. In: Proceedings of the Fifth International Symposium on Parallel and Distributed Computing, 2006. ISPDC'06, pp. 360–366. IEEE (2006)
31. Farmer, J.D., Packard, N.H., Perelson, A.S.: The immune system, adaptation, and machine learning. Physica D: Nonlin Phen. **22**(1), 187–204 (1986)
32. Bonabeau, E., Dorigo, M., Theraulaz, G.: Swarm Intelligence: From Natural to Artificial Systems, vol. 1. Oxford University Press, New York (1999)
33. Nair, S.B., Godfrey, W.W., Kim, D.H.: On realizing a multi-agent emotion engine. Int. J. Synth. Emot. (IJSE) **2**(2), 1–27 (2011)
34. Godfrey, W.W., Nair, S.B., Kim, D.H.: Towards a dynamic emotional model. In: Proceedings of IEEE International Symposium on Industrial Electronics, 2009. ISIE 2009, pp. 1932–1936. IEEE (2009)
35. Mishra, R., Srivastava, A., Bhaumik, K., Chaudhary, S.: ACTH and regulation of adrenocortical secretion: a mathematical model. Indian J. Pure Appl. Math. **13**(12), 1503–1512 (1982)
36. Matani, J., Nair, S.B.: *Typhon* - a mobile agents framework for real world emulation in prolog. In: Sombattheera, C., Agarwal, A., Udgata, S.K., Lavangnananda, K. (eds.) MIWAI 2011. LNCS (LNAI), vol. 7080, pp. 261–273. Springer, Heidelberg (2011)
37. Erdős, P., Rényi, A.: On the evolution of random graphs. Publ. Math. Inst. Hungar. Acad. Sci. **5**, 17–61 (1960)

On the Existence and Heuristic Computation of the Solution for the *Commons Game*

Rokhsareh Sakhravi[1], Masoud T. Omran[1]([✉]), and B. John Oommen[1,2]

[1] School of Computer Science, Carleton University,
Ottawa K1S 5B6, Canada
rsakhrav@connect.carleton.ca,
{mtomran,oommen}@scs.carleton.ca
[2] University of Agder, Grimstad, Norway

Abstract. It is well known that Game Theory can be used to capture and model the phenomenon of economic strategies, psychological and social dilemmas, and the exploitation of the environment by human beings. Many artificial games studied in Game Theory can be used to understand the main aspects of humans using/misusing the environment. They can be tools by which we can define the aggregate behavior of humans, which, in turn, is often driven by "short-term", perceived costs and benefits. The *Commons Game* is a simple and concise game that elegantly formulates the different behaviors of humans toward the exploitation of resources (also known as "commons") as seen from a game-theoretic perspective. The game is intrinsically hard because it is non-zero-sum, and involves multiple players, each of who can use any one of a set of strategies. It also could involve potential competitive and cooperative strategies. In the *Commons Game*, an ensemble of approaches towards the exploitation of the commons can be modeled by colored cards. This paper shows, in a pioneering manner, the existence of an optimal solution to *Commons Game*, and demonstrates a heuristic computation for this solution. To do this, we consider the cases when, with some probability, the user is aware of the approach (color) which the other players will use in the exploitation of the commons. We then investigate the problem of determining the best probability value with which a *specific* player can play each color in order to maximize his ultimate score. Our solution to this problem is a heuristic algorithm which determines (locates in the corresponding space) feasible probability values to be used so as to obtain the maximum average score. This project has also involved the corresponding implementation of the game, and the output of the new algorithm enables the user to visualize the details.

Keywords: Game theory · *Commons Game* · Tragedy of commons · Implementation of commons · Convergence of commons

Some very preliminary results of this study were published in the Proceedings of DCAI'12, The 9th International Symposium on Distributed Computing and Artificial Intelligence, March 2012, Salamanca, Spain.
B. John Oommen was partially supported by NSERC, the Natural Sciences and Engineering Research Council of Canada.

© Springer-Verlag Berlin Heidelberg 2014
N.T. Nguyen (Ed.): TCCI XIV 2014, LNCS 8615, pp. 71–99, 2014.
DOI: 10.1007/978-3-662-44509-9_4

1   Introduction

1.1   Game Theory

In Game Theory, a number of players attempt to find strategies for playing a specific game so as to lead to the best solution for a predefined goal. Although, Game Theory has been extensively studied in the field of mathematics, it also has many applications in economics, biology, engineering, politics, philosophy and computer science. In recent years, there has been a remarkable increase in research in fields that intersect game theory and computer science.

1.2   What is the *Commons Game?*

Apart from the above-mentioned domains in which Game Theory has been applied, many reported artificial games studied can be used to understand the main aspects of humans using/misusing the environment. Games can, indeed, be used as tools to model the collective behavior of humans and nations, often driven by "short-term", perceived costs and benefits. We believe that humans should demonstrate a good understanding of how to protect the global environment, and in this regard Game Theory presents a potentially useful framework for the modeling and understanding of innate aggregate behaviors of multiple parties, as related to strategies for the use of resources. The *Commons Game* basically describes how a selfish player can use an unregulated resource, and instructs us of the different strategies that humans can use to cooperatively benefit from the resources found in the environment (e.g., forest, fish, water, energy, etc.).

In order to reach a point where there is a sustainable use of the environment, humans must attempt to cooperate. Thus, for example, in the case of fisheries, it is advantageous that the relevant parties cooperate to establish a rule governing how much fish can be caught, so as to continue to protect an area from over-harvesting. In this example, a group that works cooperatively can limit the amount of fish they individually can harvest so as to sustain the fishery with the least amount of effort, although the "cheaters" may take as many fish as they can in any conceivable way. If the number of cheater fishermen are more than the number of cooperators, most of the time is spent protecting the acquired resources from these parties, and so the pool of fish resources will not be successfully maintained. Finding other parties who will cooperate with you can then be a successful strategy, since they will only interact with the cheaters once, and thus spend less time fighting over the resources. However, there must be a balance between the cooperators and the cheaters due to the costs associated with each strategy.

The commons dilemma in Hardin's "Tragedy of the Commons" [14] is "whether to reduce their individual rates of consumption, sacrificing their own desires, freedom to consume, and perhaps personal well-being for the future of the group, or to continue using the resources at the same rate, risking the common pool" [11]. Hardin describes a pasture open to all, where herdsmen can keep as many cattle as they desire. There are two choices in this commons dilemma.

Each herdsman may pursue his own interest by keeping as many cattle as he wants on the pasture and maximizing his gains. The other choice is for all herdsmen to limit the number of cattle they put on the pasture, resulting in gains for everyone. The tragedy occurs when all herdsmen pursue their own interests, and the community is harmed by the depletion of the resource, such as the overcrowding of the pasture. Hardin writes, "Each man is locked into a system that compels him to increase his herd without limit in a world that is limited. Ruin is the destination toward which all men rush, each pursuing his own best interest in a society that believes in the freedom of the commons". The Payoff for defecting behavior is higher than the Payoff for cooperative behavior [9].

The world-famous[1] example of players consuming resources is that of countries harvesting whales in the ocean. This provides a good illustration of how a commons resource works and, unfortunately, also represents the consequence of continuously and imprudently exploiting the commons resource at a high rate. In the past, whales were plentiful in the ocean, and whaling was profitable for all those nations engaged in the trade. With the growth of technology, finding, killing and the processing of whales became more proficient, and the harvests steadily increased for numerous years. Eventually, since World War II, the harvest has reduced because of the high rate of exploitation and the steady competition among nations, when, in actuality, the whale harvesting should have been cut back. Unfortunately, the parties involved have continued to keep "harvesting" the whales, and this has led to some serious problems including the near-extinction of some of the great whales (i.e., the Blue and Right whales). Apparently, many whale-hunting nations assumed that there was an "infinite" steady supply of whales, which would have led to a non-conflicting scenario.

A similar example can be cited in the harvesting of trees, and many other natural resources.

In a commons, the individual parties using it are in competition with each other. It would, however, be more beneficial for each party (person, nation) to ensure that there will always be a harvest. But to do so, everyone in the commons must trust the others to act morally if and when an agreement to restrict exploitation is made. It will not be fair if one party restricts his exploitation, while another continues to use the resources in an unrestricted manner.

The important features in a commons are thus:

1. An individual's short-term selfish actions are in conflict with his long-term best interests.
2. Each individual's actions affect the others in the commons. For example, if a person acts greedily in the short-term, he restricts not only his own long-term benefits, but also restricts the possible earnings and benefits of all the other parties, regardless of whether he acts greedily or with restraint.

The aim of this paper is to show the existence of an optimal solution to *Commons Game*, and to derive a heuristic computation for this solution.

---

[1] The reader should clearly understand that this document is not intended to initiate a political or moral dialogue on any of the related issues.

This task is far from trivial because the game is particularly difficult. First of all, it is a multi-player game which requires both competition and cooperation. Further, to augment the complexity, the various players are unaware of the moves made by the others – they merely observe the *consequences* of their respective moves. This makes the game extremely difficult to analyze, and *there is thus no known method by which one can even understand whether the game has an equilibrium point or not*. We thus believe that our results are both novel and pioneering, and that they constitute a significant contribution to the field of Game Theory, in general, and more specific to the field of socio-economic games and dilemmas which have real-life applications!

This project has also involved the corresponding implementation of the game, and the output of the new algorithm enables the user to visualize the details. The paper also describes this implementation, which can be made available to other researchers, if requested.

1.3   History of the *"Computational"* Commons Game

The introduction[2] of the problem to research in Game Theory dates back to 1968 when Hardin offered a simple application of Game Theory for the utilization of environmental resources in the so-called *Tragedy of the Commons* [14]. However, Sigmund asserted that the "Tragedy of the Commons" has been around, since, at least, the Middle Ages. Indeed, there is no direct way for humans to escape the dilemma when it concerns the use of the available (finite) resources on the earth.

With regard to designing a computational "game" to efficiently and appropriately model this scenario, Power *et al.* [18] developed one such environmental game, the *Commons Game* in 1977 which is the theme of this study. This is a group game which has to be played cooperatively. In this game, players choose their cards individually but free communication is allowed. Players are free to act independently or interdependently in such a way that they can withdraw from the commons or take part in it. Consequently, it is possible that intra groups can form so as to have control on individual actions. In this game, players have plenty of resources in the beginning which could result in greedy actions. This, in turn, has long-term consequences for all the players. In any simulation, the Payoffs must be dynamic, and changes in score should depend on how players conserve or exploit the resources. This is basically the version of the game that we use in our work.

In the *Commons Game*, the players are required to pay more attention to the so-called cost. This cost is calculated based on one's own move, the proportion of other players who play the different moves, and also *their* respective strategies. This cost is determined in such a way that if the relative number of cheaters is higher, the perceived benefit of the other players cooperating increases. Consequently, a proportion of the players must usually play cooperatively even though

---

[2] This sub-section has been included in the interest of completeness. It can be removed or abridged at the recommendation of the Referees.

the others fail to, because the success of each strategy is calculated based on the proportion of the players in the total population, using the various strategies.

The *Commons Game* has been studied and used in different applications after its initial introduction into the literature. In [1,5], Baba presented two microcomputer games that deal with serious environmental problems. We believe that these games can contribute, in an interesting and helpful manner, towards the increased awareness of environmental issues, since they operate in a dialog mode, and because they are well animated and displayed. In [17], Kirts *et al.* focused more on simulations which can be used to familiarize participants with the complexities of decision making and negotiation. They believed that computer communication strategies, coupled with simulations, present the potential for creating educationally rewarding learning experiences in a cost effective, flexible and realistic manner. Hardin [15] noted the important aspect that it is impossible to neglect the issues concerning the commons when it involves breeding. He believed that no technical solution can rescue us from what he perceived to be "the misery of overpopulation", for he believed that "freedom to breed will bring ruin to all". Marsili and Challet, in [8], discussed the minority nature of the game which shows that the minority nature of the interaction crucially depends on the expectation of the agents. In their research, they also reviewed the effect of the marketplace.

More recently, the *Commons Game*[3] has received a lot of attention due to its applicability to real-world issues. Baba *et al.* [2–4] suggested that the utilization of soft computing techniques (such as Genetic Algorithms (GAs) and Evolutionary Algorithms (EAs)) could contribute towards making the original game much more exciting. They also comparatively discussed three games, namely, the original *Commons Game*, the modified *Commons Game* utilizing GAs and Neural Networks (NNs), and the modified *Commons Game* utilizing EAs and NNs. They declared that the *Commons Game* which used EAs and NNs provided the best opportunity for letting players seriously consider the use of the commons. Brown and Vincent [6] analyzed the evolution of cooperation for a family of evolutionary games involving shared costs and benefits, with a continuum of strategies from non-cooperation to total cooperation. This cost-benefit game allows the cooperating parties to share in the benefit of the option to cooperate, and the recipients to be, in turn, burdened with a share of their cost. In [10], Dodds noted that the fundamental aspects of human beings using the environment can be explained by game theory, which demonstrates the aggregate behavior of the human species driven by perceived costs and benefits. He suggested schemes for controlling the impact of the human being on the global environment, which, in turn, must also take into consideration the basic behavioral aspects including the development of social norms and the positive feedback created. This is because resources become more valuable with increasing rarity, leading to a greater incentive for consumption. Baba and Handa [13] focused

---

[3] The game is explained, in some detail, in a subsequent section. Although a revised version of the game was introduced in [7,12], we shall deal with the original game, as explained later in this paper.

on designing the game rule by applying two EAs. The first of these, which is a Multiple-Objective EA (MOEA) generates various skilled players. By improving their skill, these players can modify the parameters of the game, i.e., the likelihood of choosing a card in the *Commons Game*.

1.4   Contributions of the Paper

In this paper:

1. We shall develop a deterministic approach to maximize the average case score of a player (Player 1) when the probability by which the other players select a color is known *a priori*.
2. While we do not claim that our solution attains the local/global optimum (which, we believe, is an intractable problem), what we endeavor to obtain is a heuristic by which a feasible solution is achieved.
3. We analyze the game data and present various interesting properties pertaining to its performance.
4. Finally, we illustrate the implementation results of executing the algorithm and provide various charts so that the reader can visualize the behavior of the game in various situations.

1.5   Paper Organization

After presenting the state-of-the-art when it concerns the *Commons Game* in Sect. 2, the mechanics of the game is described in fair detail in Sect. 2.1. The algorithm to infer the best suitable strategy to be played by Player 1 (if the knowledge of the selection probabilities of the other players is known *a priori*) is given in Sect. 3, which also includes a formal record of the solution in Sect. 3.2. Section 4 describes, in some detail, an implementation of a prototype of the game, and lists some of the salient features of the results obtained from various simulations. Section 6 concludes the paper and presents the possible avenues for future research.

2   State-of-the-Art of the *Commons Game*

The purpose of the *Commons Game* is to simulate the workings of a set of players utilizing the commons in such a way that no player has an exclusive right to the resource, while on the other hand, all the players have access to it.

In the *Commons Game*, the players can play either selfishly or cooperatively in each round. The resource is depleted gradually if the collective play is predominantly selfish, and consequently, everyone ends up with a profit less than if they had played cooperatively. On the other hand, if the play is predominantly cooperative, each player takes less than his maximum on each trial, implying that the resource is inexhaustible, and thus that they can "indefinitely" keep earning benefits from the resource.

Beside the existing alternative of individuals or nations participating in a commons, these are three additional options listed below:

1. The first alternative allows a player to withdraw from the commons if he does not like the way the game is going or if he does not fully trust the other players. Such a move earns a *small* fixed amount, but this amount is less than the amount that would be earned if he played cooperatively.
2. The second alternative is a so-called "police" response. In this case, a selfish player will not be able to earn anything in the round if a competing player chooses to police him. Instead, the selfish player loses a number of points. This move allows players to determine the effectiveness of relying on altruistic behavior, and on invoking mild sanctions so as to control the selfish behavior of others.
3. The third alternative allows players the option of rewarding others who cooperate. This choice also costs points for those who invoke it. These two options, i.e. the ones of rewarding and penalizing, permit players to have some control over their fellow players and yields explicit control "parameters" that are potentially available to members in the commons.

One study [14] shows that a novice group of players play selfishly or withdraw from the commons after several cooperative attempts. So, the literature recommends players to come back "to the table" and to continue to play the game subsequently – because players generally behave more cooperatively in their second or third games.

Hardin's article titled "The Tragedy of the Commons" [14] in the book by Hardin and Baden [16], and his film are excellent introductions to potential players of this game. Although, the game director gives some thought to the issue of the "debriefing" phase of simulating productive ideas for the resolution of commons-type dilemmas, there is no need to stress the issues of explaining the commons, or to appeal to students to behave cooperatively *prior* to the game. Neither the tragic nature of the trap nor the feeling of futility of those caught, is grasped by lecturing about the commons (even to college students) before they have played the game. When students get a chance to play, though, they will listen with effective understanding, and are also ready to spend time to enter into discussions over possible solutions.

2.1 The Original *Commons Game* Settings

The *Commons Game* aims to let players comprehend that resources are limited in the real-world, so that they must manage their exploitation of the resources carefully. Players will eventually understand that in order to benefit the most, they must think and play cooperatively. In the *Commons Game*, players try to gain points by playing different strategies represented by colored cards. When the game is started, each player should play a card simultaneously but none of them is allowed to see the card played by the other players.

In what follows, although we are working with specific numeric score values defined in the original game manual [18], *the arguments and strategies presented here work even if one changes the values such that after applying the changes, the main properties of the game remain the same.*

Each card represents an approach toward the commons. The role of each color is defined in the following:

1. **Green card:** A green card represents a high exploitation of the commons. Players who play this card can get the maximum reward. However, they get -20 points if at least one player plays a Black card in the same round. The score received by the player who plays the Green card depends on the state of the game, and the number of Red card players, as will be discussed later.

2. **Red card:** A Red card represents a careful utilization of the commons. Each Red card is worth about forty percent of the points associated with a Green card. Red card players receive 10 extra points for every Orange card played at the same round. The points allocated to the Red card again depends on the state of the game and the number of Red card players, as discussed later.

3. **Yellow card:** A Yellow card denotes a complete abstention from the utilization of the commons. Players who play this card get 6 points at anytime in the game regardless of the move made by the other players.

4. **Orange card:** An Orange card is intended to give an encouraging signal to the Red card players. Those who have played this card will lose a single point for each player in the game divided by the number of Orange cards played at that round. So, the formula to calculate the score of the player who plays an Orange card would be $\frac{N}{N_O}$, where N is the number of persons in the group and N_O is the number of players who play an Orange card in one round. As mentioned above, Orange cards are able to add 10 points to Red card players.

5. **Black card:** A Black card is used for "policing", and thus punishing Green card players. Players who play Black will get one negative point for each player in the game divided by the number of Black cards played at that round. For example, in a group of 6 persons, it will cost 6 points to play Black. When more than one player plays Black, the cost is shared equally between them. So, the formula to calculate the score of the player who plays a Black card would be $\frac{N}{N_B}$, where N is the number of persons in the group and N_B is the number of players who play a Black card in the given round. As mentioned before, by making this move, these players are able to punish Green card players by giving each of them -20 points.

While the score for Yellow, Orange, and Black card players are easy to calculate, the computation for Green and Red card players are a little more elaborate. The game has different states ranging from -8 to $+8$ (the state computation will be discussed in detail later), and for every state a so-called matrix called the Payoff matrix is specified, which assigns the score of playing Green and Red cards depending on the current state of the game. Table 1 shows all the relevant Payoff matrices.

Note that at each state, the score for both Green and Red card players is defined under the number of Red cards played. For example, in state -2, if 2 players play a Red card, the score of Red card players is 15, and that of the Green is 50.

Table 1. Payoff matrices for 6 players.

State +8				State +7				State +6				State +5		
N_R	S_R	S_G		N_R	S_R	S_G		N_R	S_R	S_G		N_R	S_R	S_G
0	–	200		0	–	198		0	–	196		0	–	194
1	90	202		1	89	200		1	88	198		1	87	196
2	92	204		2	91	202		2	90	200		2	89	198
3	94	206		3	93	204		3	92	202		3	91	200
4	96	208		4	95	206		4	94	204		4	93	202
5	98	210		5	97	208		5	96	206		5	95	204
6	100	–		6	99	–		6	98	–		6	97	–

State +4				State +3				State +2				State +1		
N_R	S_R	S_G		N_R	S_R	S_G		N_R	S_R	S_G		N_R	S_R	S_G
0	–	186		0	–	174		0	–	154		0	–	130
1	83	188		1	77	176		1	67	156		1	55	132
2	85	190		2	79	178		2	69	158		2	57	134
3	87	192		3	81	180		3	71	160		3	59	136
4	89	194		4	83	182		4	73	162		4	61	138
5	91	196		5	85	184		5	75	164		5	63	140
6	93	–		6	87	–		6	77	–		6	65	–

State 0		
N_R	S_R	S_G
0	–	100
1	40	102
2	42	104
3	44	106
4	46	108
5	48	110
6	50	–

State -1				State -2				State -3				State -4		
N_R	S_R	S_G		N_R	S_R	S_G		N_R	S_R	S_G		N_R	S_R	S_G
0	–	70		0	–	46		0	–	26		0	–	14
1	25	72		1	13	48		1	3	28		1	-3	16
2	27	74		2	15	50		2	5	30		2	-1	18
3	29	76		3	17	52		3	7	32		3	1	20
4	31	78		4	19	54		4	9	34		4	3	22
5	33	80		5	21	56		5	11	36		5	5	24
6	35	–		6	23	–		6	13	–		6	7	–

State -5				State -6				State -7				State -8		
N_R	S_R	S_G		N_R	S_R	S_G		N_R	S_R	S_G		N_R	S_R	S_G
0	–	6		0	–	4		0	–	2		0	–	0
1	-7	8		1	-8	6		1	-9	4		1	-10	2
2	-5	10		2	-6	8		2	-7	6		2	-8	4
3	-3	12		3	-4	10		3	-5	8		3	-6	6
4	-1	14		4	-2	12		4	-3	10		4	-4	8
5	1	16		5	0	14		5	-1	12		5	-2	10
6	3	–		6	2	–		6	1	–		6	0	–

Observe that in this game, there are 17 Payoff matrices $(-8, ..., -1, 0, +1, ..., +8)$. As the game proceeds, the Payoff matrix may change and this will effect the number of points earned by Red and Green card players. The change of the Payoff matrix is defined by means of the *Matrix Board*, noted with a marker peg. Every bin in the Matrix Board corresponds to a state of the game and its payoff matrix. Each bin consists of 10 holes except bin zero that has 21 holes and the payoff matrix will change if the peg moves into a different bin as depicted in Fig. 1. During the game, the Matrix Board and the peg position inform the players about the payoff matrices that are in effect. The game starts with the peg in the starting hole in the 0 matrix. The game will be improved if players do not play Green and the payoff matrices will gradually worsen if they do.

The Peg movement on the matrix board has two rules:

1. The peg moves one hole down for each Green card played.
2. The peg moves up after a random number of plays whose average is 6. The sequence of numbers which generates this random number is as follow: 2, 4, 6, 8, and 10.

The amount of upward movement of the peg is controlled by the corresponding Payoff matrix which is in effect when the resource is designated to be replenished. The schedule given in Table 2, controls the upward movements.

During the game, players keep their own score on a Record Sheet. Each player writes down the number of points earned or lost at the appropriate trial number.

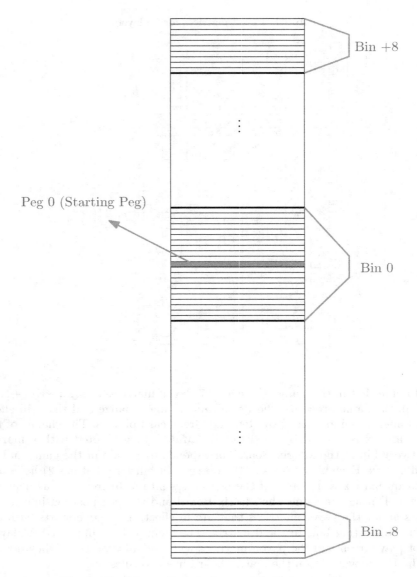

Fig. 1. The Matrix Board of a typical *Commons Game*.

The number of the points earned is shown in the Payoff matrix, which is visible to all players. The Game Director helps players to keep track of their own scores if they are in doubt. At each round the Game Director will announce the number of Green cards played, but no players is aware of the *identity* of the players who play the various cards.

Table 2. Upward movement of the peg as a function of the replenishment.

Current state	0	±1	±2	±3	±4	±5	±6	±7	±8
Peg increase	8	7	7	6	6	5	5	4	4

The state of the game mainly depends on the players' strategies. If they play in a greedy manner to exploit the commons, a faster deterioration of the commons occurs, and the state falls down faster, so that they earn less as the game continues. On the other hand, if they play cooperatively and use more Red cards, the state would go up and they would have more resources to use. The game has 60 rounds but it will finish as soon as the resources are completely used, which occurs when the game passes state -8. After every 8th round, the players have some time to discuss the status of the game. In this way, they can define their approach for the next rounds of the game. Figure 2 depicts 10 sample rounds of the game when different colors have been played by 6 players.

This describes the *Commons Game* completely.

3 Maximum Score Computation

In this section, we develop a deterministic approach to maximize the average case score of a specific player when the probability by which all the other players select a color is known *a priori*. We do not claim that our solution attains the local/global optimum. What we endeavor to obtain is a heuristic by which a feasible solution is achieved.

3.1 Problem Formulation

Suppose that for every player i, a probability vector P_i is given, which is the probability by which the player chooses a specific color. To be specific, Player i chooses color Green with probability P_{G_i}, Red with probability P_{R_i}, Yellow with probability P_{Y_i}, Orange with probability P_{O_i}, and Black with probability P_{B_i}. Let N be the number of players. We define the expected number of players that play each color as follows:

$$P_G = \sum_{i=1}^{N} P_{G_i}, \ P_R = \sum_{i=1}^{N} P_{R_i}, \ P_Y = \sum_{i=1}^{N} P_{Y_i}, \ P_O = \sum_{i=1}^{N} P_{O_i}, \ P_B = \sum_{i=1}^{N} P_{B_i}.$$

We apologize for this notation of using the same symbol to represent different concepts. However, the context of the symbols is, generally speaking, not confusing.

Figure 3 depicts the probability vectors and the expected values for $N = 6$.

As described earlier, the score of playing Green at each round is defined using the Payoff matrix, the Matrix Board, and the number of players who play Red cards. This score is in effect before invoking the consequence of playing a Black

Player	1	2	3	4	5	6
Color	G	G	R	R	O	O
Round Score	104	104	62	62	-3	-3
Total Score	104	104	62	62	-3	-3

Round	State	Replenish
1	0	0

Player	1	2	3	4	5	6
Color	G	Y	Y	R	O	R
Round Score	104	6	6	52	-6	52
Total Score	208	110	68	114	-9	49

Round	State	Replenish
2	0	0

Player	1	2	3	4	5	6
Color	G	G	G	G	B	R
Round Score	-20	-20	-20	-20	-6	40
Total Score	188	90	48	94	-15	89

Round	State	Replenish
3	0	0

Player	1	2	3	4	5	6
Color	G	B	B	O	R	G
Round Score	-20	-3	-3	-6	50	-20
Total Score	168	87	45	88	35	69

Round	State	Replenish
4	0	0

Player	1	2	3	4	5	6
Color	R	G	G	G	G	R
Round Score	42	104	104	104	104	42
Total Score	210	191	149	192	139	111

Round	State	Replenish
5	−1	0

Player	1	2	3	4	5	6
Color	G	G	G	B	O	O
Round Score	-20	-20	-20	-6	-3	-3
Total Score	190	171	129	186	136	108

Round	State	Replenish
6	0	+7

Player	1	2	3	4	5	6
Color	G	R	O	O	O	O
Round Score	102	80	-1.5	-1.5	-1.5	-1.5
Total Score	292	251	127.5	184.5	134.5	106.5

Round	State	Replenish
7	0	0

Player	1	2	3	4	5	6
Color	G	G	B	B	B	B
Round Score	-20	-20	-1.5	-1.5	-1.5	-1.5
Total Score	272	231	126	183	133	105

Round	State	Replenish
8	−1	0

Player	1	2	3	4	5	6
Color	G	G	G	Y	Y	Y
Round Score	70	70	70	6	6	6
Total Score	342	301	196	189	139	111

Round	State	Replenish
9	−1	0

Player	1	2	3	4	5	6
Color	G	G	G	G	G	G
Round Score	70	70	70	70	70	70
Total Score	412	271	266	259	209	181

Round	State	Replenish
10	−2	0

Fig. 2. 10 sample rounds of the game played by 6 players.

Player \\ Color	1	2	3	4	5	6	Expected Number of Players
Green	P_{G_1}	P_{G_2}	P_{G_3}	P_{G_4}	P_{G_5}	P_{G_6}	P_G
Red	P_{R_1}	P_{R_2}	P_{R_3}	P_{R_4}	P_{R_5}	P_{R_6}	P_R
Yellow	P_{Y_1}	P_{Y_2}	P_{Y_3}	P_{Y_4}	P_{Y_5}	P_{Y_6}	P_Y
Orange	P_{O_1}	P_{O_2}	P_{O_3}	P_{O_4}	P_{O_5}	P_{O_6}	P_O
Black	P_{B_1}	P_{B_2}	P_{B_3}	P_{B_4}	P_{B_5}	P_{B_6}	P_B
Sum	1	1	1	1	1	1	6

Fig. 3. The game information table as defined in the formulation.

card. For ease of explanation, we alter the Payoff matrix so that it allows not only a scalar number of players but also real numbers. For each state of the game we define a linear function that represents the score for playing a Green card based on the number of Red cards played. The score functions, denoted by *Payoff functions*, are obtained by connecting points on scalar representations of the Payoff matrices. Figure 4 shows the Payoff function at state -2 of the game for $N = 6$ using the data provided in Table 1. For example, if, on the average, 2.5 players play Red cards, the score for playing a Green card in State -2 of the game is 51. Similarly, the score for playing a Red card at each round is defined using the Payoff matrix, the Matrix Board, and number of players who played a Red card. Again, we use Payoff functions to evaluate the score for playing a Red card at each state of the game. Figure 5 shows the Payoff function at state -2 of the game for $N = 6$.

As before, the score of playing a Yellow card is 6, and the score of playing Orange and Black cards are $\frac{-6}{P_O}$ and $\frac{-6}{P_B}$, respectively.

In the original version of the game, "Replenishment" occurs in random rounds, and it is known that, on the average, it occurs every 6th round. Thus, to accommodate for the average computation, we consider it to occur every 6th round.

Based on the above problem setting, our goal is to compute a probability vector for a specific player to maximize his score when the probability vector for the other players is known *a priori*. Note that although we are working with the original version of the game as proposed in [18], we desire a general approach which is applicable to all problems that reflect on the basics of the "Tragedy of the Commons".

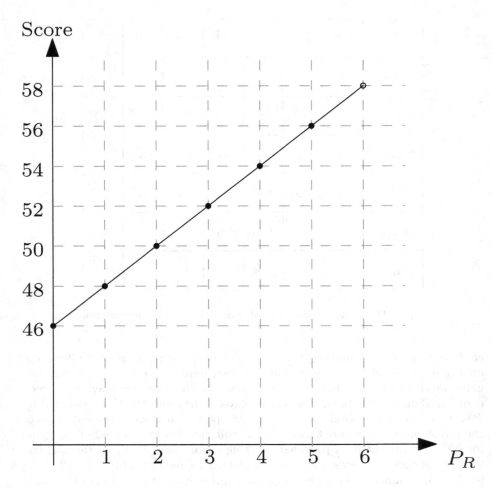

Fig. 4. The Payoff function for a Green card for State -2 of the game.

3.2   The Proposed Solution

Suppose that the probability vector P_i, $i = 2, \ldots, N$, is given, and that we are planning to determine the probability vector P_1 that maximizes the average case score of Player 1. Once P_1 has been computed, the average score of playing each color at each round is available, where we use the expected number of players playing each color to compute the scores for the round. The peg moves, which are based on the expected number of Green cards played at each round, will then, in turn, be used to obtain the corresponding Payoff function for the Green and Red players' scores. The expected value of Red card players is used to evaluate the score of Green and Red card players from the corresponding Payoff function. Also, the expected number of Orange and Black card players are all we need to obtain their score at each round. Moreover, Yellow card players always get 6

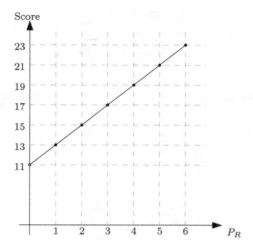

Fig. 5. The Payoff function for a Red card for State -2 of the game.

points and we assume that replenishment occurs at every 6th round. As a result, all the necessary components needed to compute all the scores are at hand, and thus, these scores are computable.

Although the scores for playing Yellow, Orange, and Black cards stay the same on different rounds, the scores of playing Green and Red cards change as a result of the change in state of the game. Once the expected numbers for all the colors have been computed, the table in Fig. 6 is used to compute the score for playing Green and Red cards at each round. Here, S_{G_i} and S_{R_i} are the scores for playing Green and Red cards in round i, $i = 1, \ldots, RN$, where RN is the total number of rounds for which the game is played.

Our approach to determine the best probability vector for Player 1 is by considering the different cases based on the structural properties of the problem. We repeat that although we are working with score values defined in the original game manual [18], the same method presented here works even if one changes the values such that after applying the changes the main properties of the game remain the same.

First of all, it is straightforward to see that playing Orange and Black cards is not beneficial toward the goal of the problem. The reason for this is that for any number of Orange and Black players, the score for those who play them is negative so that they have a *contra* effect towards maximizing the score. Consequently, the maximum advantage is obtained by setting $P_{O_1} = 0$ and $P_{B_1} = 0$.

Consider the following cases:

1. $P_B \geq 1$

   Whenever the expected number of Black card players is greater than or equal to unity, playing a Green card always leads to a score of -20 points. So, playing a Green card is not beneficial, implying that $P_{G_1} = 0$. So, the best

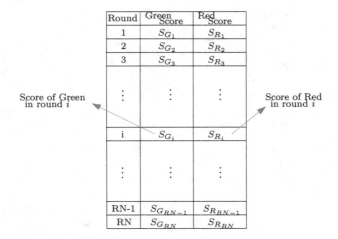

Fig. 6. Score of playing Green and Red cards in each round.

probability vector is obtained for some proportion involving P_{R_1} and P_{Y_1}, (note that $P_{R_1} + P_{Y_1} = 1$). In order to calculate the proportion, we define the average score of Red card players as the following:

$$AVG_R = \frac{\sum_{i=1}^{RN}(S_{R_i} + P_0 * 10)}{RN}, \tag{1}$$

where, for sake of convenience, we compute the time average, even though, more formally, we should have computed the ensemble average.

The following cases are possible:

- **If** $(P_{R_1} = 1) \wedge (AVG_R > 6)$. This case implies that the best probability vector is obtained by setting $P_{Y_1} = 0$ and $P_{R_1} = 1$.
- **Else If** $(P_{R_1} = 1) \wedge (AVG_R < 6)$. In this scenario, the best probability vector is obtained by setting $P_{Y_1} = 1$ and $P_{R_1} = 0$.
- **Else** $(i.e., (P_{R_1} = 1) \wedge (AVG_R = 6))$. In this scenario, either of the above solutions is the best probability vector.

The above discussion follows from the fact that decreasing P_{R_1} from its original value (equal to 1) results in a decrease in AVG_R, and so the total score will drop more as Player 1 uses less Red cards and more Yellows cards.

2. $P_B < 1$

   If the expected number of Black card players is less than unity, playing a Green card may also be beneficial. Therefore, the best probability vector is obtained for some proportion involving P_{G_1}, P_{R_1}, and P_{Y_1}, where the reader should observe that $P_{G_1} + P_{R_1} + P_{Y_1} = 1$. In order to calculate the proportion, we first consider the option of only playing Green and Red cards, and subsequently extend the solution to include playing Yellow cards.

   It should be mentioned that, for the sake of convenience, instead of computing the three point convex combination of P_{G_1}, P_{R_1}, and P_{Y_1} simultaneously, we consider P_{Y_1} separate from P_{G_1} and P_{R_1}. The reasoning behind this is a consequence of the simplifying effect of assuming that changes in P_{Y_1} are independent from changes to the values of P_{G_1} and P_{R_1}. As a result, our heuristic algorithm involves computing trivial two-point convex combinations while producing reasonable results.

We define the average score for Green card players as the following:

$$AVG_G = \frac{\sum_{i=1}^{RN}(S_{G_i} * (1 - P_B) + P_B * (-20))}{RN}.$$

Note that the average score of Red card players at each round is given by Eq. (1).

The following cases are possible when a Yellow card play is not involved:

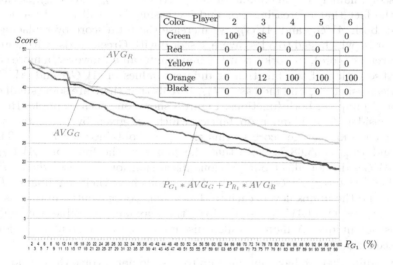

Color \ Player	2	3	4	5	6
Green	100	88	0	0	0
Red	0	0	0	0	0
Yellow	0	0	0	0	0
Orange	0	12	100	100	100
Black	0	0	0	0	0

Fig. 7. A plot of AVG_G, AVG_R, and the function $P_{G_1} * AVG_G + P_{R_1} * AVG_R$ for increasing values of P_{G_1} when $(P_{R_1} = 1) \wedge (AVG_G \leq AVG_R)$.

- **If** $(P_{R_1} = 1) \wedge (AVG_G \leq AVG_R)$. In this case, the best probability vector is obtained when $P_{R_1} = 1$ and $P_{G_1} = 0$. To show that it is true, suppose that we decrease P_{R_1} and increase P_{G_1} to get a new proportion between these probabilities. The average score of playing Red and Green drops when less Reds are used because of the increasing nature of the Payoff functions. Besides this, playing more Green cards will cause the state to drop to negative values faster, which, in turn, results in a less average score for playing both Red and Green cards. Thus, the total score will drop if we decrease P_{R_1} and increase P_{G_1} not only because the average scores are decreasing, but also because we are replacing Red cards (which have a higher average score) with Green cards which have a lesser average score. Consequently, the best probability vector is obtained when the most possible Red cards are played, namely $P_{R_1} = 1$. Figure 7 shows an example where $AVG_G = 46.82$ and $AVG_R = 46.96$ for $P_{R_1} = 1$. The results demonstrate that even for some values of AVG_G greater than AVG_R, $P_{R_1} = 1$ is the best probability vector for Player 1. More details of this are given in Sect. 4.

- **Else** $(i.e., (P_{R_1} = 1) \wedge (AVG_G > AVG_R))$. In this case the best probability vector is obtained by finding the maximum of $(P_{G_1} * AVG_G + P_{R_1} * AVG_R)$ for all possible values of P_{R_1} and P_{G_1}, where one should observe that $P_{G_1} + P_{R_1} = 1$. Here, in order to find the maximum possible average score, we decrease P_{R_1} from its original value, 1, by some value Δ and increase P_{G_1} (initially equal to 0) by Δ and compute $(P_{G_1} * AVG_G + P_{R_1} * AVG_R)$. The highest value is the resultant maximum possible average score, namely the maximum of $(P_{G_1} * AVG_G + P_{R_1} * AVG_R)$. Because of the fact that decreasing P_{R_1} and increasing P_{G_1} will lead to a decrease in both AVG_G and AVG_R, we increase the total score by replacing Red cards (which lead to a less average score) with Green cards (with a greater average score), to work towards a maximum value. However, a more careful observation of the function at different values of AVG_G and AVG_R by decreasing P_{R_1} and increasing P_{G_1} reveals that there are some small drops and jumps in both functions. Figure 8 shows one such example. Here, we consider $\Delta = 1$ and probabilities which are given by percentages. The maximum average score in this example is obtained for $P_{G_1} = 34.32\%$ and $P_{R_1} = 65.68\%$. Note that the jumps in the functions AVG_G and AVG_R do not affect our previous discussion for the case where $(P_{R_1} = 1) \wedge (AVG_G \leq AVG_R)$ since both functions have their maxima for $P_{G_1} = 0$, and the jumps never reach to that value. Consequently, in the case that $((P_{R_1} = 1) \wedge (AVG_G > AVG_R))$, the maximum possible average score is not unique. A more detailed discussion of the different cases for this scenario is presented in Sect. 4.

The results that we have obtained up to now do not involve the consideration of playing Yellow cards. We now consider the case where a Yellow card can also be played. We define the joint average score of playing Green and Red cards (defined earlier) as the following:

$$AVG_{GR} = P_{G_1} * AVG_G + P_{R_1} * AVG_R.$$

The following cases are possible when Yellow cards are also involved:

- **If** $AVG_{GR} > 6$. In this case, playing a Yellow card together with Green and Red cards is not beneficial, implying that $P_{Y_1} = 0$ (see Fig. 8). To prove this assertion, by way of contradiction, suppose that if we decrease P_{G_1} by some value Δ and increase P_{Y_1} by Δ, we can obtain a greater total score. If this is true we could, instead of increasing P_{Y_1}, increase P_{R_1} by Δ and get an even higher total score. But this contradicts the fact that AVG_{GR} is the maximum possible joint average score for playing Green and Red cards. Also, it is easy to see that decreasing P_{R_1} by some

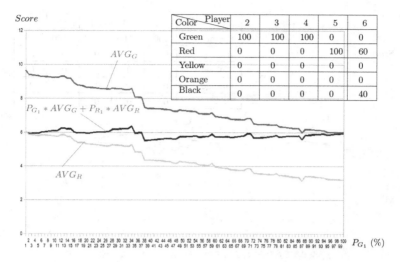

Color Player	2	3	4	5	6
Green	100	100	100	0	0
Red	0	0	0	100	60
Yellow	0	0	0	0	0
Orange	0	0	0	0	0
Black	0	0	0	0	40

Fig. 8. A sample probability vector, AVG_G, AVG_R, and the function $P_{G_1} * AVG_G + P_{R_1} * AVG_R$, for increasing values of P_{G_1}.

value Δ and adding Δ to P_{Y_1} will not increase the total score since we are replacing values greater than 6 by 6, and at the same time AVG_{GR} gets decreased as both AVG_G and AVG_R fall. So, the best probability vector would be obtained by the same probabilities as we had before.

– **Else If** $AVG_{GR} < 6$. In this case, the best probability vector is obtained when $P_{G_1} = 0$, $P_{R_1} = 0$, and $P_{Y_1} = 1$ (see Fig. 9 for a clarification). This is true because, for any combination of Green, Red, and Yellow cards, if $P_{Y_1} \neq 0$, the joint average score of playing Green and Red cards is less than AVG_{GR} obtained earlier. As a result, the best probability vector is obtained when we use all Yellow cards which, in turn, yields the greatest possible total score.

– **Else** (i.e., $AVG_{GR} = 6$). In this setting, either of the above cases would lead to an equal total score, and this would be the best probability vector for Player 1.

The above algorithm leads the maximum average score for Player 1 when the probability vectors for the other players are given *a priori*. Observe that the solution is unique other than for some special cases discussed above.

Note that although we presented our arguments by considering the original version of the game presented by Powers *et al.* [18], our solution also works for other improved versions of the game. Indeed, as one can notice, there is nothing "special" about the original setting of the game and the specified scores. For example, we have considered the case when the use of Black card causes the Green card players to lose 20 points. Since our solution is not based on the specific values of these points, it could be replaced with any desired value in the formula. The only factor that our solution is based on is the foundational

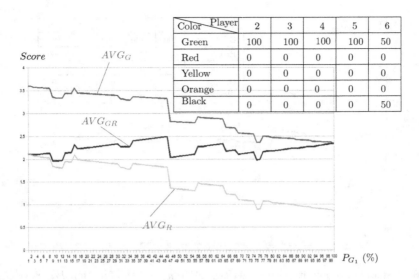

Color \ Player	2	3	4	5	6
Green	100	100	100	100	50
Red	0	0	0	0	0
Yellow	0	0	0	0	0
Orange	0	0	0	0	0
Black	0	0	0	0	50

Fig. 9. A sample game setting for which $AVG_{GR} < 6$.

concept of the *Commons Game* which must remain the same for all versions of the game, namely the increasing nature of the Payoff function as number of Red card players increases, and the faster fall of the state as more Green cards are used.

Algorithm 1 is the formal presentation of the algorithm we informally described above.

4 *Commons Game* Implementation and Analysis

This section illustrates the results obtained by implementing the algorithm discussed in the previous section. We provide various charts so that the reader can visualize the behavior of the game in various situations. We have also analyzed the game data and enumerated interesting properties of the results.

4.1 Implementation

We have implemented the *Commons Game* in order to visualize and analyze the details of the game, and to test the effectiveness of our algorithm in attaining the average maximum score. Our implementation of the game is based on the manual published by Powers *et al.* [18]. It includes two major JAVA classes named *CommonsGame* and *UserInterface*. The *CommonsGame* class contains all the details of the game, and the *UserInterface* class is the graphical user interface which obtains the user's data, and presents the processed results to the user. The *CommonsGame* class mainly consists of a number of methods by which

Algorithm 1. Maximum Score Computation

Input: P_G, P_R, P_Y, P_O, P_B: Expected number of players playing each color

RN: Number of rounds

S_{R_i}, S_{G_i}: Score of playing Green and Red in round i

Output: $P_{G_1}, P_{R_1}, P_{Y_1}, P_{O_1}, P_{B_1}$

Method:

1: $P_O = 0$
2: $P_B = 0$
3: $AVG_R = \frac{\sum_{i=1}^{RN}(S_{R_i}+P_O*10)}{RN}$
4: $AVG_G = \frac{\sum_{i=1}^{RN}(S_{G_i}*(1-P_B)+P_B*(-20))}{RN}$
5: $P_{G_1} = 0$
6: $P_{R_1} = 1$
7: $P_{Y_1} = 0$
8: **if** $P_B \geq 1$ **then**
9:    **if** $AVG_R < 6$ **then**
10:       $P_{R_1} = 0$
11:       $P_{Y_1} = 1$
12:    **end if**
13: **else**
14:    **if** $AVG_G > AVG_R$ **then**
15:       $P_{G_1}, P_{R_1} = P_{G_1}, P_{R_1} \cdot$ $(P_{G_1} * AVG_G + P_{R_1} * AVG_R)$ is Maximized
16:    **end if**
17:    **if** $P_{G_1} * AVG_G + P_{R_1} * AVG_R < 6$ **then**
18:       $P_{G_1} = 0$
19:       $P_{R_1} = 0$
20:       $P_{Y_1} = 1$
21:    **end if**
22: **end if**
23: **return** $P_{G_1}, P_{R_1}, P_{Y_1}, P_{O_1}, P_{B_1}$

End Algorithm

the user can perform a variety of tasks such as playing different game types, score computations, game state monitoring, and the preparation of results.

In our implementation, the game can be played in two ways: *random* and *manual*. If the player selects the "random play" option, the user has to enter a value between 0 to 100 for each color under that player. These numbers are the respective probabilities (given in percentages) with which the player selects each color in each round of the game, and the sum of these probabilities must be unity. On the other hand, if the user selects to play the game manually, he will be given the opportunity to choose his desired color at each round of the game. An snapshot of the game's main user interface window is shown in Fig. 10.

The program provides information about the game even as players are playing it. Once the player types have been defined, pressing the **Play** button will run

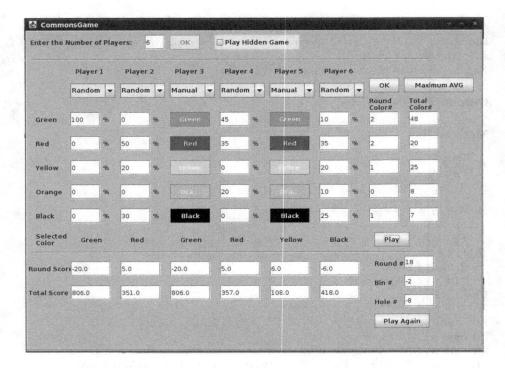

Fig. 10. A screen snapshot of the user interface of the game.

one round of the game. While the color of the card played by random type players is defined based on the given probabilities, the card played by manual players should be specified by the user. After each round of the game the score of the round and the total score up to the current round will be both computed and displayed. Additionally, the number of cards of each color played in the current round, and the total number of cards of each color played up to the current round are also displayed to the user. In order to virtually build the game environment for the users, they have the choice of playing it with information that is hidden or with all the information being visible. If the user opts to play it with the information being hidden, only the number of Green cards played in each round and their total number is visible to the users.

We have also implemented the average maximum score computation algorithm presented in Sect. 3. Once the probability vectors for all the players other than Player 1 is defined, pressing the **Maximum AVG** button would compute the best probability vector based on the proposed algorithm and places the probabilities in the corresponding boxes. The user can then start playing the game using the computed probabilities.

5   Analysis

Our implementation illustrates some of the structural properties of the *Commons Game* and those of the new maximum score computation algorithm. The new algorithm proposed here computes the maximum possible score that Player 1 can earn (on average) by working with the average number of players that play each color in each round. The principle motivation of the new algorithm is to simplify the behavior of the game using its structural properties, which is captured by the two functions defined earlier, namely AVG_G and AVG_R. Since the Green and Red card moves are related to each other in different ways and toward the score computation, they effect the final score inter-dependently. Therefore, in our algorithm which computes the average maximum score, we first compute the joint average score of playing Green and Red cards, denoted by AVG_{GR}, and use this quantity to obtain the ultimate result.

A desirable property of the variation of the indices AVG_G and AVG_R, as a function of P_{G_1}, is its decreasing nature. As we use more Green cards and less Red cards the average score of playing both Green and Red cards will drop because of both the faster decrease in the game states and the increasing nature of the Payoff functions. As shown earlier, these functions are not always decreasing but have some small drops and jumps. Two examples of these functions are shown in Fig. 11.

The following properties are observable in the AVG_G and AVG_R functions:

1. Both functions are almost always decreasing, except at a few drop and jump points. The drops in the AVG_G and AVG_R functions are the result of the changes at the points at which replenishment and state changes occur.
2. Both functions decrease at about the same rate, although the rate of decrease of AVG_G is slightly more than that of the AVG_R function. The difference in the decrease rates is due to the fact that, in all Payoff functions, the score for playing a Green card is more than the corresponding score for playing a Red card. Thus, the degradation to lower states effects the score of Green card players more than that of Red card players.
3. The points at which drops and jumps occur are mostly the same in both functions, and the functions look quite similar. Note that the major reason for these drop and jump changes in AVG_G and AVG_R is the state change which affects the scores of the Green and Red cards at the same junctures.

The drops and jumps in the AVG_G and AVG_R functions also effect the quantity AVG_{GR}. Apart from this, we also record the following properties, noticeable in the AVG_{GR} function:

1. The AVG_{GR} function starts from where the AVG_R starts and ends where the AVG_G ends.
2. If both the function AVG_G and AVG_R were strictly decreasing, AVG_{GR} would have possessed a unique maximum value. Because of the drops and jumps in both AVG_G and AVG_R, the maximum value for AVG_{GR} is not

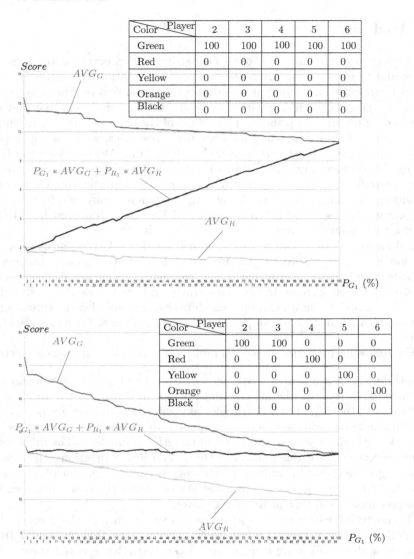

Fig. 11. Typical graphs of the indices AVG_G, AVG_R, and AVG_{GR} as a function of P_{G_1}.

unique. Figures 12, 13, and 14 show examples in which the maximum values for AVG_{GR} occur for two different values of P_{G_1}. Figure 15 depicts an example where the maximum occurs for 3 different values of P_{G_1}, and Fig. 16 is an example showing the case when the maximum occurs for many values of P_{G_1}.

3. The higher the value of the maximum AVG_{GR}, the smoother is the shape of the functions AVG_G, AVG_R, and AVG_{GR}. Thus, the shape of the function would be more like the one that is sought for. This is because of the fact that

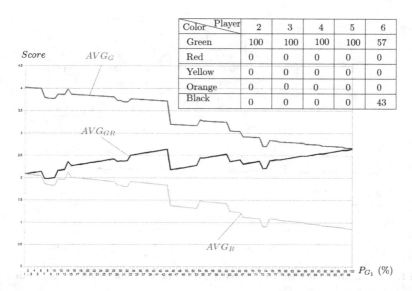

Fig. 12. This figure shows that the maximum value of the function AVG_{GR} is obtained for both $P_{G_1} = 42$ and $P_{G_1} = 100$.

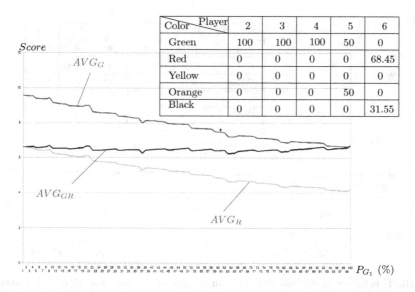

Fig. 13. This figure shows that the maximum value of the function AVG_{GR} is obtained for both $P_{G_1} = 9$ and $P_{G_1} = 100$.

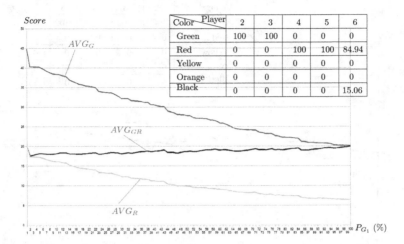

Fig. 14. This figure shows that the maximum of the function AVG_{GR} is obtained for both $P_{G_1} = 0$ and $P_{G_1} = 100$.

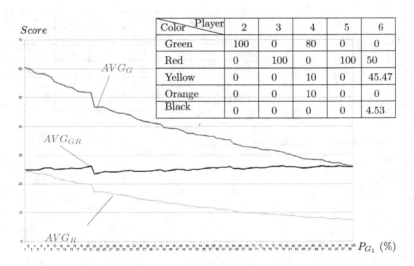

Fig. 15. This figure shows that the maximum value of the function AVG_{GR} is obtained for $P_{G_1} = 21$, $P_{G_1} = 91$ and $P_{G_1} = 96$.

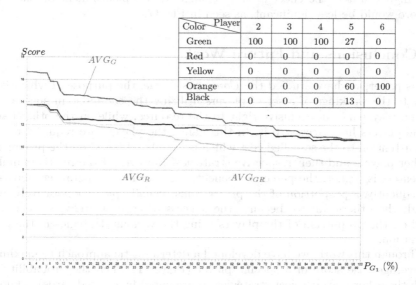

Color \ Player	2	3	4	5	6
Green	100	100	100	27	0
Red	0	0	0	0	0
Yellow	0	0	0	0	0
Orange	0	0	0	60	100
Black	0	0	0	13	0

Fig. 16. This figure shows the case when the maximum value of the function AVG_{GR} is obtained for many values of P_{G_1} between 0 and 4.

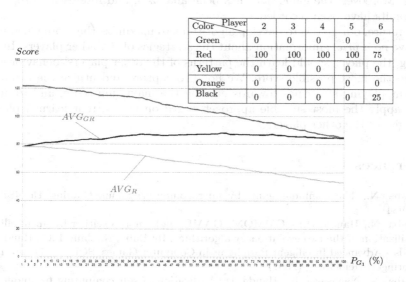

Color \ Player	2	3	4	5	6
Green	0	0	0	0	0
Red	100	100	100	100	75
Yellow	0	0	0	0	0
Orange	0	0	0	0	0
Black	0	0	0	0	25

Fig. 17. An example showing the case that the maximum of AVG_{GR} occurs at higher scores.

in higher states, the effect of state changes and replenishment on the total score would be less significant, as seen in Fig. 17.

6   Conclusions and Future Work

In this paper, we have studied the *Commons Game*, the purpose of which is to simulate the workings of a set of players utilizing the commons in such a way that no player has an exclusive right to the resource, while on the other hand, all the players have access to it. In this game, the players are required to pay more attention to the so-called cost which is calculated based on the proportion of other players and their respective strategies. However, if the relative number of cheaters is higher, the perceived benefit of the others cooperating increases. Consequently, a proportion of the players must usually play cooperatively even though the others fail to, because the success of each strategy is calculated based on the proportion of the players using the various strategies in the total population.

Through this work, we have developed a deterministic approach to maximize the average case score of a specific player (Player 1) when the probability by which the other players select strategies (represented by colored cards) is known *a priori*. We do not claim that our solution attains the local/global optimum. What we endeavor to obtain is a heuristic by which a feasible solution is achieved. We have illustrated the implementation of the algorithm and provided various charts so that the reader can visualize the behavior of the game in various situations. Moreover, the game data has been analyzed, and interesting properties and results have been recorded.

In future, our goal is to develop algorithms to maximize the score when players have no *a priori* information about the strategies of the other players. In this setting, the player should learn the patterns of the other players' behavior so as to gain the most possible score. We hope to capture and utilize the results of different playing strategies towards earning the maximum score, and to adaptively apply the most suitable approach based on the current learned playing strategies of the other players.

References

1. Baba, N.: The commons game by microcomputer. Simul. Gaming **15**, 487–492 (1984)
2. Baba, N., Handa, H.: COMMONS GAME made more exciting by an intelligent utilization of the two evolutionary algorithms. In: Baba, N., Jain, L.C., Handa, H. (eds.) Advanced Intelligent Paradigms in Computer Games. SCI, vol. 71, pp. 1–16. Springer, Heidelberg (2007)
3. Baba, N., Nagasawa, K., Handa, H.: Utilization of soft computing techniques for making environmental games more exciting –toward an effective utilization of the COMMONS GAME. In: Lovrek, I., Howlett, R.J., Jain, L.C. (eds.) KES 2008, Part II. LNCS (LNAI), vol. 5178, pp. 411–417. Springer, Heidelberg (2008)

4. Baba, N., Sakurai, Y., Matsuda, A., Kawachi, T.: Soft computing techniques for making game playing exciting. pp. 132–135 (2005)
5. Baba, N., Sawaragi, Y., Takahashi, H., Nakamura, E., Machida, K.: Two microcomputer based games. Technical report, WP-86-79 (1986)
6. Brown, J.S., Vincent, T.L.: Evolution of cooperation with shared costs and benefits. Proc. Roy. Soc. B: Biol. Sci. **275**(1646), 1985–1994 (2008)
7. Brunovský, P.: The commons game. Ekon. Cas. **55**(8), 811–814 (2007)
8. Challet, D., Marsili, M., Zhang, Y.C.: Modeling market mechanism with minority game. Phys. A: Stat. Mech. Appl. **276**(1), 284–315 (2000)
9. Dawes, R.M.: Social dilemmas. Annu. Rev. Psychol. **31**(1), 169–193 (1980)
10. Dodds, W.K.: The commons, game theory and aspects of human nature that may allow conservation of global resources. Environ. Values **14**(4), 411–425 (2005)
11. Edney, J.J.: The commons problem: alternative perspectives. Am. Psychol. **35**(2), 131–150 (1980)
12. Faysse, N.: Coping with the tragedy of the commons: game structure and design of rules. J. Econ. Surv. **19**(2), 239–261 (2005)
13. Handa, H., Baba, N.: Evolutionary Computations for Designing Game Rules of the Commons Game, pp. 334–339. IEEE, Los Angeles (2007)
14. Hardin, G.: The tragedy of the commons. Science **162**(3859), 1243–1248 (1968)
15. Hardin, G.: Essays on science and society: extensions of "the tragedy of the commons". Science **280**(5364), 682–683 (1998)
16. Hardin, G., Baden, J.: Managing the Commons. Freeman, San Francisco (1977)
17. Kirts, C.A., Tumeo, M.A., Sinz, J.M.: The commons game: its instructional value when used in a natural resources management context. Simul. Gaming **22**(1), 5–18 (1991)
18. Powers, R.B., Duss, R.E., Norton, R.S.: THE COMMONS GAME Manual (1977)

Method of Constructing the Cognitive State for Context-Dependent Utterances in the Form of Conditionals

Grzegorz Skorupa[✉]

Institute of Computer Science,
Wroclaw University of Technology, Wroclaw, Poland
grzegorz.skorupa@pwr.wroc.pl

Abstract. During the last few years we have been working on a theory for the grounding of semiotic symbols in artificial agents. So far the theory allows for the grounding of statements that summarize a speaker's knowledge generally without limiting the time or space related denotations of the utterance. The aim of this work is to propose an exemplary method for the grounding of context-dependent utterances. The implementation of this method should allow for the grounding of conditional statements about (describing) the current (last) environmental observation. To solve this task, a method for constructing a context-dependent model of a cognitive state is proposed. An agent's knowledge is partitioned into a few disjoint subsets. This division is the result of a classification of past environmental observations. The classification process utilizes some known data exploration and feature selection methods which pick the environmental observations that seem relevant to the described situation.

Keywords: Cognitive agent · Language grounding · Conditional sentences · Modal conditionals · Context-dependent utterance

1 Introduction

The grounding theory [9–12,21,22] provides means of grounding[1] a given class of natural language statements within the environmental observations made by a cognitive agent. The statements are encoded as formal modal formulas. Conjunctions, alternatives [9–12] and in particular conditionals [21,22] are considered. Formulas may be extended with auto-epistemic modal operators of possibility (I find it possible that), belief (I believe that) and knowledge (I know that).

Statement grounding within the theory is achieved by the careful construction of a link between the environmental observations gathered by the agent and the natural language statements encoded as formal modal formulas. We say the formula can be grounded only when this link can be constructed. Every grounded

---

[1] The grounding problem itself has been broadly described in [7,18,19,24,25].

© Springer-Verlag Berlin Heidelberg 2014
N.T. Nguyen (Ed.): TCCI XIV 2014, LNCS 8615, pp. 100–119, 2014.
DOI: 10.1007/978-3-662-44509-9_5

formula can (but does not have to) eventually be translated to the respective natural language statement and uttered. It has been proven that the solution proposed in the grounding theory meets a series of common-sense constraints. These constraints are related to the conventional criteria of natural language statement usage. As a result the grounding theory guarantees that a grounded statement can be eventually uttered sustaining its conventional natural language meaning. Such a meaning includes typical denotations and implicatures [1,5] of the natural language statements.

The formal conditions for modal statement grounding are validated against an agent's empirical knowledge in the form of past partial environmental observations. Depending on the type of statement, empirical knowledge is divided between 2 or 4 subsets called grounding sets. Each grounding set contains previous experiences which support or neglect a statement. For example, to ground the statement $Bel(p \wedge q)$ (I believe that p and q) one has to extract four grounding sets, each corresponding to one of four mutually exclusive situations: $p \wedge q$, $p \wedge \neg q$, $\neg p \wedge q$ and $\neg p \wedge \neg q$. The statement can be grounded only when the distribution of empirical knowledge between the grounding sets (their cardinalities) meets the predefined formal criteria [9,11].

The grounding theory, in its raw form [9–12], constructs grounding sets using all the empirical knowledge. Relevance of used knowledge is not evaluated against any context-specific information. In such an approach, the agent is able to describe its knowledge generally, without reference to any specific observational context. When the agent says: $Pos(p)$ (I find it (generally) possible that p.), it simply means that p can hold or not. The agent has observed in past situations where there was p and where there was not p. Based on that, it states that p may hold. There is no prioritization of past observations that are more important in the considered case (observational context). Such an approach is said to be *context-free*, as it results in utterances that generally summarize the agent's knowledge. Such statements are not 'absolutely' context-free as they are built in relation to the agent's subjective knowledge. They are context-free in the sense that the agent does not limit their reference to any particular space or time except the ones resulting from obvious limitations in the agent's knowledge base.

The same utterances may also be used to describe some chosen observation from one particular time point. The form of such an utterance may be the same, but its meaning changes (see [23] for a discussion on that matter). The exemplary formula: $Pos(p)$ (I find it possible that p (now).) changes its denotation as it describes p at a particular time point. Such utterances are said to be *context-dependent* as the time point determines a specific context. Assumed understanding of the context is close to the definition of the context of thought [20], as it matters what the speaker knows or can deduce about the current time point.

As a result the mental representation of the environmental state when speaking generally is different than when speaking about the current time. The empirical knowledge used to ground the statement is chosen with respect to the specific knowledge related strictly to the current time point. That choice of knowledge results from the agent's intentions and point of focus on the current time point.

This forces the agent to use as much information specific for this time point as possible and discard information that is unrelated or even contradictory to its knowledge about the world state at this moment.

In order to contextualize utterances, some simple strategies for filtering empirical knowledge have been proposed. For example, [13] proposes a distance function to pick the most similar observations to the current observation (the observation being described). Work [17] summarizes traffic density based on live-data gathered from various traffic nodes. To summarize traffic for one crossing, only data gathered at that crossing is considered. In that sense the described crossing forms the spatial context of the utterance and limits the data that should be used. Other data is simply not relevant.

The proposed simple solutions [13,17] can be greatly improved. In the grounding theory, the context can be taken into account on the level of the cognitive state model. Some previous environmental observations should be included within the grounding sets as important in the considered context, while others should be excluded as unsuitable to it. There is a need to partition empirical material that is included in the grounding of statements. To achieve this, the agent needs to be able to construct its cognitive state with respect to the current observation. Such a cognitive state should encode the agent's subjective knowledge about the current situation. This model has to be constructed autonomously and use only the agent's knowledge (i.e. previous environmental observations). This in turn requires the agent to be able to reason and learn from empirical knowledge. The agent should search for various patterns in the knowledge. Learned patterns should determine the contents of the grounding sets.

The aim of this paper is to provide an exemplary method for constructing the cognitive state model. The cognitive state model is constructed in the context of the last observation and is based on previous empirical observations. To construct the cognitive state model, the agent is equipped with some fundamental reasoning and data analysis mechanisms. Firstly the agent learns from the empirical knowledge by finding associative rules among it. Secondly the agent fills the cognitive state model with past observations directly related to the learned rules in the context of the current observation. The proposed method consists of two strategies. Firstly the agent tries to crisply determine as much as possible about the current observation. Secondly, if the first approach does not provide desirable results, the agent searches for empirical material most similar to the current observation.

In the next section the grounding theory is briefly explained. In Sect. 3 a motivational example is presented. Section 4 provides necessary data definitions and formally defines the task of constructing the cognitive state according to the context. Within Sects. 5 and 6 the exemplary method which constructs the cognitive state is defined and described. Section 7 provides a computational example.

2   A Short Introduction to the Grounding Theory

The symbol grounding problem [7,18,19,24,25] is about the need for a connection between an environment and the symbols (for example statements) describing it. To ground a symbol is to find its relation to environmental observations.

Such a relation has to satisfy postulates that in turn result from an assumed meaning (semantics) of the symbol.

The grounding theory [9,10,12,17,21,22] addresses the symbol grounding problem for a predefined class of modal formulas representing natural language statements. Exemplary considered statements and formulas are 'I find it possible that p' ($Pos(p)$), 'I believe p or not q' ($Bel(p \vee \neg q)$), 'I know not p and q' ($Know(\neg p \wedge q)$). The semantics of formulas are defined with respect to an agent's knowledge[2]. Furthermore, the semantics are assumed to be consistent with the conventional meaning of the associated natural language statements[3]. Such an approach, for example, requires that the agent does not know that p holds when it says p is possible.

The grounding theory consists of a series of steps that allow for grounding modal formulas. Firstly an empirical knowledge base is defined. It holds observations from the current and past time points. Secondly a cognitive state is presented. This cognitive state is meant to partition the observations from the empirical knowledge base with respect to the agent's focus of attention. Thirdly grounding conditions are formally encoded and defined in the form of epistemic satisfaction relations. Each formula type has its own definition of the epistemic relation. Only when this relation holds can the formula be grounded. The epistemic relation is validated against the cognitive state.

The further paragraphs present the crucial components of the grounding theory.

2.1   The Empirical Knowledge Base

An agent's empirical knowledge consists of a series of temporarily ordered environmental observations. The agent is unable to observe the whole environment, hence the observations contain only partial information about the state of the environment. An agent's empirical knowledge contains perceptions of physical environmental properties. We assume a simple model of knowledge where each observation consists of binary properties that may hold, not hold or be unknown.

Definition 1. *Let the agent's empirical knowledge base be defined as a tuple:*
$TB = \langle P, T, V, R \rangle$, *where:*

$$
\begin{aligned}
&\mathcal{P} = \{p_1, p_2, ..., p_K\} && \text{is a set of attributes} \\
&T = \{1, 2, ..., N\} && \text{is a set of time points} \\
&V = \{-1, 0, 1\} && \text{is a set of attribute values} \\
&R : T \times \mathcal{P} \to V && \text{is a relation assigning values} \\
& && \text{to attributes at different time points}
\end{aligned}
$$

The relation R defines the observed values of attributes at particular time points. Let $t \in T$ and $p \in P$. Attribute values V have the following interpretation:

---

[2] Semantics differ from classical approaches based on truth tables. They are defined according to the agent's partial knowledge, not to the physical (often unknown) state of the world.

[3] For details on semantics please refer to the grounding theory.

- $R(t, p) = 1$ - attribute p was observed to hold in t (shortly: p holds).
- $R(t, p) = -1$ - attribute p was observed NOT to hold in t (shortly: $\neg p$).
- $R(t, p) = 0$ - attribute p is unknown in observation t (was not observed).

The *observation* at time point t shall be denoted by a vector:

$$R(t) = \langle R(t, p_1), R(t, p_2), ..., R(t, p_K) \rangle$$

Observation $R(t)$ contains all data observed at time point t. The empirical knowledge base can also be represented as a series of observations: $R(1), R(2), ..., R(N)$, where $R(N)$ is the current observation.

2.2 The Cognitive State Model

The cognitive state model (Definition 2) represents the state of an agent's mind at some time point. The model consists of previous time points that are divided between two layers: conscious (or working memory) and unconscious (or permanent memory). One can partition past observations according to the time points from sets $\overline{CS}$ and $\underline{CS}$. The fundamental partition is based on time points where the whole observation is classified as one of the layers. In the grounding theory, empirical knowledge is later divided again according to observed attributes. In such a way grounding sets are formed. The grounding sets form models for mental representations [16].

Definition 2. *An agent's cognitive state CS is defined as a partition $CS = \overline{CS} \cup \underline{CS}$, being a subset of set T such that*

$$CS = \overline{CS} \cup \underline{CS} \subseteq T \text{ and } \overline{CS} \cap \underline{CS} = \emptyset$$

Sets $\overline{CS}$ and $\underline{CS}$ are called the conscious and unconscious layers of the cognitive state respectively.

Intuitively the conscious layer represents past observations that are crucial in the reasoning process performed by the agent. For example, it includes the observations that are most similar to the current observation and contain knowledge on the attributes the agent is interested in. The unconscious layer represents observations that are not so important but construct an influential background for the agent's reasoning. For example, it includes the observations where some of the interesting attributes were known[4]. The model of the cognitive state can be aligned with fundamental assumptions from the models of the mind from non-technical literature [3, 4, 15].

The cognitive state model also has many similarities to mental models in the theory of mental models and possibilities [8] from Johnson. He proposed that some mental models should be divided into two types: explicit and implicit.

---

[4] For more information on the cognitive state model and its two layer architecture please refer to the grounding theory.

His explicit models can be considered as residing in the conscious area and implicit models reside in the unconscious area.

The Definition 2 is a bit different from the one in the grounding theory. It has been changed specifically for the purpose of this paper. The grounding theory provides a definition where $\overline{CS} \cup \underline{CS} = T$. Such an approach results in using all the empirical knowledge (either consciously or unconsciously) to ground a statement. After a slight change ($CS = \overline{CS} \cup \underline{CS} \subseteq T$) some of the knowledge can be omitted in the grounding process. Of course it is not yet said which part of knowledge can be omitted, as choosing it is the core aspect of this paper. Intuitively knowledge unsuitable for the analysis of the current observation should be omitted. Suppose the agent is considering only situations where p holds. In such a case all the observations where p does not hold should be neither in $\overline{CS}$, nor in $\underline{CS}$.

Finally the cognitive state is verified against the formal grounding constraints. If the cognitive state meets them, a statement can be grounded.

2.3 Formulas Representing Conditional Statements

This paper deals only with conditional statements which are represented by the formulas:

- $\phi \rightarrow M(\psi)$
- $M(\phi \rightarrow \psi)$

where $\phi \in \{p, \neg p\}$, $\psi \in \{q, \neg q\}$ and $M \in \{Pos, Bel, Know\}$.

The formulas have been assigned intuitive semantics:

- If ϕ then I find it possible / I believe / I know, that ψ.
- I find it possible / I believe / I know, that if ϕ then ψ.

The semantics of the formulas are defined with respect to the speaker (the agent). Such semantics impose some constraints resulting from rational language usage patterns. For example one of such constraints requires the agent not to know the state of the antecedent ϕ as otherwise there is no need to use a conditional 'If ϕ ...' at all[5].

For example: $p \rightarrow Bel(\neg q)$ means: 'If p, then I believe, that not q'. The statement should be read literally as a natural language indicative conditional used to express the agent's knowledge. Similarly the modal operator of belief 'Bel' has the conventional natural language meaning of belief. One should not treat these formulas as any form of formal implication in logic.

3 Motivational Example

The meaning of a statement depends on when it is uttered and why it is uttered. A statement 'If ϕ then I believe ψ' may generally summarize the speaker's

---

[5] Please refer to [5, 21, 22] for more information on this subject. Here we count for the reader's intuitive understanding of the conventional meaning.

knowledge or only refer to the current observation (speak about it, describe it). The listener decides how to interpret the same statement depending on the conversational context. The conversational context itself is not considered within this paper. The knowledge used to ground the statement depends on the chosen time bounds. When one wishes to obtain a general summary then all of the past observations (empirical knowledge) should be equally considered and the cognitive state should be set to: $CS = \overline{CS} = T$, $\underline{CS} = \emptyset$. In the second case only relevant observations should be considered, so CS is some proper subset of T. Obviously it is not trivial to decide which observations are relevant. The grounding theory does not provide any method for partitioning empirical knowledge, it simply acknowledges the existence of such a partition.

Suppose that an agent's knowledge contains only observations, such that when there was p_1 and p_2 there also was q. Attributes p_1, p_2 and q have sometimes held and sometimes they have not held. Always when p_1 and p_2 held, q also held. From such knowledge the agent can learn that p_1 and p_2 imply q.

When speaking generally (summarizing all the knowledge), the agent may say: 'If p_1 and p_2, then q', but should not say: 'If p_1, then q'. It should not use the second statement because p_1 alone does not guarantee q to hold.

Now consider a situation where the agent is saying something about the current observation. Assume that the agent has currently observed p_1 but was unable to observe p_2 and q. In such a situation the statement 'If p_1 and p_2, then q' is still valid as a material implication but is no longer a reasonable answer[6]. The agent already knows that p_1 currently holds, so it is pointless to say 'If (currently) p_1 ...'. On the other hand one is expecting the utterance 'If p_2, then q'. When p_1 is known to hold, p_2 is the only missing ingredient for q to hold, so the expected utterance seems reasonable according to the agent's knowledge. When it comes to statement grounding, the chosen context (the current situation), should change the cognitive state. The agent still has to refer to past observations but now only the ones where p_1 holds are relevant.

As a second example let us assume the agent has observed p_1 and p_2 but was unable to observe q. In such a situation no indicative conditional statement about q is suitable. The agent should simply deduce q and say that it knows q holds although it has not been directly observed.

These examples show that the current observation, as a set of observed attributes, defines the context and should influence the choice of observations taking part in the statement grounding process. The current observation is not the only element of the context. Another element is related to the agent's focus of attention. The choice of past observations also depends on the attributes that the agent is interested in. In the examples above, the observation of p_1 played an important role in the choice of the content of the cognitive state. The observation of p_1 was important because it influenced q. Attribute q was dependent on p_1 because empirical knowledge provided evidence for that. One can think of some other attribute p_3 that is independent of p_1 (empirical knowledge does not

---

[6] The utterance is unreasonable because it conventionally implies that the speaker does not know whether p_1 holds or not [21, 22].

suggest any correlation between p_1 and p_3). For p_3 it is irrelevant if p_1 holds or not. The fact that the agent is interested in q, not p_3, has an impact on the contents of the cognitive state. In conclusion, the agent's focus of attention (what attributes it is currently interested in) plays an important role.

From this simple example one can conclude that the choice of an utterance highly relies on the current observation and the agent's focus of attention. It is believed that in the grounding theory context-dependent behavior can be successfully achieved by the proper limitation of the empirical knowledge taking part in the statement grounding process. This limitation should directly depend on the current observation (what was observed (not) to hold) and the agent's focus of attention (what it is currently interested in).

At the same time the distribution of the empirical knowledge chosen for the cognitive state highly depends on the agent's past empirical knowledge (all of it). This happens because the same empirical knowledge provides evidence of what is important for the considered context. To choose what is important, the agent is required to be equipped with some cognitive abilities. Namely the agent must be able to learn from the data in order to construct higher level, more general knowledge. The analysis of the empirical knowledge may result in a discovery of various correlations, associative rules, classifications, trends etc. The discovered knowledge should later be used to choose observations for the cognitive state. The choice of particular learning and data analysis methods relies on the environment model. Intuitively the better suited methods within the agent, the more appropriate empirical material shall be chosen.

The aim is to implement the ability to construct the context-dependent cognitive state within the agent. As a result the agent should be able to choose a reasonable utterance about the current observation.

4   The Task Definition

4.1   Additional Notation

Before the task is defined some additional notation is needed:

Definition 3. *Let $\overline{R} : T \times \mathcal{P} \rightarrow V$ denote an extended relation assigning attribute values to observations such that:*

$$\forall t \in T, p \in \mathcal{P} : R(t, p) \neq 0 \rightarrow \overline{R}(t, p) = R(t, p)$$

The extended relation $\overline{R}$ is equivalent to relation R on all known attribute values. The extended relation may have some additional attribute values fixed as known. In the presented approach the extended relation is used to hold predictions of unobserved attribute values.

Definition 4. *Let $c(p, v)$ where $p \in \mathcal{P}$ and $v \in V$ be a condition denoting that the attribute p takes the value v. Let $\mathcal{C}$ be a set of all such conditions. Let $\mathcal{C}_k \subset \mathcal{C}$ be a set of all conditions where $v \in \{-1, 1\}$.*

A condition presents a requirement, that some observations may meet or not. The set $\mathcal{C}$ contains all such conditions. The set $\mathcal{C}_k$ holds all conditions where we require the property to be known ($v \neq 0$).

Definition 5. *Let an observation t be informative with respect to property $p \in \mathcal{P}$ iff*

$$R(t, p) \neq 0$$

Let $t \in T$ be informative with respect to set $P \subseteq \mathcal{P}$ iff it is informative with respect to every property $p \in P$.

An observation t is *informative* with respect to some property p if the agent has observed it. One can find a set of all observations within the agent's knowledge base that are informative with respect to p:

Definition 6. *Let $Tk(p)$ denote a set of all observations informative with respect to p:*

$$Tk(p) = \{t \in T : R(t, p) \neq 0\}, \quad p \in \mathcal{P}$$

and let $Tk(P)$ denote a set of all observations informative with respect to all properties from $P \subseteq \mathcal{P}$

$$Tk(P) = \bigcap_{p \in P} T_k(p), \quad P \subseteq \mathcal{P}$$

Definition 7. *Let the observation t be consistent with a condition $c(p, v)$ iff*

$$R(t, p) = v$$

Let the observation t be consistent with a set of conditions $C \subseteq \mathcal{C}$ iff it is consistent with every condition $c \in C$.

An observation t is *consistent* with some condition $c(p, v)$, if property p holds (for $v = 1$), does not hold (for $v = -1$) or is unknown (for $v = 0$). One can find a set of all observations within the agent's knowledge base that are consistent with respect to c:

Definition 8. *Let $Tv(c(p, v))$ denote a set of all observations consistent with a condition $c(p, v)$.*

$$Tv(c(p, v)) = \{t \in T : R(t, p) = v\}$$

and let $Tv(C)$ denote a set of all observations consistent with respect to a set $C \subset \mathcal{C}$ of conditions.

$$Tv(C) = \bigcap_{c \in C} Tv(c), \quad C \subseteq \mathcal{C}$$

4.2   Input and Desired Output Data

The aim is to model the ability to choose a conditional statement which conventionally describes the current observation from the agent's perspective. It is assumed that the conditional statement should contain p as the antecedent and q as the consequent. The input data consists of:

Input data

- the empirical knowledge base TB of previous observations,
- the current observation at time point N (the context),
- two attributes p and q considered by the agent (the context, the agent's focus of attention).

The current observation and attributes $p, q \in P$ form the only considered context. To choose conditional statements suitable to this context, the contents of the cognitive state have to be chosen so that they contain only relevant observations.

The intermediate aim is to fix sets $\overline{CS}, \underline{CS}$ (construct the cognitive state) so that they are suited to the current observation N, p and q. These sets should contain empirical knowledge relevant to the assumed context. Section 4.3 defines how to understand relevant empirical knowledge.

Later, the obtained cognitive state is passed to methods of the grounding theory [21, 22] in order to decide which conditional statements can be grounded and eventually uttered in the assumed context.

Desired output data: A subset of a set of all possible modal conditional formulas holding only statements that can be grounded in the context[7]. In layman's terms: all conditional statements that the agent can use to describe its knowledge about p and q at the current moment.

4.3   Intuitive Postulates

Observations can be divided between sets $\overline{CS}$ and $\underline{CS}$ in many ways, meaning that there are many possible cognitive states. The aim is to carefully choose the contents of $\overline{CS}$ and $\underline{CS}$. The contents should exemplify the agent's knowledge on p and q (being the considered antecedent and consequent respectively). This knowledge should be chosen in accordance to the assumed context. As mentioned in the motivational example, the agent must be able to learn and reason, in order to choose a reasonable partition. The better the learning and reasoning algorithms, the better the results. The agent should be able to learn from data at least as effectively as humans do. Unfortunately we are unable to implement all of the cognitive abilities of humans. That is why only an exemplary solution is proposed. This solution assumes the agent has two fundamental abilities. Firstly the agent can find 100 % confidence associative rules and reason using them. Secondly the agent can measure the similarity of past observations to the current observation. For such an ability the cognitive state should meet the following intuitive postulates:

---

[7] According to the grounding theory.

The agent should consider the current observation:

1. If the antecedent p is known $(R(N,p) \neq 0)$ then the cognitive state should not contain past observations contradictory to it. (If the agent knows that $R(N,p) = 1$ / $R(N,p) = -1$, it should only consider past observations where p holds / does not hold respectively).
2. Similarly, if the consequent q is known $(R(N,q) \neq 0)$, then the cognitive state should not contain past observations contradictory to it.

Postulates 1 and 2 require the agent to reason in accordance to the current observation. If some of the considered attributes have been observed directly, the agent should not consider observations which are contradictory in that aspect. Considering such observations could lead to purely hypothetical reasoning - the reasoning of what p or q would be if it were not as it had been observed.

The postulates 1 and 2 refer to situations where p or q is directly observed. When it is not observed the agent should try to reason from the learned rules to determine as much as possible about the current observation. Each of such rules is learned from empirical knowledge. Some of the observations in past empirical knowledge provide information about the rule. For example, a rule $p_1, p_2 \rightarrow p_3$ is learned from all past observations where the three attributes were known. Some of such observations are consistent with the current observation (with respect to attributes in the rule). These observations form the source of knowledge that can be used to crisply determine p or q.

The agent should use the learned rules to reason about the current observation:

3. If some rule allows for deductions on p or q, then the cognitive state should contain observations that the rule was learned from.

Postulate 3, formulated above, requires the agent to use learned rules in the choice of past observations. If some rule allows for deductions on p or q the agent should consider it. The empirical knowledge the rule is based on should be included in the cognitive state. In other words: the observations related to the rule provide a justification for the deduction of p or q.

The agent may fail to deduce the value of p or q. Such a situation can happen when learned rules do not allow for a crisp deduction. In such a case the agent must fix the cognitive state using a different strategy. This strategy should meet postulate 4.

4. If some properties influence p or q (according to the agent), then the agent should favor the past experiences most similar to the current observation with respect to those properties.

These postulates have been chosen in accordance to previously assumed and limited cognitive (learning and reasoning) abilities of the agent. These postulates define the common-sense criteria of choosing the past observations that should go into conscious and unconscious areas. It is not claimed the method will work efficiently and correctly in any complex environment and with any empirical knowledge characteristics. The aim is to provide an *exemplary* solution to this very complex and general problem.

5 Pre-existing Methods Used Within the Proposed Solution

5.1 The Idea of Jumping Emerging Patterns

We are given a set of transactions D where each transaction d is a subset of a given set of items $\mathcal{I} = \{i_1, i_2, ..., i_n\}$. The transactions are divided into two partitions: D_1 and D_2 with respect to some binary decision attribute.

The idea of Jumping Emerging Patterns [2,14] can be used to quickly find all item-sets $I \subseteq \mathcal{I}$ existing in D_1 but not in D_2. Each such item-set I may be used to classify transaction d. If $I \subseteq d$, then d belongs to D_1 and does not belong to D_2.

From all found item-sets, one can choose the ones that are minimal. An item-set is minimal if removing any of the items does not guarantee the correct classification of known transactions to D_1.

Furthermore, found minimal item-sets may be used to construct associative rules, where items from item-sets construct an antecedent and D_1 is in the consequent ($I \Rightarrow D_1$). Each such associative rule has 100 % confidence and non-zero support in D. When using consecutive items $i \in \mathcal{I}$, one can find all associative rules of the form: $I \Rightarrow i$ ($I \subset \mathcal{I}$ and $i \in \mathcal{I} \setminus I$), where the attribute i is a decision.

MDB-LLborder [2,14] is a fast algorithm designed to find all JEPs in a transaction base $D = D_1 \cup D_2$. We use this algorithm to find rules with 100 % confidence and non-zero support of the form: $X \Rightarrow c$ where $c = c(p, v) \in C_k$, $X \subset C_k \setminus \{c\}$. When it comes to 100 % confidence and non-zero support rules, MDB-LLborder is much faster than the A-priori algorithm.

The definitions of algorithm and input data have been modified to suit the needs of this paper. Instead of transactions there are observations. Each observation, instead of items, is represented by a set of conditions $X \subset C_k$ (please notice that we do not add conditions related to lack of knowledge). An algorithm is run multiple times for every condition $c \in C_k$ as a decision to find rules of the form $X \Rightarrow c$. When dealing with a condition $c(p, v)$, observations where the value of p is unknown (where $R(t, p) = 0$) are ignored.

Unfortunately most found rules using MDB-LLborder are a result of data overfitting. They have a very low support and have happened simply by chance. To conquer the overfitting problem, minimal support S_{min} for found rules is required[8]. From all found rules only the ones with at least a support of S_{min} observations shall be later used.

---

[8] The support is understood here as the amount of observations, not a percentage value. The choice of S_{min} value is a separate matter outside the scope of this paper.

5.2   Feature Selection

A feature selection problem is the problem of finding relevant features $P \subseteq \mathcal{P}$ useful in the context of some classification. Often features are selected using statistical measures such as correlation. The most common usage of feature selection is for the reduction of the dimensionality of input data. This data is usually later passed to a classification algorithm.

Feature selection is utilized to find attributes influencing one fixed attribute q (the consequent). Later these attributes are used to construct an attribute-dependent similarity measure. The idea is to find past observations most similar to the current observation, but to do it in the context of predicting q.

Within the method the greedy algorithm introduced in [6] is used (one can choose different algorithms). Given some attribute q, the algorithm finds relevant attributes from $\mathcal{P} \setminus \{q\}$ that influence the value of q.

5.3   The Distance that Depends on Attributes

A distance function expresses the similarity between the current observation and previous observations. The distance is dependent on some non-empty subset of properties $P \subseteq \mathcal{P}$. Distance is defined as:

$$D_P(t) = \frac{\sum_{p \in P} (\overline{R}(N, p) - R(t, p))^2}{4 \cdot card(P)} \tag{1}$$

Distance $D_P(t)$ is a normalized metric which takes values from interval $[0, 1]$. If distance equals 0, all the attributes within P have the same values (they both hold, do not hold or are unknown) within $\overline{R}(N, p)$ and observation for time point t. If it is equal to 1 all the attributes within P have contradictory values.

If one chooses $P = \mathcal{P}$, distance is measured using all properties (general distance). If one chooses only one property $P = \{p_i\}$, where $p_i \in \mathcal{P}$, distance is measured between the values of only this property.

The distance function shall be used to find the most similar past observations in the context of the current observation and interesting property q. Set P shall be chosen to hold important attributes being a result of the feature selection algorithm.

6   Proposed Method

The method of constructing the cognitive state consists of two separate strategies. Firstly the agent tries to find 'crisp' associative rules within the empirical knowledge base. Those rules are used as material implications to perform 'crisp' reasoning and hopefully determine p or q.

The second strategy is applied if the first one fails. In such a case the agent uses the feature selection algorithm to search for attributes influencing q. Those attributes are later used in the relative distance function to find the most similar past observations that are in turn put into the cognitive state.

Finally the cognitive state is verified according to the epistemic relations of the grounding theory. This results in the grounding of conditional formulas which describe the current observation.

6.1 Strategy 1

Step 1 (discover associative rules): For every condition $c(p_i, v) \in C_k$ find all minimal sets of conditions $X \subseteq C_k \setminus \{c(p_i, v)\}$ such that:

- $card(Tv(X) \cap Tv(c(p_i, v))) \geq S_{min}$ (minimal support)
- $Tv(X) \cap Tk(p_i) \subseteq Tv(c)$ (100 % confidence).

To find all such sets one can use a modified version of the MDB-LLborder algorithm [2,14]. As a result one obtains a set of rules Rs of the form: $X \Rightarrow c$. These rules form the discovered crisp knowledge about the environment.

Step 2 (use rules to determine attribute values): The learned rules Rs are treated as logical implications describing the environment. The implications are used to reason and determine as many attribute values as possible.

Initially set $\overline{R} := R$. Compare found rules Rs against $\overline{R}(N)$.

For every rule $X \Rightarrow c(p_i, v)$, such that: $\overline{R}(N)$ is consistent with X and $\overline{R}(N, p_i) = 0$, set $\overline{R}(N, p_i) = v$. Repeat this procedure until no rules can be used to further change $\overline{R}(N)$. As a result one obtains $\overline{R}(N)$ hopefully having more attribute values determined than $R(N)$.

Step 3 (has p or q been determined?): Run this step only if p or q is known in $\overline{R}(N)$.[9]

If p or q is known in $R(N)$ (meaning it has been observed directly):

  Fix $\overline{CS} = \{N\}$ and $\underline{CS} = \emptyset$.

Otherwise, if q is known:

  Find a rule from step 2 that determined q ($X \Rightarrow c(q, v)$).

Otherwise:

  Find a rule from step 2 that determined p ($X \Rightarrow c(p, v)$).

Fix the conscious set to $\overline{CS} = Tv(X)$. Fix the unconscious set to $\underline{CS} = \emptyset$.

Return the obtained cognitive state and finish. In this case the cognitive state either simply consists of the current observation (when the attributes have been observed directly) or it contains observations consistent with the antecedent within the rule.

Step 4 (assuming p was known, search for rules that determine q): Search set Rs for rules such, that all three conditions are met:

- $X \rightarrow c(q, v)$ (q in the consequent).
- $c(p, 1) \in X$ or $c(p, -1) \in X$ (there is p in the antecedent).
- $\forall c(p_i, v) \in X \setminus \{c(p, 1), c(p, -1)\} : \overline{R}(N, p_i) = v$ (all other properties are known and consistent with the current observation).

---

[9] In this case, according to the grounding theory, no epistemic relation for a conditional statement shall be met. The conditional statement can not be grounded and hence uttered, because it is required by the grounding theory that neither the antecedent, nor the consequent q is known.

For every found rule, take past observations: $Tv(X \setminus \{c(p, 1), c(p, -1)\})$. These observations are directly related to the considered rule and the current observation. The observations form the source of the discovered knowledge on p and q. Add found observations to the conscious area of the cognitive state: $\overline{CS} = Tv(X \setminus \{c(p, 1), c(p, -1)\})$. Fix the unconscious set to $\underline{CS} = \emptyset$.

As a result of strategy 1, one obtains the cognitive state consisting of observations providing crisp knowledge on q (or p). Either one of the attributes has been determined or a rule joining p and q has been found. If no crisp knowledge (rules) can be found, both conscious and unconscious sets remain empty.

6.2   Strategy 2

If after running strategy 1: $\overline{CS} = \emptyset$ and $\underline{CS} = \emptyset$, the agent was unable to find any crisp dependencies on p and q. Strategy 1 failed to provide useful results. In such a case the agent proceeds to step 5 and applies a different strategy to further analyze the current observation.

Step 5 (discover important attributes): Find attributes influencing q. Put found attributes to set Rel (Rel is never an empty set). The attributes are discovered using the feature selection algorithm.

Step 6 (calculate relative distance): For every observation $t \in T$ calculate the distance $D_{Rel}(t)$. Previously found attributes Rel as used to measure distance. The distance considers only important attributes in the context of q.

Step 7 (construct the cognitive state): Put all observations such that $D_{Rel}(t) \leqslant d_{cMax}$ into $\overline{CS}$. Put all observations such that $d_{cMax} < D_{Rel}(t) \leqslant d_{sMax}$ into $\underline{CS}$.

Distance thresholds d_{cMax} and d_{sMax} are fixed so that: $0 \leqslant d_{cMax} < d_{sMax} \leqslant 1$. The greater their values, the more observations shall be included within the cognitive state.

7   Computational Example

To test the proposed method, randomly generated data was used. The data consisted of 5 attributes and 500 observations. Data was generated in accordance with conditional probabilities provided by Eq. 2.

$$
\begin{aligned}
&P(p_2) = 0.5 \quad P(p_1|\neg p_2) = 1, \; P(p_1|p_2) = 0.5 \\
&P(p_4) = 0.3 \quad P(p_3|p_1 \wedge p_4) = 0.8, \; P(p_3|\neg p_1 \vee \neg p_4) = 0.2 \\
&\qquad\qquad P(p_5|p_1 \wedge p_4) = 1, \; P(p_5|\neg p_1 \vee \neg p_4) = 0.5
\end{aligned} \tag{2}
$$

Attributes p_2 and p_4 are independent. Other attributes directly or indirectly depend on p_2 or p_4. Value $\neg p_2$ implies p_1. Values p_1 and p_4 imply p_5. Attribute p_3 strongly relies on p_1 and p_4.

Data was randomly masked so that about 20 % of the values were unknown to the agent. Please notice the data is missing at random and the observations are independent between time points. This case ensures that there are no dependencies between the attributes outside the scope of the agent's learning abilities. The agent can learn everything there is to learn about the data.

Distance thresholds were set to $d_{cMax} = 0.25$ and $d_{sMax} = 0.5$. The last observation (for $t = 500$) was chosen as the current observation. This observation and a few exemplary past observations are given in Table 1. Within the last observation, the agent observed that not p_2 ($p_2 = -1$). All other attributes were not observed.

Table 1. Data used for empirical knowledge consisting of 500 observations. Only 7 of them are shown in the table. First row ($t = 500$) contains the current observation.

t	p_1	p_2	p_3	p_4	p_5
500	0	−1	0	0	0
499	1	1	−1	−1	1
498	0	1	0	−1	1
...		...			
4	−1	1	1	−1	−1
3	1	−1	0	1	1
2	1	0	0	1	1
1	0	0	1	1	1

Table 2. Learned 100 % confidence rules

R1	$p_2 = -1 \Rightarrow p_1 = 1$
R2	$p_1 = 1 \wedge p_4 = 1 \Rightarrow p_5 = 1$
R3	$p_2 = -1 \wedge p_4 = 1 \Rightarrow p_5 = 1$
R4	$p_4 = 1 \wedge p_5 = -1 \Rightarrow p_1 = -1$
R5	$p_1 = -1 \Rightarrow p_2 = 1$
R6	$p_4 = 1 \wedge p_5 = -1 \Rightarrow p_2 = 1$
R7	$p_1 = 1 \wedge p_5 = -1 \Rightarrow p_4 = -1$
R8	$p_2 = -1 \wedge p_5 = -1 \Rightarrow p_4 = -1$

The work-flow of the method can be described as follows:

In step 1 the agent utilizes the JEP idea to find the associative rules with 100 % confidence and enough support. The found rules are presented in Table 2. The found rules match the ones that were used to construct artificial random data.

In step 2, from the rule R1 (see Table 2) the agent concludes that $p_1 = 1$ in observation 500. The agent sets the observation $\overline{R}(500, p_1) = 1$:

$$\overline{R}(500, p_1) = 1, \ \overline{R}(500, p_2) = -1, \ \overline{R}(500, p_3) = 0, \ \overline{R}(500, p_4) = 0, \ \overline{R}(500, p_5) = 0$$

There are no further rules to use, because the attributes in the antecedent are either unknown within $\overline{R}$ or contradictory to it.

Steps 1 and 2 are independent of the agent's focus of attention but it must be fixed in the further steps. Assume the agent focuses on p_4 and p_5 being the candidates for the antecedent and the consequent of a conditional formula. These attributes are put to the context (the method's input). The agent does not know the values of p_4 and p_5, so it skips step 3. In step 4 the agent once more searches through the rules to find any relations concerning p_4 and p_5. It searches for rules such that p_5 is in the rule's consequent and p_4 is within the rule's antecedent. All other conditions must be known in $\overline{R}(500)$ and consistent with it. Rules R2 and R3 meet these conditions.

From R2 the agent knows that p_1 and p_4 determine p_5. Attribute p_1 is already known to hold. The agent searches for previous observations such that $p_1 = 1$ and puts them into the conscious area of the cognitive state. These observations form the source of knowledge on the considered rule R1 with respect to the current observation. Similarly for R3 the agent searches for previous observations such that $p2 = -1$ and puts them into the conscious area of the cognitive state.

As a result the conscious area of the cognitive state consists of a total of 221 observations (out of a possible 500). The cardinalities related to 4 mutually exclusive cases concerning p_4 and p_5 are as follows:

- 51 observations where $p4 = 1$ and $p5 = 1$,
- 0 observations where $p4 = 1$ and $p5 = -1$,
- 87 observations where $p4 = -1$ and $p5 = 1$,
- 83 observations where $p4 = -1$ and $p5 = -1$.

There are no observations such that $p4 = 1$ and $p5 = -1$ in the constructed cognitive state. Such observations (a total of 14) exist in empirical knowledge base TB. These observations have been excluded from the agent's reasoning as inapplicable to the current context.

The agent does not apply strategy 2 because the strategy 1 has succeeded. For such a cognitive state (utilizing the grounding theory [21, 22]) the agent may utter:

1. $p_4 \rightarrow Know(p_5)$: "If p_4, then I know, that p_5" (now).
2. $Know(p_4 \rightarrow p_5)$: "I know, that if p_4, then p_5" (now).
3. $\neg p_4 \rightarrow Pos(\neg p_5)$: "If not p_4, then I find it possible, that not p_5" (now).

This answer is about the current observation and intuitively consistent with it. The agent does not summarize the whole knowledge base, only the current situation (based on past observations). The direct observation of $p_2 = -1$ has had an important impact on the reasoning. This reasoning is based on the learned rules R1, R2 and R3.

For a second example let the agent focus on attributes p_4 and p_3. The focus of attention is changed to p_4 and p_3 respectively. The conditional probabilities used to generate data on p_3 and p_4 were: $P(p_3|p_4 \wedge p_1) = 0.8$ and $P(p_3|\neg p_4 \vee \neg p_1) = 0.2$. This implies a strong relation between p_1, p_4 and p_3. When both p_1 and p_4 hold, p_3 has a much greater chance of holding.

Steps 1 and 2 stay unchanged as they are independent from the focus of attention. At $t = 500$ the agent knows neither p_3, nor p_4. The found rules stay the same (Table 2). Again, the agent discovers $p_1 = 1$ from rule R1. As a result the agent knows that p_1 holds and p_2 does not hold.

Because there are no rules with p_3, strategy 1 fails. The agent switches to strategy 2. In step 5 the agent uses the feature selection algorithm, which returns p_2 as the only property influencing p_3. Actually we were expecting p_1 and p_4, so at first glance p_2 does not seem a valid result. On the other hand both p_1 and p_4 rely on p_2 (see rules R1, R5 for p_1 and rules R3 and R6 for p_4). So p_2 may be not such a bad result after all.

Later the agent uses the distance function (see Eq. 1) and chooses the most similar past observations to the conscious and the unconscious areas of the cognitive state. Because p_2 has been chosen as the property influencing p_3, past observations where $p_2 = -1$ are selected as the most similar to the current one. Indirectly the agent favors p_1 because of rule R1. As a result of strategy 2 the cognitive state consists of:

- 32 observations where $p4 = 1$ and $p3 = 1$,
- 10 observations where $p4 = 1$ and $p3 = -1$,
- 30 observations where $p4 = -1$ and $p3 = 1$,
- 118 observations where $p4 = -1$ and $p3 = -1$.

Most of these observations are placed within the conscious area. Such a cognitive state, when passed to the methods of the grounding theory, results in utterances:

1. $p_4 \rightarrow Bel(p_3)$ "If p_4, then I believe that p_3" (now).
2. $\neg p_4 \rightarrow Bel(\neg p_3)$ "If not p_4, then I believe that not p_3" (now).

The returned statements form a common-sense result, being in accordance with our conventional understanding of conditionals. When p_4 holds, the chance for p_3 is high. When p_4 does not hold that chance is low.

For a third short example let the agent focus on p_2 and p_1. For such a case the agent gives no answer. The cognitive state contains only experiences where p_2 holds (see step 3). For such a case, when p_2 is already known to hold, there is no point in uttering an indicative conditional. Again the result is in accordance with common-sense.

8 Conclusions

An exemplary method of providing empirical knowledge for grounding modal conditional statements in the context of the current observation has been presented. The method has proven to work well for the provided simple data case. Utilizing the grounding theory, it was able to produce results which complied with common-sense and suited the provided context (current observation).

The proposed method uses an exemplary learning algorithm (MDB-LLBorder) and a simple feature selection algorithm to learn higher level knowledge from empirical knowledge. This learned knowledge is later used to choose past observations applicable in the context of an utterance. The proposed intuitive postulates (see Sect. 4.3), met by the proposed method, ensure the proper grounding of conditional statements.

The proposed method is only an exemplary solution to the complex problem of contextualization. The results of this method greatly depend on the characteristics of the provided data and the agent's cognitive capabilities.

Acknowledgments. This paper was partially supported by Grant no. N N519 444939 funded by Polish Ministry of Science and Higher Education (2010–2013). Fellowship co-financed by European Union within European Social Fund.

References

1. Davis, W.: Implicature. In: Zalta, E.N. (ed.) The Stanford Encyclopedia of Philosophy. Fall 2012 edn. (2012)
2. Dong,G., Li, J.: Efficient mining of emerging patterns: discovering trends and differences. In: Proceedings of the 5th ACM SIGKDD Conference on Knowledge Discovery and Data Mining, pp. 43–52 (1999)
3. Freeman, W.: Comparison of brain models for active vs. passive perception. Inf. Sci. **116**(2), 97–107 (1999)
4. Freeman, W.J.: A neurobiological interpretation of semiotics: meaning, representation, and information. Inf. Sci. **124**, 93–102 (2000)
5. Grice, H.P.: Meaning. Philos. Rev. **66**, 377–388 (1957)
6. Hall, M.A.: Correlation-based feature selection for machine learning. Ph.D. thesis, The University of Waikato (1999)
7. Harnad, S.: The symbol grounding problem. Physica D **42**, 335–346 (1990)
8. Johnson-Laird, P., Savary, F.: Illusory inferences: A novel class of erroneous deductions. Cognition **71**(3), 191–229 (1999)
9. Katarzyniak, R.: Grounding atom formulas and simple modalities in communicative agents. In: Applied Informatics'03, pp. 388–392 (2003)
10. Katarzyniak, R.: The language grounding problem and its relation to the internal structure of cognitive agents. J. Univ. Comput. Sci. **11**(2), 357–374 (2005)
11. Katarzyniak, R.: On some properties of grounding nonuniform sets of modal conjunctions. Int. J. Appl. Math. Comput. Sci. **16**(3), 399 (2006)
12. Katarzyniak, R.: On some properties of grounding uniform sets of modal conjunctions. J. Intell. Fuzzy Syst. **17**(3), 209–218 (2006)
13. Katarzyniak, R., Pieczyńska-Kuchtiak, A.: Grounding and extracting modal responses in cognitive agents: 'and' query and states of incomplete knowledge. Int. J. Appl. Math. Comput. Sci. **14**, 249–263 (2004)
14. Li, J., Dong, G., Ramamohanarao, K.: Making use of the most expressive jumping emerging patterns for classification. In: Terano, T., Liu, H., Chen, A.L.P. (eds.) PAKDD 2000. LNCS, vol. 1805. Springer, Heidelberg (2000)
15. Paivio, A.: Mental Representations. Oxford University Press, Oxford (1990)
16. Pitt, D.: Mental representation. In: Zalta, E.N. (ed.) The Stanford Encyclopedia of Philosophy. Winter 2012 edn. (2012)

17. Popek, G.: Integration of modal and fuzzy methods for agent's knowledge representation. Ph.D. thesis, Wroclaw University of Technology, Swunburne University of Technology (2012)
18. Ogden, C.A., Richards, I.A.: The Meaning of Meaning. Harvest/ HBJ, San Diego (1989)
19. Roy, D., Reiter, E.: Connecting language to the world. Artif. Intell. **167**, 1–12 (2005)
20. Schlenker, P.: Context of thought and context of utterance: a note on free indirect discourse and the historical present. Mind Lang. **19**(3), 279–304 (2004)
21. Skorupa, G., Katarzyniak, R.: Applying possibility and belief operators to conditional statements. In: Proceedings of the 14th Conference on Knowledge-Based and Intelligent Information and Engineering Systems: Part I, pp. 271–280 (2010)
22. Skorupa, G., Katarzyniak, R.: Modelling relationship between antecedent and consequent in modal conditional statements. In: Jedrzejowicz, P., Nguyen, N.T., Hoang, K. (eds.) ICCCI 2011, Part II. LNCS, vol. 6923, pp. 120–129. Springer, Heidelberg (2011)
23. Stanley, J.: Context and logical form. Linguist. Philos. **23**(4), 391–434 (2000)
24. Steels, L.: The symbol grounding problem has been solved. so what's next. In: de Vega, M. (ed.) Symbols and Embodiment: Debates on Meaning and Cognition, pp. 223–244. Oxford University Press, Oxford (2008)
25. Vogt, P.: Anchoring of semiotic symbols. Robot. Auton. Syst. **43**, 109–120 (2003)

Conflict Compensation, Redundancy and Similarity in DataBases Federation

Germano Resconi[✉]

Department of Mathematics, Brescia Catholic University, Brescia, Italy
resconi@speedyposta.it

Abstract. Integration of several databases is a complex process, in which it is needed to specify if two databases with entities and relationship are similar or strong equivalents or weak equivalent. Data bases that are strong equivalent became identical with suitable change of entities without change the relationship. In this situation in the federation of databases we have a lot of strong redundant databases that can be changed in only one prototype. The week equivalence or week redundant databases are more difficult to discover because in the federation of databases change the entities but also the relationship. For example images on the sphere are week equivalent to the projected image that is a locally distortion of the original images. In this paper we give the algorithm to discover the week redundant databases and also how to create the local compensation in a way to transform all the different databases in only one prototype. This is a useful method to solve conflicts among agents as databases.

Keywords: Data base · Strong equivalence · Week equivalence · Redundant databases · Compensation process · Similarity · Conflicts

1 Introduction

A system of distribute database locate data in different databases. Any independent database has entities and relationship as referential integration for which any entity or table with its primary key has foreign key that point to another entity with its primary key. Entities are connected by primary and foreign keys. Independent data base are not always completely different but in many case are partially equivalent with different degree of equivalence or strong or week equivalents with possible local distortions. When two database are equivalent means that when we solve a query in one data base is possible to solve similar or equivalent query in another database. When we want to know where is the minimum distance between two cities in the earth, we can solve the query by the geographic map on a plane and after we compensate the distortion and found the minimum distance in the database given by map on the sphere. From the data in the sphere and on the two dimensional plane there is a week equivalence and one point in the sphere has one point on the plane and we have always the compensation process to move from the plane to the sphere to eliminate the distortion. The main job of this paper is to found methods or algorithm to discover where and how two or more given database are equivalents. In many cases without a method is impossible to compare two or more database that at the first superficial impression appear completely

© Springer-Verlag Berlin Heidelberg 2014
N.T. Nguyen (Ed.): TCCI XIV 2014, LNCS 8615, pp. 120–135, 2014.
DOI: 10.1007/978-3-662-44509-9_6

different one from the others. Equivalent relation without distortion can be obtained with simple change of the names of the entities with the same relationship. Equivalent relation with distortion or week equivalence is obtained by local distortions of the original database. In the equivalent relation we can activate a compensation process to restore original database with elimination of any distortion. When two database are not equivalent in a strong or week we can found the part of the new database that is not equivalent to the old database and the part where are equivalent. To organize data base to study equivalent relation we built hypercube in multi dimension space where nodes are database and connection are equivalent relations. Different orders of conceptual integration are possible. At the zero order we have only one database. At the first order we have two databases with and equivalent (strong or week) relation. At the order two a square of four data bases are connected by four equivalent relations. At the third order eight data bases are connected by equivalent relation. At the fourth order sixteen data bases are connected and so on. Data base conceptual structure is organize in different dimension hypercube, one dimension hypercube, two dimension hypercube (square of data base) three dimension of hypercube (ordinary cube of data base), fourth dimension hypercube,...., n dimension hypercube. In conclusion we can discover the structure of equivalence for independent database in a way to control query and answer in a set of database as in the federation of database without a physical integration but only by the conceptual integration where different data bases strong or week equivalents can be transformed in only one prototype database.

2 Entity and Relationship at the Zero Order

We know that any data base is defined by entity and relation in this usual way (Fig. 1)

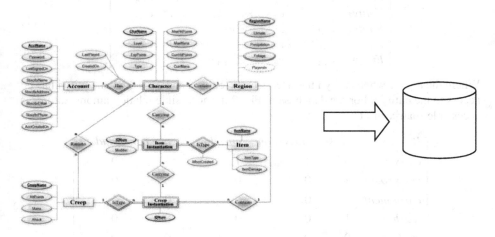

Fig. 1. Ordinary database Entity, Relation structure.

Where the entities in the color green are Account, Character, Region, Item, Creep instantiation. Any entity in green is represented by a table of files in rose. All the entities are represented by a relationship (Wikipedia). For our purposes we study a more simple database with Entity and Relationship which example is given by the graph in Fig. 2.

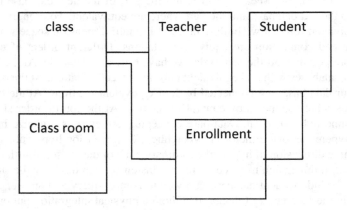

Fig. 2. Simple Entity Relation data base

2.1   Accessible Matrix for Entity Relation in Database

In general any relationship in data base can write in this matrix way

$$\begin{bmatrix} R & Entity_1 & Entity_2 & Entity_3 & .... & Entity_n \\ Entity_1 & e_{1,1} & e_{1,2} & e_{1,3} & \cdots & e_{1,n} \\ Entity_2 & e_{2,1} & e_{2,2} & e_{2,3} & \cdots & e_{2,n} \\ Entity_3 & e_{3,1} & e_{3,2} & e_{3,3} & \cdots & e_{3,n} \\ .... & \cdots & \cdots & \cdots & \cdots & \cdots \\ Entity_n & e_{n,1} & e_{n,2} & e_{n,3} & \cdots & e_{n,n} \end{bmatrix} \quad (1)$$

Where the $e_{i,j} = 1$ when entity i has access to the entity j and $e_{i,j} = 0$ when entity i has no access to the entity j. For the data base in Fig. 2 the accessible relation among entities is accessible matrix in (1) is

$$\begin{bmatrix} R & class & class\,room & enrollment & teacher & student \\ class & 0 & 1 & 1 & 1 & 0 \\ class\,room & 1 & 0 & 0 & 0 & 0 \\ enrollment & 1 & 0 & 0 & 0 & 1 \\ teacher & 1 & 0 & 0 & 0 & 0 \\ student & 0 & 0 & 1 & 0 & 0 \end{bmatrix} \quad (2)$$

And the matrix of the relationship is

$$R = \begin{bmatrix} 0 & 1 & 1 & 1 & 0 \\ 1 & 0 & 0 & 0 & 0 \\ 1 & 0 & 0 & 0 & 1 \\ 1 & 0 & 0 & 0 & 0 \\ 0 & 0 & 1 & 0 & 0 \end{bmatrix}$$

So we have in (3) the initial entities and final entities vectors of the accessible entities

$$Rv = \begin{bmatrix} 0 & 1 & 1 & 1 & 0 \\ 1 & 0 & 0 & 0 & 0 \\ 1 & 0 & 0 & 0 & 1 \\ 1 & 0 & 0 & 0 & 0 \\ 0 & 0 & 1 & 0 & 0 \end{bmatrix} \begin{bmatrix} class \\ classroom \\ enrollment \\ teacher \\ student \end{bmatrix} = \begin{bmatrix} (classroom, enrollment, teacher) \\ class \\ (class, student) \\ class \\ enrollment \end{bmatrix}$$

(3)

The data base relationship (3) connect five entities in this way. For the initial entity or principal key class* we have three foreign keys or vectors of final entities as (class room, enrollment, teacher). Now we can ask where is the room of the class "mathematics" the teacher "Charles" is the teacher of the class "mathematics" where the students that are enrolled in the class "mathematics". At the entity class we associate a table of data where are locate the foreign key and the principal key in this way (Fig. 3)

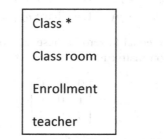

| Class * |
| Class room |
| Enrollment |
| teacher |

Fig. 3. The field with asterisk is the principal key the other three fields are the foreign key

The formal description of the principal key and foreign key can be repeated for all the other initial entities in (3). We conclude that with the matrix R we have the formal description of the relationship in a way that we can make mathematical computation to compare the databases one with the others. Given two databases with the same number of entities, different names and different relations, to compare the two databases first we put the same name at the two databases. After with permutations of the colons and rows of one database we try to obtain the second database. If from the first data base we obtain the second the two data base are equivalent in a strong or week way. If they are not equivalent we can try the same process for a part of the first and the second database. With the equivalent relations we can eliminate a huge number of databases that are all similar and redundant.

2.2   Change One Accessible Matrix in Another by Permutation Matrix

To change the accessible matrix in another equivalent matrix we create the permutation matrix in this way. Given the permutation of the n entities

$$P = \begin{pmatrix} 1 & 2 & 3 & \cdots & n-1 & n \\ p_1 & p_2 & p_3 & \cdots & p_{n-1} & p_n \end{pmatrix}.$$

The permutation matrix is

$$a_{h,k} = \delta_{h,p_k}, where \begin{cases} \delta_{k,p_k} = 1 \\ \delta_{h,p_k} = 0, h \neq k \end{cases} \tag{4}$$

For example given the permutation

$$P = \begin{pmatrix} k = 1 & k = 2 & k = 3 \\ p_1 = 2 & p_2 = 1 & p_3 = 3 \end{pmatrix} \tag{5}$$

And the permutation matrix A_{k,p_h} is

$$A = \begin{bmatrix} a_{1,p_1} & a_{1,p_2} & a_{1,p_3} \\ a_{2,p_1} & a_{2,p_2} & a_{2,p_3} \\ a_{3,p_1} & a_{3,p_2} & a_{3,p_3} \end{bmatrix}$$

$$k = 1, p_1 = 2 \text{ we have } a_{1,2} = 1$$
$$k = 2, p_2 = 1, \text{ we have } a_{2,1} = 1$$
$$k = 3, p_3 = 1, \text{ we have } a_{3,1} = 1$$

All other elements of A are equal to zero because are not included in the permutation operator. So the permutation matrix is

$$A = \begin{bmatrix} 0 & 1 & 0 \\ 1 & 0 & 0 \\ 0 & 0 & 1 \end{bmatrix}$$

Given the accessible relation in the matrix form

$$R = \begin{bmatrix} e_{1,1} & e_{1,2} & e_{1,3} \\ e_{2,1} & e_{2,2} & e_{2,3} \\ e_{3,1} & e_{3,2} & e_{3,3} \end{bmatrix}$$

When we multiply R with the permutation matrix A at the left we permute the colons of R. In fact

$$RAE = \begin{bmatrix} e_{1,1} & e_{1,2} & e_{1,3} \\ e_{2,1} & e_{2,2} & e_{2,3} \\ e_{3,1} & e_{3,2} & e_{3,3} \end{bmatrix} \begin{bmatrix} 0 & 1 & 0 \\ 1 & 0 & 0 \\ 0 & 0 & 1 \end{bmatrix} \begin{bmatrix} E_1 \\ E_2 \\ E_3 \end{bmatrix} = \begin{bmatrix} e_{1,2} & e_{1,1} & e_{1,3} \\ e_{2,2} & e_{2,1} & e_{2,3} \\ e_{3,2} & e_{3,1} & e_{3,3} \end{bmatrix} \begin{bmatrix} E_1 \\ E_2 \\ E_3 \end{bmatrix}$$

The new relation R A is the composition of the permutation matrix A of the entities E and after the accessible relation on AE. So we permute the set of initial entities without change the accessibility relation. For example for the database in (2) we have

$$RAE = \begin{bmatrix} 0 & 1 & 1 & 1 & 0 \\ 1 & 0 & 0 & 0 & 0 \\ 1 & 0 & 0 & 0 & 1 \\ 1 & 0 & 0 & 0 & 0 \\ 0 & 0 & 1 & 0 & 0 \end{bmatrix} \begin{bmatrix} classroom \\ class \\ enrollment \\ teacher \\ student \end{bmatrix} = \begin{bmatrix} (class, enrollment, teacher) \\ classroom \\ (classroom, student) \\ classroom \\ enrollment \end{bmatrix}$$

When we multiply R with the permutation matrix A at the right we permute the rows of R. In fact

$$ARE = \begin{bmatrix} 0 & 1 & 0 \\ 1 & 0 & 0 \\ 0 & 0 & 1 \end{bmatrix} \begin{bmatrix} e_{1,1} & e_{1,2} & e_{1,3} \\ e_{2,1} & e_{2,2} & e_{2,3} \\ e_{3,1} & e_{3,2} & e_{3,3} \end{bmatrix} \begin{bmatrix} E_1 \\ E_2 \\ E_3 \end{bmatrix} = \begin{bmatrix} e_{2,1} & e_{2,2} & e_{2,3} \\ e_{1,1} & e_{1,2} & e_{1,3} \\ e_{3,1} & e_{3,2} & e_{3,3} \end{bmatrix} \begin{bmatrix} E_1 \\ E_2 \\ E_3 \end{bmatrix}$$

At the begin we use the relation R to compute the accessible entities and after we use the permutation matrix A to obtain the final results. For example in the database in Fig. 2 we have

$$ARv = \begin{bmatrix} 1 & 0 & 0 & 0 & 0 \\ 0 & 1 & 1 & 1 & 0 \\ 1 & 0 & 0 & 0 & 1 \\ 1 & 0 & 0 & 0 & 0 \\ 0 & 0 & 1 & 0 & 0 \end{bmatrix} \begin{bmatrix} class \\ classroom \\ enrollment \\ teacher \\ student \end{bmatrix} = \begin{bmatrix} class \\ (classroom, enrollment, teacher) \\ (class, student) \\ class \\ enrollment \end{bmatrix}$$

2.3 Isomorphism Between Data Base by Permutations

When we have the commutative identity

$$AR = GA$$

$$G = ARA^{-1}$$

G and R are strong equivalent or isomorphic. In given the permutation matrix

$$Permutation = \begin{bmatrix} class & classroom & enrollment & teacher & student \\ classroom & class & enrollment & teacher & student \end{bmatrix}$$

$$and \; A = \begin{bmatrix} 0 & 1 & 0 & 0 & 0 \\ 1 & 0 & 0 & 0 & 0 \\ 0 & 0 & 1 & 0 & 0 \\ 0 & 0 & 0 & 1 & 0 \\ 0 & 0 & 0 & 0 & 1 \end{bmatrix}$$

We can compute G by the permutation by A^{-1} of the colons and after by the permutation A of the rows. So we have

$$RA^{-1} = RA = \begin{bmatrix} 1 & 0 & 1 & 1 & 0 \\ 0 & 1 & 0 & 0 & 0 \\ 0 & 1 & 0 & 0 & 1 \\ 0 & 1 & 0 & 0 & 0 \\ 0 & 0 & 1 & 0 & 0 \end{bmatrix}, G = A(RA^{-1}) = \begin{bmatrix} 0 & 1 & 0 & 0 & 0 \\ 1 & 0 & 1 & 1 & 0 \\ 0 & 1 & 0 & 0 & 1 \\ 0 & 1 & 0 & 0 & 0 \\ 0 & 0 & 1 & 0 & 0 \end{bmatrix}$$

and

$$Gv = \begin{bmatrix} 0 & 1 & 0 & 0 & 0 \\ 1 & 0 & 1 & 1 & 0 \\ 0 & 1 & 0 & 0 & 1 \\ 0 & 1 & 0 & 0 & 0 \\ 0 & 0 & 1 & 0 & 0 \end{bmatrix} \begin{bmatrix} class \\ classroom \\ enrollment \\ teacher \\ student \end{bmatrix} = \begin{bmatrix} classroom \\ (class, enrollment, teacher) \\ (classroom, student) \\ classroom \\ enrollment \end{bmatrix}$$

If in G we substitute "class" with "classroom" we came back to the original accessible relation R. The accessible relation G has the same relationship of R when we permute the entities class and classroom. In a graphic way we

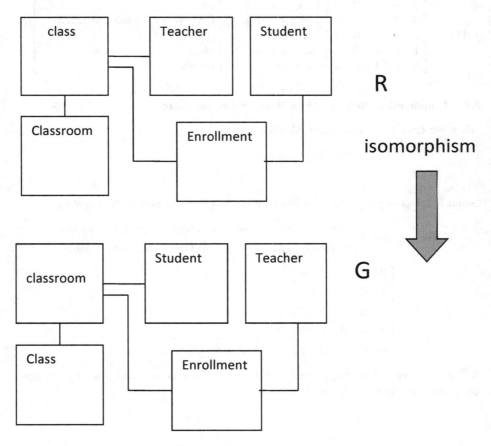

The isomorphism can write by the commutative diagram (Fig. 4).

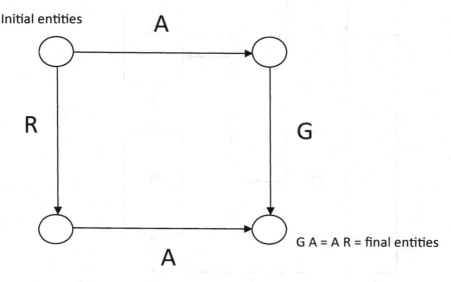

Fig. 4. Commutative diagram in the category theory for isomorphic data base

We remark that the equivalent accessible relation G can write in this way

$$ARA^{-1} = G$$

So given R and G if we can change R by the same permutation for the rows and the colons of R in a way to generate G, G is equivalent to R. If this is impossible we can found a G′ relation equivalent to R and at the minimum distance to G. Given the two different relationships R and G (Fig. 5)

The accessible matrices are

$$
\begin{bmatrix}
R & 1 & 2 & 3 & 4 \\
1 & 0 & 1 & 1 & 0 \\
2 & 0 & 0 & 0 & 1 \\
3 & 0 & 0 & 0 & 1 \\
4 & 0 & 0 & 0 & 0
\end{bmatrix}
,
\begin{bmatrix}
G & 1 & 2 & 3 & 4 \\
1 & 0 & 0 & 0 & 1 \\
2 & 1 & 0 & 0 & 1 \\
3 & 0 & 1 & 0 & 0 \\
4 & 0 & 0 & 0 & 0
\end{bmatrix}
$$

Now we permute in the same way the rows and colons of R to be nearest to G. We start with R and we take G as a target so we fix the in G the relation (2, 1) we permute R in a way to have the relation (2, 1)

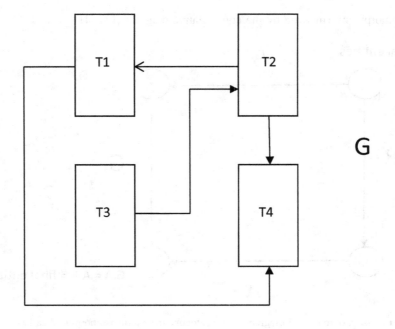

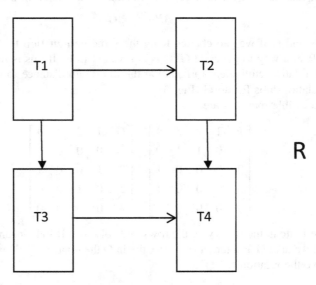

Fig. 5. G and R are two non equivalent data bases

$$
\begin{bmatrix}
R & 1 & 2 & 3 & 4 \\
1 & 0 & 1 & 1 & 0 \\
2 & 0 & 0 & 0 & 1 \\
3 & 0 & 0 & 0 & 1 \\
4 & 0 & 0 & 0 & 0
\end{bmatrix}
\Rightarrow
\begin{bmatrix}
R' & 1 & 2 & 3 & 4 \\
1 & 0 & 0 & 1 & 0 \\
2 & 1 & 0 & 0 & 1 \\
3 & 0 & 0 & 0 & 1 \\
4 & 0 & 0 & 0 & 0
\end{bmatrix}
$$

R and R' are equivalent and R' is the nearest relation to G equivalent with R. We see that R' and G have two arrows in common. Because the isomorphism relation have a lot of constrains we enlarge the meaning of the equivalence to the more general equivalence denoted homotopy for which two accessible relations are part of the same type also if they are not isomorphic.

2.4 Isomorphism with Distortion, Homotopy, Gauge Transformation, Week Equivalence and Compensation by Permutation

To explain the meaning of the homotopy or relations with the same type, we take as example the projection operator of the sphere into a plane. In the geographic data base we have two principal data of the earth geography. The first is locate on a sphere and the other is the projection of the geography information on a plane. Now we know that the two data base are relate but we also know that are not isomorphic because when we project from the sphere one image the new image on the plane has a distortion. In fact map projection make distortion of a sphere is not a developable solid, transfer from 3D globe to 2D map must result in loss of one or global characteristics as

Shape, Area, Distance, Direction, Position

The distance is equidistance between sphere and plane projection. All the other elements are distorted. Given a path on the sphere we project the initial point and the final point of the path into the plane. The path on the plane change in different way from one part of the sphere to another. The same path at the north polo has a little dimension but at the equator is more or less the same on the sphere. We have no global transformation that change paths from the sphere to the plane. We have only local transformation (gauge) that change point by point in the sphere. This local transformation or gauge is due to the impossibility to have the curvature property of the sphere into the plane. Given a sphere with many isomorphic circles (same circle but in different positions on the sphere). When we project this sphere on the plane the circles are deformed as we can see in Fig. 6.

In the projection operation we have a weak equivalence for which objects have the same basic "shape". For example the Africa image in the sphere and Africa image in the projection plane are object that are not similar but have the same basic "shape" so are week equivalent. The projection operation generate distorted image so is a gauge transformation. Compensation of the distorted image restore the original image on the sphere. For example in Fig. 6 we can compensate the deformation of the circles in ellipses in a way to come back to the original circle. Another example of homotopy is given by a set of trajectories that pass from the same two points (same types) as we can see in Fig. 7.

Fig. 6. Equal circles on the sphere are distorted in ellipses by projection from three to two dimensions. Circles are week equivalent to the ellipses after the projection

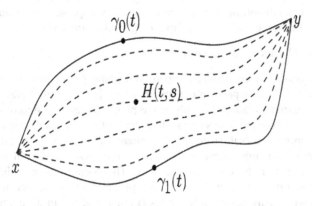

Fig. 7. Homotopy set of trajectories that are week equivalent or homotopy because the different trajectories have same basic shape (pass from the same two points x and y)

The paths H (t, s) = γs (t) are all different one from the other and also are not connected by an isomorphism. The transformation that move from one path to another is a continuous transformation that is different from different points on the path. This homotopy can be denoted isomorphism with continuous distortion for which length and direction is different from the different points in the path s in compare with the path s = 0. Another example of equivalence is in formal language theory, weak equivalence of two grammars means they generate the same set of strings, i.e. that the formal language they generate is the same with different semantic interpretations. In compiler theory the notion is distinguished from strong (or structural) equivalence which additionally means that the two parse trees are reasonably similar in that the same semantic interpretation can be assigned to both. Compensation in biology is denoted adaptation that is a process by which we compensate distortion, in biological DNA project, given by the environment.

2.5   Week Equivalence in Data Base

Given the accessible relation R and two different permutation matrices A and B when

$$AR = GB$$

$$G = ARB^{-1}$$

R and G are not strong equivalent but are week equivalents or homotopics. In fact for the two permutations

$$A = \begin{bmatrix} class & classroom & enrollment & teacher & student \\ classroom & class & enrollment & teacher & student \end{bmatrix}$$

$$B = \begin{bmatrix} class & classroom & enrollment & teacher & student \\ enrollment & classroom & class & teacher & student \end{bmatrix}$$

We have

$$RB^{-1} = RB = \begin{bmatrix} 1 & 1 & 0 & 1 & 0 \\ 0 & 0 & 1 & 0 & 0 \\ 0 & 0 & 1 & 0 & 1 \\ 0 & 0 & 1 & 0 & 0 \\ 1 & 0 & 0 & 0 & 0 \end{bmatrix}, G = A(RB^{-1}) = \begin{bmatrix} 0 & 0 & 1 & 0 & 0 \\ 1 & 1 & 0 & 1 & 0 \\ 0 & 0 & 1 & 0 & 1 \\ 0 & 0 & 1 & 0 & 0 \\ 1 & 0 & 0 & 0 & 0 \end{bmatrix}$$

the accessible relation G is

$$Gv = \begin{bmatrix} 0 & 0 & 1 & 0 & 0 \\ 1 & 1 & 0 & 1 & 0 \\ 0 & 0 & 1 & 0 & 1 \\ 0 & 0 & 1 & 0 & 0 \\ 1 & 0 & 0 & 0 & 0 \end{bmatrix} \begin{bmatrix} class \\ classroom \\ enrollment \\ teacher \\ student \end{bmatrix} = \begin{bmatrix} enrollment \\ (class, classroom, teacher) \\ (enrollment, student) \\ enrollment \\ class \end{bmatrix}$$

We remark that G is of the same type of R in fact the number of accessible relations from on entity in G and is the same as in R. But G is not strong equivalent to R because in R we have no self loop that are present in G. For example enrollment as access to itself in G but not in R. So R and G have only week equivalence. Now given G we always can came back to the original relation R. In fact

$$AR = GB$$

$$R = A^{-1}RB$$

The week equivalence means that G and R are not equivalent in a strong way but one is connected to the others so from R we can go to G and reverse. The week equivalence can draw by the commutative diagram in the category theory

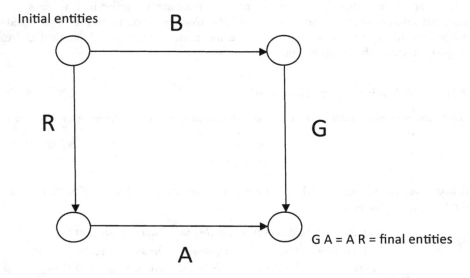

3   Level of Equivalence Among Data Base

Hierarchy of relationship First order relationship (Table) Relationship (Table) Second order relationship an equivalent bond between relationship Third order relationship an equivalent bond between second order relationship Fourth order relationship an equivalent bond between third order relationship and so on. The traditional database is make by tables (Entities) which colons are fields and relationship between tables. Query are possible paths among fields in the tables and answers are all possible data that is in agreement with the given path. In our model we represent table as entities at the order zero and tables with relationship as entities at the order one. So we have an initial conceptual hierarchy between tables as the bottom and simple database as the top of the hierarchy. Now we can go at another level by a new type of database or entity at the order two where we have database at the level one and a relationship between data base. Database and relation between database is another entity which order is two. In this way we can create a tower of entities at high order. As example of entity at the second order is the federation of the data warehouse (Fig. 8).

Now we will show that when we move from one order to another appear new type of integration identities that we must solve to avoid conflicts and inconsistency. In fact a distribute set of database generate a lot of problems for the risk to loss coherence and integration. In fact to solve this problem we use a new entity or data base manager which work is to control the coherence of the database itself. Now we think that the description in a formal way of the order of data base give us a solid description of the possible risk to built complex federations of database.

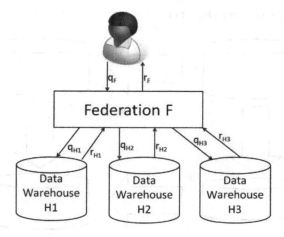

Fig. 8. Federation of database

So at the zero order we have (Fig. 9)

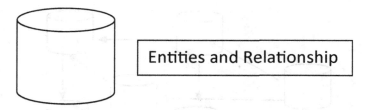

Fig. 9. Zero order, or basic order, with simple data base make by entities and relationship

At the first order we have (Fig. 10)

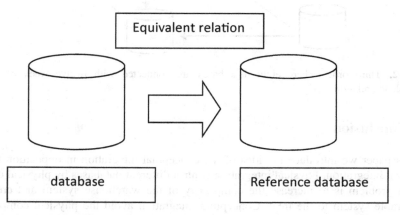

Fig. 10. First order with an equivalence week or strong between data base

At the second order we have (Fig. 11)

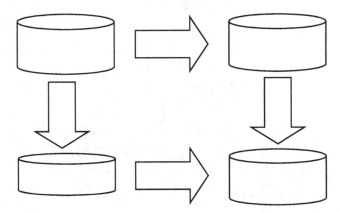

Fig. 11. Second order of equivalence with four databases and four equivalent relations

A the third order of equivalent relations we have the eight databases (Fig. 12)

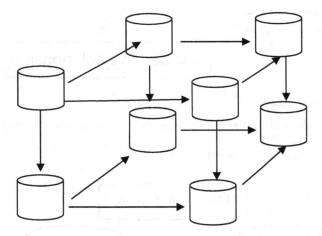

Fig. 12. Third order where eight data bases are connected with twelve week or strong equivalence relations

4   Conclusion

In this paper we introduce the idea of the conceptual integration in opposition to the physical integration. Physical integration control different databases by physical devise which problem is to increase the complexity of the warehouse system and create a vulnerable system to the treat. Conceptual integration avoid the physical complexity with the deeper knowledge of the equivalent relation and compensation between databases. When we know the strong or weak equivalence we can create suitable transformations or compensation for any database in a way to reduce all different databases to only prototype. In this way similarity became identity and disappear the necessity to integrate different databases in one because all are week or strong equivalent to one prototype databases. So is only necessary to know the transformation to compare different databases. In this way when we found rules in one databases we can project this rules in other databases. In this way at the physical integration with physical control network, we can substitute a pure conceptual control and network by week or strong equivalence. We overcame the physical complexity and problems to solve conflicts and luck of consensus for a set of databases. We argue that the translation from one language and another with weak and strong equivalence can be improved by conceptual integration.

References

1. Nguyen, N.T.: Advanced Methods for Inconsistent Knowledge Management. Springer, London (2008)
2. Resconi, G., Jain, L.: Intelligent Agents. Springer, Heidelberg (2004)
3. Eilenberg, S., Mac Lane, S.: General theory of natural equivalences. Trans. Am. Math. Soc. **58**, 231–294 (1945)
4. Kelly, G.M.: Many-variable functorial calculus I. In: Kelly, G.M., Laplaza, M., Lewis, G., Mac Lane, S. (eds.) Coherence in Categories, pp. 66–105, Lecture Notes in Mathematics 281. Springer, Heidelberg (1972)
5. Kelly, G.M.: Basic concepts of enriched category theory. London Mathematical Society Lecture Note Series 64. Cambridge University Press, Cambridge (1982)
6. Lawvere, F.W., Schanuel, S.H.: Conceptual mathematics. Cambridge University Press, Cambridge (1997)
7. Mac Lane, S.: Categories for the Working Mathematician. Springer, New York (1971)

Extended Learning Method for Designation of Co-operation

Edyta Kucharska$^{(\boxtimes)}$ and Ewa Dudek-Dyduch

Department of Automatics and Biomedical Engineering,
AGH University of Science and Technology, 30 Mickiewicza Av.,
30-059 Krakow, Poland
{edyta, edd}@agh.edu.pl

Abstract. The aim of the paper is to present a new machine learning method for determining intelligent co-operation at project realization. The method uses local optimization task of a special form and is based on learning idea. Additionally, the information gathered during a searching process is used to prune non-perspective solutions. The paper presents a formal approach to creation of constructive algorithms that use a sophisticated local optimization and are based on a formal definition of multistage decision process. It also proposes a general conception of creation local optimization tasks for different problems as well as a conception of local optimization task modification on basis of acquired information. To illustrate the conceptions, the learning algorithm for NP-hard scheduling problem is presented as well as results of computer experiments.

Keywords: Machine learning · Learning in scheduling · Algebraic-logical model (ALM) · Learning based on ALM · Local search techniques · Optimization of co-operation · Project management · Multistage decision process

1 Introduction

The paper is related to the development of a new machine learning method that can be applied to discrete optimization problems (also scheduling) and especially co-operation problems. Intelligent co-operation is defined as an accurate assignment of executors to tasks that form a project. On the one hand, a particular executor is supposed to realize tasks that it is best suited for, on the other, the selection of tasks and their ordering needs to take into account optimal (suboptimal) realization of tasks by other executors.

The aim of the article is to present a new heuristic method for determining intelligent co-operation at project realization. The method uses a local optimization task of a special form and is based on learning ideas. Additionally, the information acquired during a searching process is used to prune non-perspective solutions.

A project is composed of a number of tasks that need to be performed by various executors. The term executor may refer to people and/or machines characterized by a number of differentiating features. Executors should aim towards achieving a common target, which is the realization of a project at minimal costs, and meet restrictions which most often refer to execution time, costs and ordering of particular tasks. The execution time of particular tasks most frequently depends on the assigned executor and the

© Springer-Verlag Berlin Heidelberg 2014
N.T. Nguyen (Ed.): TCCI XIV 2014, LNCS 8615, pp. 136–157, 2014.
DOI: 10.1007/978-3-662-44509-9_7

extent of the tasks performed so far (the set of performed tasks). This is caused by the fact that some of the already realized tasks may facilitate or accelerate other task realization. The completed tasks may become the resources for realization of other tasks. Thus, such problems can be treated as scheduling problems with increasing resources which depend on the project state.

One must determine such an ordering of tasks and assignment of these to particular executors which would minimize the total project cost and meet the restrictions.

The fact that resources depend on the project state makes solving this class of problem additional difficult and is the cause for developing a new heuristic method presented in this article.

A lot of combinatorial problems correspond to the co-operation problem presented above, e.g. task scheduling for multiple machines, especially task scheduling with state dependent resources. Researches in this area are conducted in two main directions: developing algorithms for particular problems and developing general solution methods. The latter includes research devoted to meta-heuristics and software tools implementing them. The paper also belongs to the second group of research as well.

The paper [11] presents a conception of software tools based on agent team approach and mainly improvement algorithms. Improvement algorithms can be applied only when the solution type can be defined a priori (for example, it is a permutation, set, vector, etc.). However, there are a number of problems for which type of solution cannot be determined a priori and consequently it is impossible to apply the improvement algorithm (see an example below). Then, it is necessary to apply a constructive approach.

The authors' research is related to methods based just upon this constructive approach. The paper presents developing of learning method given in [5, 7]. Its aim is twofold:

- to present a general conception of a new method for different co-operation and scheduling problems; the method is based on learning process connected with pruning non-perspective solutions,
- to present an application of the extended learning method for NP-hard co-operation problem (scheduling problem with state dependent resources).

Many types of learning have been explored for scheduling: rote learning, inductive learning (ID3), neural network learning [17], case-based learning, classifier systems, and others [14]. Particular methodology offers positive and negative features. However, none of the mentioned learning concept use of a mathematical model of a problem to be solved. Novelty of the presented in the paper machine learning is fact that this method is based on a special mathematical model of problem, named algebraic-logical model (in short ALM). The model is presented in Sect. 2. A formal approach to creation of constructive algorithms that use a local optimization and are based on the formal model of a multistage decision process is presented in Sect. 3. It is clear that efficiency of any learning method strongly depends on: an amount of the provided knowledge, a type of knowledge representation that should be convenient to processing, a way of acquiring and usage of additional acquired knowledge. Better knowledge representation makes more effective machine learning algorithms. Because the fundamental knowledge for the presented learning method is given by mathematical model ALM, the presented method is named as learning method based on ALM.

It may be underlined, that the presented ideas of learning algorithm significantly differ from ideas for learning algorithms given in [12, 15].

2   Algebraic-Logical Model of a Multistage Decision Process

An admissible way of a project realization, and in particular assigning executors to tasks, can be determined with the help of simulation experiments. A single experiment establishes a sequence of decisions related to the assignment of executors (resources) to tasks and task realization ordering. It is impossible to provide a sensible sequence of decisions a priori. It needs to be established in the simulation course.

Simulation course of project realization consists in determining a sequence of process states and the related time instances. The new state and its time instant depend on the previous state and the decision that has been realized (taken) then. The decision determines the task to be performed, resources, transport unit, etc.

Generation of the state sequence is terminated if the new state is a goal state (state we want the process to be at the end), a non-admissible state, or state with an empty set of possible decisions. The sequence of consecutive process states from a given initial state to a final state (goal or non-admissible) form a process trajectory.

The paper and the presented method are based on the formal model of multistage decision process defined by Dudek-Dyduch E. in [3, 4]. The model is called the algebraic-logical model of multistage decision process. Let's recall its definition.

Definition 1. Algebraic-logical model of multistage decision process (MDP) is defined by the sextuple $MDP = (U, S, s_0, f, S_N, S_G)$ where U is a set of decisions, $S = X \times T$ is a set named a set of generalized states, X is a set of proper states, $T \subset \Re^+ \cup \{0\}$ is a subset of non-negative real numbers representing the time instants, $f: U \times S \rightarrow S$ is a partial function called a transition function, (it does not have to be determined for all elements of the set $U \times S$), $s_0 = (x_0, t_0)$, $S_N \subset S$, $S_G \subset S$ are respectively: an initial generalized state, a set of not admissible generalized states, and a set of goal generalized states, i.e. the states in which we want the process to take place at the end.

The transition function is defined by means of two functions, $f = (f_x, f_t)$ where f_x: $U \times X \times T \rightarrow X$ determines the next state, $f_t: U \times X \times T \rightarrow T$ determines the next time instant. It is assumed that the difference $\Delta t = f_t(u, x, t) - t$ has a value that is both finite and positive.

Thus, as a result of the decision u, that is taken or realized at the proper state x and the moment t, the state of the process changes for $x' = f_x(u, x, t)$ that is observed at the moment $t' = f_t(u, x, t) = t + \Delta t$.

Because of the fact that not all decisions defined formally make sense in certain situations, the transition function f is defined as a partial one. As a result, all limitations concerning the decisions in a given state s can be defined in a convenient way by means of so-called sets of possible decisions $U_p(s)$, and defined as:

$$U_p(s) = \{u \in U : (u, s) \in Dom f\}.$$

In the most general case, sets U and X may be presented as a Cartesian product $U = U^1 \times U^2 \times \ldots \times U^m$, $X = X^1 \times X^2 \times \ldots \times X^n$ i.e. $u = (u^1, u^2, \ldots, u^m)$, $x = (x^1, x^2, \ldots, x^n)$. Particular u^i represents separate decisions that must or may be taken at the same time and relate to particular executor (resources). There are no limitations imposed on the sets; in particular they do not have to be numerical. Thus values of particular co-ordinates of a state may be names of elements (symbols) as well as some objects (e.g. a finite set, sequence etc.). The sets S_N, S_G, and U_p are formally defined with the use of logical formulae. Therefore, the complete model constitutes a specialized form of algebraic-logic model of multistage decision process and will be denoted as ALM of MDP or simply ALM.

For a problem instance, an algebraic-logical model represents a set of its trajectories that starts from the initial state s_0. It is assumed that no state of a trajectory, apart from the last one, may belong to the set S_N or has an empty set of possible decisions. Only a trajectory that ends in the set of goal states is admissible. The control sequence determining an admissible trajectory is an admissible decision sequence. The task of optimization lies in the fact of finding such an admissible decision sequence $\tilde{u}$ that would minimize a certain criterion Q.

The ALM of MDP can be easily applied as a model of project realizations. The ALM can represent all potential possibilities of a project realization. According to its structure, the knowledge on a project is represented by coded information on U, S, s_0, f, S_N, S_G. The admissible trajectory corresponds to the admissible project realization.

Using a formal model allows to present an optimization method on a general level (high level of abstraction). It is also able to define strictly properties of the problem, for which this method can be applied. In particular, the ALM of MDP allows to define the approximate distance in state space, even though the state space is not a numerical space. In [3, 8] co-author has proposed application of semi-metrics to this aim.

3 Extended Learning Method

Let us consider co-operation scheduling problem when some previously performed tasks may become resources. To solve the problem one should determine assigning tasks to executors and order of task performing. An admissible solution (an admissible project realization) corresponds to admissible trajectory. The best admissible trajectory defines the best co-operation.

To determine the best cooperation, we presented the learning method in [9]. In this paper the authors propose an "Extended learning method" based on learning method and additionally using pruning of non-perspective solutions. Therefore, this method strives during calculations to get and afterwards use much more information, which could accelerate finding the best solution.

The idea of the extended learning method is as follow. The method consists in generation of consecutive solutions (trajectory), analyzing them and remembering the relevant information obtained from the analysis. This information is used to generate more and better solutions (trajectories). In the course of generating the trajectory, a local optimization task is used to choose decision in a particular state. Particularly, this task may use the semi-metrics term in the state space. Learning is realized in such a way that gathered during the trajectory generation information is used to change the coefficients and/or a local optimization task form. The precise mode of learning will be described later in this paper. Additional collected information is used to prune non-perspective trajectories. Thus, the presented method combines learning with pruning and is an extension of the method presented in [9].

The characteristic elements of the method, so as a technique to generate the trajectory, the creation of a local optimization task, trajectory analysis and pruning non-perspective solutions will be described below.

3.1 Generating a Single Trajectory

The presented method consists in the consecutive construction of whole trajectories, started from the initial state $s_0 = (x_0, t_0)$.

Trajectory generation process using algebraic-logic model is as follows. In each newly designated process state s we have to take decision and this decision is chosen from a set of possible (sensible) decisions in the given state. Then, for considered state and chosen decision new process state $s' = (x', t')$ is determined, both the process of proper state and the corresponding moment of time. They are calculated using the transition function of the process. If the new state belongs to the set of goal states S_G, the generation of the trajectory is completed successfully, and we can make its assessment. If the new state or the corresponding moment of time do not meet the limitations, then this process state belongs to the set of not admissible generalized states S_N. Then the trajectory generation is stopped (the trajectory is non-admissible).

During the trajectory generation, the characteristic parameters (attributes) can be calculated and saved for each generated state. The values of particular parameters can be analyzed and then they can be used to make an additional assessment of the generated trajectory.

3.2 Local Optimization of Decision Choice

The literature presents a heuristic method of discrete optimization problems using local optimization. They are a search methods and are based on partial generating and searching of states graph [1]. But in these methods local optimization was only based on minimization (maximization) of the local increase of quality criterion.

In contrast to methods based on the states graph, presented method is based on algebraic-logical model of multistage decision process (ALM of MDP). This model takes into account much more information about the optimization problem than the states graph. As a result, it is able to design a much better search method [5, 6, 13], and also to present them in a formal way. In particular, ALM allows to create sophisticated local optimization criteria, which takes into account much more information than only just about the increase of the criterion.

The trajectory generation is connected with a choice of decision in subsequent states. It is very important to take adequate decision among all possible decisions in given state, it has a significant impact on ability to generate an admissible solution.

There are different ways of selecting a decision at the $u \in U_p(s)$. In the simplest case, we can choose randomly one decision from all possible decisions in this state. Another way is to choose the decision using the probability distribution, which takes into account certain preferences. But most often, choice of the best decision in given state is connected with a local optimization criterion. Its quality has great influences on the ability to generate an admissible solution faster.

Characteristic element of the extended learning method is the choice of the decision with a specially designed local optimization task, using the idea of semi-metric. Below it is presented in detail.

The local optimization task lies in the choice of such a decision among the set of possibilities in the given state $U_p(s)$, for which the value of a specially constructed local criterion is the lowest. The form of the local criterion and its weight coefficients are modified in the process of solution search. The coefficients are modified as a result of learning process.

The special local optimization criterion consists of three parts and is created in the following way. The first part concerns the value of the global index of quality for the generated trajectory. It consists of the increase of the quality index resulting from the realization of the considered decision and the value related to the estimation of the quality index for the final trajectory section, which follows the possible realization of the considered decision. This part of the criterion is suitable for problems, which quality criterion is additively separable and monotonically ascending along the trajectory [3].

The second part consists of components related to additional limitations or requirements. The components estimate the distance in the state space between the state in which the considered decision has been taken and the states belonging to the set of non-admissible states S_N, as well as unfavorable states or distinguished favorable states. Since the results of the decision are known no further than for one step ahead, it is necessary to introduce the "measure of distance" in the set of states, which will aid to define this distance. For that purpose, any semimetrics can be applied. As it is known, semimetrics, denotes here by ψ, differs from metrics in that it does not have to fulfill the condition $\psi\,(a,b) = 0 \Leftrightarrow a = b$.

The third part includes components responsible for the preference of certain types of decisions resulting from problem analysis.

The basic form of the local criterion $q(u,x,t)$ can be then represented as follows:

$$q(u,x,t) = \Delta Q(u,x,t) + {}^{\wedge}Q(u,x,t) + a_1 \cdot \varphi_1(u,x,t) + \ldots + a_i \cdot \varphi_i(u,x,t) + \ldots + a_n \cdot \varphi_n(u,x,t)$$
$$+ b_1 \cdot \rho_1(u,x,t) + \ldots + b_j \cdot \rho_j(u,x,t) + \ldots + b_m \cdot \rho_m(u,x,t)$$

$$(1)$$

where

- $\Delta Q(u,x,t)$ - increase of the quality index value as a result of decision u, undertaken in the state $s = (x,t)$,
- ${}^{\wedge}Q(u,x,t)$ - estimation of the quality index value for the final trajectory section after the decision u has been realized,

- $\varphi_i(u,x,t)$ - component reflecting additional limitations or additional requirements in the space of states, $i = 1,2,...,n$,
- a_i - coefficient which defines the weight of i-th component $\varphi_i(u,x,t)$,
- $\rho_j(u,x,t)$ - component responsible for the preference of certain types of decisions that are responsible for co-operation, $j = 1,2,...,m$,
- b_j - coefficient, which defines the weight of j-th component $\rho_j(u,x,t)$.

The significance of particular local criterion components may vary. The more significant a given component is, the higher value of its coefficient is. It is difficult to define optimal weights a priori. They depend both on the considered optimization problem as well as the input date for the particular optimization task (instance). The knowledge gathered in the course of experiments may be used to verify these coefficients. On the other hand, coefficient values established for the best trajectory represent aggregated knowledge obtained in the course of experiments.

The form of local criterion can by modified also in the course of trajectory generation. This is another characteristic element of presented method. Modification of the local criterion may result from the fact that during the generation of the same trajectory, some limitations lose sense and should be ignored. An example would be the case when the trajectory reaches the state from which it is definitely not able to pass to the non-admissible states or other distinguished unfavorable subsets of states. Then the coefficient of the adequate component should be equal to zero. So in addition to changes in the coefficients before the generation of the trajectory, there is a possibility of changing values of this coefficients during the generation of the same trajectory. This additional change takes place in the states belonging to certain distinguished subsets of states, for which certain limitations are inactive or less important. These subsets can be identified a priori, based on analysis of algebraic-logical model of problem or may be specified by the experts.

It is important that verification, whether the state belongs to a distinguished subset of states, should require the minimum or possibly a small amount of calculation, for example, checking only one or a few coordinates of state.

It should be emphasized that during the creation of a local criterion we need to consider some additional aspects. On one hand, the quality of the local criterion it should be good (criterion form should be good to choice the best decision). On the other hand, we must take into account the complexity and computation time of determining the value of a local criterion. Unfortunately, these postulates are often contradictory. Of course a simpler form of a local criterion is computationally easier to process. However, this form usually includes less information and thus choice of decisions may be less beneficial.

3.3   Intelligent Pruning Non-perspective Trajectory

Intelligent pruning of non-perspective trajectories can be realized if optimization criterion is additively separable and monotonically ascending along each trajectory of MDP. This properties have been defined in [3, 4]. Let's recall these definitions.

Let us denote: P—a fixed multistage decision process,

S^P—set of all states of trajectories of the process,

$d(\tilde{s})$—number of the last state of a finite trajectory $\tilde{s}$,

$\tilde{U}$—set of all decision sequences of the process P.

Definition 2. Criterion Q is a *separable* for the process P, if for every control $\tilde{u} \in \tilde{U}$ can be recursively calculated as follows:

Q_0 = const., in particular $Q_0 = 0$
$Q_{i+1} = f_Q(Q_i, u_i, s_i)$ for $i = 0, 1, \ldots, d(\tilde{s}) - 1$

where: Q_i for $i > 0$ denotes partial value of criterion Q calculated for i-th state of the considered trajectory, defined as follows:

- $Q_i = Q(\tilde{u}')$, where $\tilde{u}' = (u_0, u_2 \ldots u_{i-1})$ is the initial part of the sequence $\tilde{u}$,
- f_Q is some partial function $f_Q : \Re \times U \times S \rightarrow \Re$ such that:

$$Dom f_Q = \{(a, u, s) \in \Re \times U \times S : \quad s \in S^P, \ u \in U_P(s), \quad a \in \Re\} \qquad (2)$$

Separability is a property of an algorithm which calculates quality criterion for a sequence of decisions $\tilde{u}$, and thus for designated by him trajectory $\tilde{s}$. Criterion is separable if we can calculate its value for the next state of trajectory knowing its value in the previous state and the decision taken at that time.

Particularly useful are the property of additive separability of criterion. Let Q be separable criterion and ΔQ_i be the increase of criterion in the i-th state of a fixed trajectory of the process P:

$$\Delta Q_i = f_Q(Q_i, u_i, s_i) - Q_i \qquad (3)$$

Definition 3. Separable criterion Q is additive if ΔQ_i depends only on u_i and s_i (is independent of Q_i) for each $i = 0, 1, \ldots, d(\tilde{s})$ for each trajectory $\tilde{s}$

so:

$$Q_{i+1} = Q_i + \Delta Q_i(u_i, s_i) \qquad (4)$$

Definition 4. Separable criterion Q is monotonically ascending along each trajectory of the process P if $Q_{i+1} \geq Q_i$ for each decision sequence $\tilde{u} \in \tilde{U}$. If $Q_{i+1} \leq Q_i$ for each $\tilde{u} \in \tilde{U}$ we say that Q is monotonically descending.

This property can be used in our extended learning method for co-operation.

After finding the first admissible trajectory, the algorithm can execute pruning the final parts of the next trajectories. We realize pruning as follows: during the generation of a single trajectory we calculate the value of a quality criterion for each admissible state but which is not a goal state. This value we compare with the earlier obtained quality criterion value for the best admissible solution (the best admissible trajectory). If quality criterion values of the current state is larger than the quality criterion value for the best admissible solution, the generation of the current trajectory is interrupted. In this way, the trajectories with a worse quality index are eliminated and number of calculations is reduced.

3.4 Idea of Learning Method

The learning method consists in generation of consecutive solutions (trajectory). Each generated trajectory is analyzed. If it is not admissible, the reasons of the failure are examined. For example, it is examined through which subsets of not advantageous states the trajectory has passed. A role of the criterion components connected with these subsets should be strengthened for the next trajectory i.e. the weights (priorities) of these components should increase. When the generated trajectory is admissible, the role of the components responsible for the trajectory quality can be strengthened, i.e. their weights can be increased.

Every pruning, partial trajectory is analyzed. In particular, we test the state in which pruning was realized. Also we determine the distances between the trajectory states and states belonging to the set of not admissible generalized states. Pruning trajectories are thus a source of information that is used to modify the coefficients of a local criterion.

Based on the gained information, the local optimization task is being improved during simulation experiments. This process is treated as learning or intelligent searching algorithm.

The process of determining a solution based on the extended learning method may be terminated if one of the following conditions is fulfilled:

- we generate the number of trajectories, which was requested before the start of the simulation experiment,
- we obtain a satisfactory admissible solution (with a sufficiently good value of quality criterion),
- significant improvement of obtained admissible solutions for subsequent trajectories are not observed - there is no longer learning,
- all the trajectories of the process P was constructed (in most cases this situation does not happen in real size of problem).

3.5 Preliminary Analysis of Information

As we have noted above, the gathering and analyzing information during the consecutive generation of the trajectory is an important aspect of extended learning method. Equally important may be to analyze the input data before starting essential part of solutions searching.

Preliminary data analysis has two main purposes. The first aim is verification whether it is possible to exclude the existence of admissible solution. There is no point in searching this solution (starting generation of any trajectory) when on the basis of data analysis we have determined that an admissible solution of the considered problem instance does not exist. So, it eliminates unnecessary calculations. However, on the basis of this analysis it is not always possible to conclude that any admissible solution exists. Then algorithm execute the next steps, in spite of that the admissible trajectory may not be determined at all.

The second aim of the initial data analysis of considered problem (actually instances of the problem) is to define its characteristics. The results of analysis may enable to classify task to sub-problem, for which algorithm determining the best results has been previously developed. In particular, they can help to set an initial values of coefficients of a local criterion for decision choice.

Information obtained from the preliminary data analysis may be very useful for the further the algorithm execution. However, this analysis couldn't be very complicated. Its range and complexity should be such that the cost and time of its using does not exceed the cost and time of solutions determination by the algorithm.

3.6 Schema of Learning Algorithm with Pruning

Based on the extended learning method we can create a lot of algorithms for solving different problems of cooperation. Figure 1 shows a general scheme of the algorithm that represents a class of algorithms based on the presented method.

In scheme, fragments that characterize the class of considered algorithms were shown: a preliminary analysis, the choice of the decision with using the local criterion, pruning trajectory, analysis of data and obtained information. A following designations are used in scheme:

- $Q_{tr}(s)$ - value of quality index in state s for tr-th trajectory,
- Q_{min} - the best value of the global quality index of previously generated admissible trajectories (upper bound).

4   Scheduling Problem with State Dependent Resources

The presented learning method is very useful for difficult scheduling problems especially for problems with state dependent resources. Managing projects, especially software projects, belongs to this class.

To illustrate an application of the extended learning method, let us consider a specific, very difficult scheduling problem that takes place during scheduling preparatory works in mines. The set of headings in the mine must be driven in order to render the exploitation field accessible. The headings form a net formally, represented by a non-oriented multigraph $G = (W, C, P)$ where the set of branches C and the set of nodes W represent the set of headings and the set of heading crossings respectively, and relation $P \subset (W \times C \times W)$ determines connections between the headings (a partial order between the headings).

There are two types of working groups. Each of them use driving machines that differ in efficiency, cost of driving, and necessity of transport. Machines of the first type (set $M1$) are more effective but their cost of driving is much higher than of the second type (set $M2$). Additionally, the first type of machines must be transported when driving starts at a different heading crossing than the one in which the machine is placed, while the second type of machines needs no transport. Driving a heading cannot be interrupted before its completion and can be done only by one machine at a time.

There are given due dates for some of the headings. They result from the formerly prepared plan of field exploitation. One must determine the order of heading driving and kind of working group which each heading should be driven by, so that the total

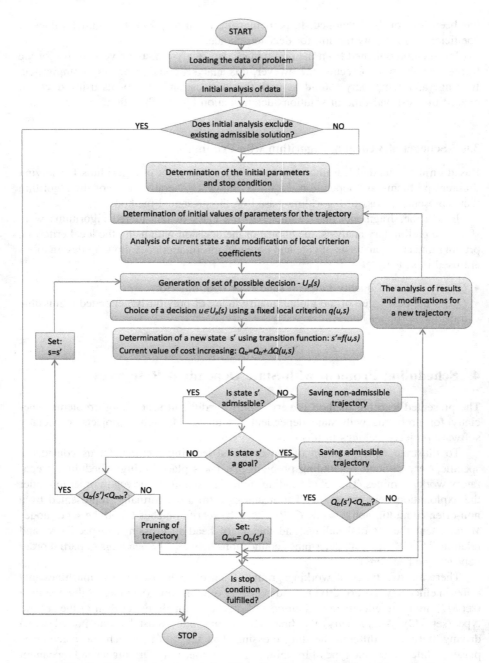

Fig. 1. Schema of proposed algorithms based on extended learning method

cost of driving is minimal and each heading complete before its due date. There are given the following: lengths of the headings $dl(c)$, efficiency of both types of machines $V_{Dr(m)}$ (driving length per time unit), cost of a length unit driven for both kinds of machines, cost of the time unit waiting for both kinds of machines, speed of machine transport $V_{Tr(m)}$ and transport cost per a length unit.

Let us notice that the driven headings become the transport ways and may accelerate realization of other headings (tasks). Thus, it is problem with state dependent resources. It is NP-hard [13].

4.1   Formal Model of Problem

The process state at any instant t is defined as a vector $x = (x^0, x^1, x^2, ..., x^{|M|})$, where $M = M1 \cup M2$. A coordinate x^0 describes a set of headings (branches) that has been driven to the moment t.

The other coordinates x^m describes state of the m-th machine, where $m = 1, 2, ..., |M|$. A structure of the machine state is as follows:

$$x^m = (p, \omega, \lambda) \tag{5}$$

where

- $p \in C \cup \{0\}$ - represents the number of the heading assigned to the m-th machine to drive;
- $\omega \in W$ - the number of the crossing (node), where the machine is located or the number of the node, in which it finishes driving the assigned heading c;
- $\lambda \in [0, \infty)$ - the length of the route that remains to reach the node $\omega = w$ by the m-th machine (in particular $\lambda > dl(c)$ meaning that the machine is being transported to the heading, the value λ is the sum of the length of heading c and the length of the route until the transportation is finished).

A state $s = (x, t)$ belongs to the set of non-admissible states if there is a heading which driving is not complete yet and its due date is earlier than t. The definition S_N is as follows:

$$S_N = \{s = (x, t) : (\exists c \in C, \ c \notin x^0) \wedge d(c) < t\} \tag{6}$$

where $d(c)$ denotes the due date for the heading c.

A state $s = (x, t)$ is a goal if all the headings have been driven. The definition of the set of goal states S_G is as follows:

$$S_G = \{s = (x, t) : s \notin S_N \wedge (\forall c \in C, \ c \in x^0)\} \tag{7}$$

A decision determines the headings that should be started at the moment t, machines which drive, machines that should be transported, headings along which machines are to be transported and machines that should wait. Thus, the decision $u = (u^1, u^2, ..., u^{|M|})$ where the co-ordinate u^m refers to the m-th machine and $u^m = C \cup \{0\}$. $u^m = 0$ denotes continuation of the previous machine operations (continuation of driving with possible transport or further stopover). $u^m = c$ denotes the number of heading c that is assigned to be driven by machine m. As a result of this decision, the machine starts driving the heading c or is transported by the shortest way to the node of the heading c.

Obviously, not all decisions can be taken into the state (x, t). The decision $u(x, t)$ must belong to the set of possible (reasonable) decisions $U_p(x, t)$. For example, a decision $u^m = c$ is possible only when the c-th heading is neither being driven nor completed and is available, i.e. there is a way to transport machine to the one of the heading crossing adjacent to the c-th heading or machine is standing in the one of the heading crossings adjacent to the c-th heading.

Moreover, in the given state $s = (x, t)$, to each machine waiting in the node w, (it has not assigned a heading to perform), we can assign an available heading or it can be decided that it should continue to wait. However, each machine which has been previously assigned a heading and is currently driving it or it is being transported to that heading, can be only assigned to continue the current activity.

Based on the current state $s = (x, t)$ and the decision u taken in this state, the subsequent state $(x', t') = f(u, x, t)$ is generated by means of the transition function f.

Firstly, it is necessary to determine the moment t' when the subsequent state occurs, that is the nearest moment in which at least one machine will finish driving a heading. For that purpose, t_m time of completion of the realized task needs to be calculated for each machine. The subsequent state will occur in the moment $t' = t + \Delta t$, where Δt equals the lowest value of the established set of t_m.

Once the moment t' is known, it is possible to determine the proper state of the process at the time.

The first coordinate x^0 of the proper state, that is the set of completed headings, is increased by the number of headings whose driving has been finished in the moment t':

$$ x^{0'} = x^0 \cup \left\{ c : \quad \underset{m \in M}{\exists} \quad x^m(s) = (p, \omega, \lambda) \ \wedge \ p = c \ \wedge \ t_m = \Delta t \right\} \qquad (8) $$

Afterwards, the values of subsequent coordinates in the new state are determined $x^{m'} = (p', \omega', \lambda')$, for $m = 1, 2 ... |M|$, which represent the states of particular machines.

Particular parameters of the coordinate of the new machine state are determined in the way described in Table 1, where $w_k(c)$ is the node adjacent to the heading c, in which the machine will finish driving, and $|r_{min}(m, c)|$ is the length of the shortest transportation route to the heading c for the machine m.

4.2   Learning Algorithm

An algorithm based on extended learning method for the considered problem is proposed in this section. This algorithm generates consecutive trajectories using the special local optimization task. A trajectory generation is interrupted when in the newly generated state we obtain quality index which is worse than a quality index for the best founded solution. The information gained as a result of the trajectory analysis is used to modify the local optimization task for the next trajectory. This approach is treated as a learning without a teacher.

Table 1. Particular parameters of the coordinate of the new machine state.

for the decision to continue the activity of the machine $u^m = 0$:
$$p' = \begin{cases} p & \text{for} & t_m > \Delta t \\ 0 & \text{for} & t_m = \Delta t \end{cases}$$
$$\omega' = \omega$$
$$\lambda' = \begin{cases} \lambda - V_{Tr(m)} \cdot \min\left(\dfrac{\max(\lambda - dl(c),0)}{V_{Tr(m)}}, \Delta t\right) - V_{Dr(m)} \cdot \max\left(\Delta t - \dfrac{\max(\lambda - dl(c),0)}{V_{Tr(m)}}, 0\right) & \text{for } m \in M1 \\ \lambda - V_{Dr(m)} \cdot \Delta t & \text{for } m \in M2 \end{cases}$$
for the decision to assign a new task to the machine $u^m = c$:
$$p' = \begin{cases} c & \text{for} & t_m > \Delta t \\ 0 & \text{for} & t_m = \Delta t \end{cases}$$
$$\omega' = w_k(c)$$
$$\lambda' = \begin{cases} |r_{\min}(m,c)| + dl(c) - V_{Tr(m)} \cdot \min\left(\dfrac{|r_{\min}(m,c)|}{V_{Tr(m)}}, \Delta t\right) - V_{Dr(m)} \cdot \max\left(\Delta t - \dfrac{|r_{\min}(m,c)|}{V_{Tr(m)}}, 0\right) & \text{for } m \in M1 \\ dl(c) - V_{Dr(m)} \cdot \Delta t & \text{for } m \in M2 \end{cases}$$

A preliminary analysis of data is made as a first step of the algorithm. The purpose of this analysis is to determine some characteristic quantities, which are useful in grouping heading networks (the instances of the problem) with similar parameters. They may also be useful for creating or matching the local optimization task. The analysis gives the following information: the length of shortest heading, the length of the longest heading, the average length of headings, the total length of all headings, the number of headings with due date, the earliest due date and the latest deadline.

Additionally, a simple analysis is performed for a time limitation. Firstly, we verify if the time limitation are active for the considered problem instance. This is true when one team uses a slower machines (without transport) can drive all headings before the earliest due date. Secondly, it can be concluded: if for any heading with due date the team with the fastest machine doesn't manage to drive heading and the shortest path which leads to it from the initial node before its due date, then time limitation are not fulfilled. Then at once (without unnecessary simulation calculations) we can say that admissible solution doesn't exist.

The local optimization task is defined in the next step of algorithm. The local criterion takes into account a component connected with cost of work, a component connected with necessity for trajectory to omit the states of set S_N and a component for preferring some co-operation decisions. Thus, the local criterion is of the form (a_1, b_1 - weights of particular components):

$$q(u,x,t) = \Delta Q(u,x,t) + {}^{\wedge}Q(u,x,t) + a_1 \cdot E(u,x,t) + b_1 \cdot F(u,x,t) \qquad (9)$$

where $\Delta Q(u, x, t)$ denotes the increase of work cost as a result of realizing decision u and ${}^{\wedge}Q(u, x, t)$ the estimate of the cost of finishing the set of headings matching the final section of the trajectory. The third component $E(u, x, t)$, connected with the necessity for the trajectory to omit the states of set S_N, is defined by means of a semimetrics. The fourth component is aimed at reduction of machine idleness time and at performing transport ways. Since the model considers the possibility that the machines will stand idle in certain cases, it seems purposeful to prefer decisions which will engage all machines to for most of the time. It is therefore necessary to reduce the probability of selecting the decision about machine stopover when headings are available for driving and machines could be used for work. This may be realized by using an additional auxiliary criterion $F(u, x, t)$, which takes into consideration penalty for a decision about a stopover in the case when a machine could have started another work/task.

In the course of trajectory generation, the local optimization task may be changed. Problem analysis reveals that the moment all headings with due dates are already finished, it is advisable to use only cheaper machines. Formally, this corresponds to the limitation of the set of possible decisions $U_p(s)$. Moreover, it is no longer necessary to apply the component $E(u, x, t)$ in the local criterion. The modified criterion is as follows: $q(u, x, t) = \Delta Q(u, x, t) + {}^{\wedge}Q(u, x, t) + b_1 \cdot F(u, x, t)$.

In order to select a decision in the given state s, it is necessary to generate and verify the entire set of possible decisions in the considered state $U_p(s)$. For each decision u_k, it is necessary to determine the state the system would reach after realizing it. Such a potentially consecutive state of the process will be represented as $s_{p\_k} = (x_{p\_k}, t_{p\_k})$. Afterwards, the criterion components are calculated. The increase of cost $\Delta Q(u_k, x, t)$ is the sum of costs resulting from the activities of particular machines in the period of time $t_{p\_k} - t$. The estimate of the cost of the final trajectory section ${}^{\wedge}Q(u_k, x, t)$ can be determined in a number of ways. One of these is to establish the summary cost of finishing previously undertaken decisions, which realization has not been completed yet, and the cost of a certain relaxed task, realized in the cheapest way. Taking into consideration that the estimate should take place with the lowest number of calculations, there has been proposed relaxation which would include omitting temporal limitations and the assuming the least expensive procedure for finishing the remaining headings; this would involve using the least expensive machines.

The component $E(u_k, x, t)$ uses the value of the estimated "distance" between the state s_{p_k}, and the set of inadmissible states. The distance is estimated with the help of semimetrics $\psi(s, S_N) = min\{\psi(s, s'): s' \in S_N\}$.

Assuming that the speed of transporting the "fastest" machine is significantly higher than its speed of performance, and this one in turn significantly exceeds the speed of performance of the remaining machines, it is possible to omit the time of transporting of the fastest machine. For the sake of simplicity, let us assume that there is just one fastest machine.

One of the methods of determining $E(u_k, x, t)$ is to calculate the time reserve $rt_c(s_{p\_k})$ for each not realized and not assigned heading c with due date.

Taking into consideration these assumptions $rt_c(s_{p\_k})=d(c) - t_{p\_k} - \tau(c) - t_{end}$, where $d(c)$ denotes due date for the heading c, $\tau(c)$ denotes time necessary to drive heading c and all the headings situated along the shortest route from the heading c to the so-called realized area in the given state, by the fastest machine, t_{end} denotes time necessary to finalize the current activity of the fastest machine.

The parameters t_{end} and $\tau(c)$ results for following situations. First, "the fastest" machine may continue the previously assigned task to drive another heading. Second, heading c may be inaccessible and it might be necessary to drive the shortest route to this spot from the realized area, involving already excavated headings as well as those assigned for excavation together with relevant crossings. For the period of time when the fastest machine finishes the excavation of the previously assigned heading, a fragment of this distance may be excavated by the fastest of the remaining machines. When the heading is accessible the time equals the time of excavating the length of the heading with the fastest machine.

Finally, this component is as follow:

$$E(u_k, x, t) = \begin{cases} \infty & \text{for } \min rt_c(s_{p\_k}) < 0 \\ \dfrac{1}{\min rt_c(s_{p\_k})} & \text{for } \min rt_c(s_{p\_k}) > 0 \end{cases} \tag{10}$$

As a result, the decision to be taken, from the set of considered decisions, is the one for which the subsequent state is most distant from the set of non-admissible states.

Component $F(u_k, x, t)$ in certain cases should make it purposeful to prefer decisions which will engage all machines for most of the time. It is therefore necessary to reduce the probability of selecting the decision about machine stopover when headings are available for driving and machines could be used for work, especially for transport ways performance. For that purpose, a penalty may be imposed for the stopover of each machine that could potentially start driving an available heading. The proposed form is $F(u_k, x, t)=R \cdot i_{waiting}$ where R denotes the penalty for machine stopover, (calculated for the decision about stopover when there are still headings available for work), $i_{waiting}$ denotes the number of machines that are supposed to remain idle as a result of such a decision.

The values a_1 and b_1 are respectively coefficients defining the weight of particular components and reflect current knowledge about controls, whilst their values change in the course of calculations. The higher the weight of a given parameter, the higher its value.

If the generated trajectory is non-admissible, then for the subsequent trajectory, the value of weight a_1 should be increased; which means the increase of the weight of the component estimating the distance from the set of non-admissible states and/or the increase of weight b_1 value, which would result in lower probability of machine stopover. If the generated trajectory is admissible, then for the subsequent trajectory the values of coefficients may be decreased.

It is easy to prove that the criterion Q is monotonically increasing along each trajectory. Thus, the pruning of non-perspective parts of trajectory may be applied.

During the generation of a single trajectory we calculate the value of a quality criterion for each admissible state but which is not a goal state. This value we compare with the quality criterion value for the best admissible solution (the upper bound). If quality criterion values of the current state is larger than the quality criterion value for the best admissible solution, the generation of the current trajectory is interrupted. Then coefficients of local criterion are modified. The weight of coefficients responsible for optimization quality criterion increase.

Let's estimate the algorithm computational complexity. It is equal to the product of a trajectory generation algorithm complexity $comp(\tilde{s})$ and established, by a stop condition, number of trajectories to be generated.

Complexity of a trajectory generation algorithm $comp(\tilde{s})$ is equal to product of number of the trajectory states $d(\tilde{s})$, complexity of the transition function step, complexity of local optimization task procedure, complexity of the pruning procedure in a state s and the procedure verifying if a state s belongs to the set S_G or S_N.

The maximal number of any trajectory states $d(\tilde{s})$ is equal to a number of jobs. Complexity of transition function is polynomial. It is so, the number of state as well as decision coordinates depend polynomially on numbers of machines and the procedure modifying the state coordinates is polynomial. Obviously, both the pruning procedure and the verifying one are polynomial, because they depend on number of state/decision coordinates only.

Complexity of local optimization task algorithm in the worst case depends on the cardinality of $U_p(s)$. Although, cardinality of a set $U_p(s)$ can't be estimated by a polynomial but it is of order (n^m) where m is relatively small. Moreover, cardinality of $U_p(s)$ strongly decreases for consecutive states of a trajectory.

4.3   Experiments

Optimal executor co-operation results in the best possible value of global cost. In considered problem, the fact that some executors (machines) perform the job that enables work for another one is the essence of cooperation. In particular, in the case of little time reserve of some heading (small value of semi-metric) some executors may prepare transport way for fast executor which should perform that heading to deadline. Component $F(u,x,t)$ corresponds with it. The aim of experiments was to verify the effectiveness of proposed method for executor co-operation (especially form of local criterion and applying the components $E(u, x, t)$ and $F(u, x, t)$).

The research was conducted for the set of 8 heading networks. Each network is represented by a planar graph, in which the vertex degrees equal from 1 to 4. The lengths of headings are numbers from the range [19, 120]. The number of headings with due dates is approximately 25 % of all headings. Two machines are used to perform the task, one of the first type and one of the second type. Parameters of machines are given in the Table 2. The symbols GI and GII denote regular and irregular structure of the network respectively.

Firstly, the effectiveness of component $E(u, x, t)$ was tested. For each network 40 trajectories was constructed with the changing value of coefficient a_1 and zero value of coefficient b_1.

Table 2. Parameters of the machines.

Parameter	Machine of M1 type	Machine of M2 type
Efficiency [m/h]	10.0	5.0
Transport speed [m/h]	100.0	Unspecified
Driving cost [$/h]	200.0	50.0
Transport cost [$/h]	100.0	0.0
Waiting cost [$/h]	30.0	5.0

The first trajectory was always generated when coefficient a_1 was equal to zero. Then the criterion does not include the component $E(u, x, t)$. Depending on the previously obtained result this coefficient has been changing for the next trajectory.

Characteristic parameters are determined after generating each subsequent trajectories: the time margin for headings with due date (the period of time between time of finishing of driving the heading and its due date), the minimal time margin and average time margin for all heading with due date. These parameters illustrate how far process trajectory passes from the non-admissible state. Values of these parameters are helpful to determine the value of coefficient a_1.

Table 3 shows results for one of the networks: GI-1. It is typical results for all networks. A value of coefficient a_1, the obtained total cost and time of network performing are given. The symbol "*" indicates that admissible solution was not obtained. In addition, the time margin for heading with due date is given. A negative value indicates how many time due date has been exceeded. The symbol "*" means that driving a heading with due date was not stated. It is also given minimum time margin for all headings and the value of average time margin when we have obtained an admissible solution.

Based on the obtained results for all network, it can be concluded that increasing the value of $E(u, x, t)$ increases the probability of obtaining an admissible solution. When the component $E(u, x, t)$ was omitted, an admissible solution was not found. In performed experiments we observed that increasing the weight of this component in the local criterion (by increasing the value of the coefficient a_1) allows to find an admissible solution. A relatively low value of coefficient a_1 causes the solution of low total cost. Further increase in the share value of this component in local criterion causes that the more expensive technology is engaging for heading driving. Therefore founding solutions has a higher total cost.

Secondly, component $F(u, x, t)$ influence on the total cost was tested. For each network trajectories were constructed with the changing value of coefficient a_1. In most cases, the increase of weight of this component resulted in increased total costs, but at the same time the probability of finding an admissible solution was higher.

To evaluate the effectiveness of the proposed algorithm one has compared the obtained results with the optimal solution. A complete review algorithm for all considered heading network has been applied. Optimal solution was found only for network GI-2. In other cases, the calculations were interrupted after more than 2 days. Only for four networks an admissible solution has been found, while for the other

Table 3. Results of applying the components $E(u,x,t)$ for the networks: GI-1.

Value of coeff. a_1	Best found cost	Time margin for head. 7	Time margin for head. 9	Time margin for head. 15	Time margin for head. 18	Time margin for head. 20	Min. time margin	Average time margin
0	*	32,67	21,00	*	*	*	*	*
1	*	32,67	21,00	*	*	*	*	*
10	*	32,67	21,00	0,46	−7,77	*	*	*
50	*	32,67	21,00	2,90	*	*	*	*
250	*	32,67	21,00	2,90	−6,83	*	*	*
500	*	32,67	21,00	2,90	2,83	*	*	*
750	*	32,67	21,00	2,90	2,83	*	*	*
2500	*	32,67	21,00	0,46	*	*	*	*
5000	*	32,67	21,00	0,46	*	*	*	*
7500	*	32,67	21,00	6,10	1,10	−3,60	*	*
25000	*	32,67	21,00	6,10	−4,00	1,20	*	*
50000	17221,10	15,30	18,50	21,90	3,73	9,00	3,73	13,69
1000000	17249,10	37,40	6,10	22,20	1,08	6,35	1,08	14,63

networks an acceptable solution has not been found at this time. Table 4 presents the summary of performed experiments. The second column contains the optimal cost for network GI-2 and the best found total cost by a complete review algorithm for which calculation was stopped after 2 days. The symbol "*" means that any admissible solution has not been found during 2 days. The next columns respectively contains the best found total cost by a proposed algorithm, value of coefficient a_1 and value of coefficient b_1 for this cost. Moreover, percentage of the cost of using machine $M1$ in the total cost and percentage of the length headings which was made by machine $M1$ in total driving work is given.

Table 4. Results of applying the components $E(u,x,t)$ and $F(u,x,t)$.

Network	Best found cost by complete review alg.	Best found cost by proposed alg.	Value of coeff. a_1	Value of coeff. b_1	Cost of using machine $M1$[%]	Length made by machine $M1$[%]
GI-1	16480,00	16922,00	50000	2	70 %	50 %
GI-2	16524,40	17284,10	55555	2	75 %	58 %
GI-3	17448,90	16359,90	25000	0	61 %	41 %
GII-4	23132,40	22665,17	500000	0	61 %	35 %
GII-5a	*	30946,32	250000	0,5	65 %	42 %
GII-5b	*	30888,33	250000	0	62 %	37 %
GII-6	31142,54	30662,31	5000	0	60 %	35 %
GII-7	*	77288,44	250000	1	72 %	52 %

The result of experiments shows that the difference between sub-optimal cost and the best found by the learning algorithm is small and in the worst case is 4.59 %. Percentage difference of cost is calculated as (LAcost-RAcost)/RAcost where LA, RA denote best cost calculated by proposed algorithm and completed review algorithm respectively. It can be stated that presented algorithm finds a better solution in most cases. It should be also pointed that its calculation time was very short (a several seconds). Moreover, using trajectory pruning reduced the number generated states, and thus solutions were found faster.

Based on the obtained results, it can be concluded that the application of the proposed algorithm for the presented problem yields very positive results. Results of another experiment are given in [13].

5 Conclusions

The paper presents a novel extended machine learning method for working out co-operation for project realizations. The method is a hybrid one. It joins primary learning method based on ALM given in [5, 7] and developed in [9] with pruning method.

To illustrate the extended learning conception, some NP-hard problem, namely a scheduling problem with state dependent resources is considered and the learning algorithm for it is presented. Results of computer experiments confirm the efficiency of the algorithm.

Novelty of machine learning method based on ALM is a fact that it is based on a formal algebraic-logical model of multistage decision processes (ALM of MDP). Thus, initial knowledge is delivered by means of a formal model of the problem. Then the additional knowledge is being acquired and gathered during successive experiments which consist in generation of subsequent trajectories.

The method uses a sophisticated structure of local optimization task. The structure as well as parameters of the task are modified during search process. It is done on a basis of acquiring information during previous iterations.

Using a formal model allows to present an optimization method on a general level (high level of abstraction). It is also able to define strictly the properties of the problem, for which this method can be applied. In particular, the ALM of MDP allows to define the approximate distance in state space, even though the state space is not a numerical space. It is done by means of semimetric. The semimetric is used to define the local optimization task.

Novelty of the extended learning method consist in integration of primary learning method based on ALM with pruning method. The introduced extension consists in acquiring of additional knowledge which is referred to quality criterion of generated trajectories and this knowledge is using to prune non-perspective parts of state tree.

Comparing our method with methods of machine learning [2, 10], presented approach has similarities to reinforcement learning [16]. However, it is not its typical example.

A large number of difficult combinatorial problems can be efficiently solved by means of the presented method. Especially, the method is very useful for difficult scheduling problems with state depended resources. Managing projects, especially software projects belong to this class. The problems of this type don't belong to the classical scheduling problems. Thus, It is difficult to compare the proposed method with others. The authors intend to compare the proposed method with the other (nature inspired algorithms, evolutionary algorithms) for simpler known problems in the later research stages.

References

1. Bolc, L., Cytowski, J.: Search Methods for Artificial Intelligence. Academic Press, London (1992)
2. Cherkassky, V., Mulier, F.: Learning from Data: Concepts, Theory, and Methods. Wiley, New York (2007)
3. Dudek-Dyduch, E.: Formalization and analysis of problems of discrete manufacturing processes. Automatics, vol. 54, (in Polish) (1990) (Scientific bulletin of AGH University)
4. Dudek-Dyduch, E.: Control of discrete event processes - branch and bound method. In: Proceedings of IFAC/Ifors/Imacs Symposium Large Scale Systems: Theory and Applications, Chinese Association of Automation, vol. 2, pp. 573–578 (1992)
5. Dudek-Dyduch, E.: Learning based algorithm in scheduling. J. Intell. Manuf. **11**(2), 135–143 (2000)
6. Dudek-Dyduch, E., Dutkiewicz, L.: Substitution task method for NP-hard scheduling problems. Automatics vol. 143, pp. 57–66 (in Polish) (2006) (Scientific bulletin of Silesian University of Technology)
7. Dudek-Dyduch, E., Dyduch, T.: Learning algorithms for scheduling using knowledge based model. In: Rutkowski, L., Tadeusiewicz, R., Zadeh, L.A., Żurada, J.M. (eds.) ICAISC 2006. LNCS (LNAI), vol. 4029, pp. 1091–1100. Springer, Heidelberg (2006)
8. Dudek-Dyduch, E., Fuchs-Seliger, S.: Approximate algorithms for some tasks in management and economy. Syst. Model. Control. **1**(7), 148–152 (1993)
9. Dudek-Dyduch, E., Kucharska, E.: Learning method for co-operation. In: Jędrzejowicz, P., Nguyen, N.T., Hoang, K. (eds.) ICCCI 2011, Part II. LNCS(LNAI), vol. 6923, pp. 290–300. Springer, Heidelberg (2011). ISSN 0302-9743, ISBN 978-3-642-23937-3
10. Flach, P.: Machine Learning: The Art and Science of Algorithms that Make Sense of Data. Cambridge University Press, Cambridge (2012)
11. Jędrzejowicz, P.: A-teams and their applications. In: Nguyen, N.T., Kowalczyk, R., Chen, S. M., et al. (eds.) ICCCI 2009. LNCS, vol. 5796, pp. 36–50. Springer, Heidelberg (2009)
12. Kolish, R., Drexel, A.: Adaptive Search for Solving Hard Project Scheduling Problems. Naval Research Logistics, vol.42 (1995)
13. Kucharska, E.: Application of an algebraic-logical model for optimization of scheduling problems with retooling time depending on system state. Ph.D. thesis (in Polish) (2006)
14. Priore, P., de la Fuente, D., Puente, J., Parreño, J.: A comparison of machine-learning algorithms for dynamic scheduling of flexible manufacturing systems. Eng. Appl. Artif. Intell. **19**(3), 247–255 (2006)
15. Sprecher, A., Kolish, R., Drexel, A.: Semiactive, active and not delay schedules for the resource constrained project scheduling problem. Eur. J. Oper. Res. **80**, 94–102 (1993)

16. Śnieżyński, B.: Resource management in a multi-agent system by means of reinforcement learning and supervised rule learning. In: Shi, Y., van Albada, G.D., Dongarra, J., Sloot, P. M.A. (eds.) ICCS 2007, Part II. LNCS, vol. 4488, pp. 864–871. Springer, Heidelberg (2007)
17. Tadeusiewicz, R.: New trends in neurocybernetics. Comput. Meth. Mater. Sci. **10**(1), 1–7 (2010)

Methods of Prediction Improvement in Efficient MPC Algorithms Based on Fuzzy Hammerstein Models

Piotr M. Marusak[✉]

Institute of Control and Computation Engineering, Warsaw University of Technology,
ul. Nowowiejska 15/19, 00-665 Warszawa, Poland
P.Marusak@ia.pw.edu.pl

Abstract. Two methods of prediction improvement in Model Predictive Control (MPC) algorithms utilizing fuzzy Hammerstein models are proposed in the paper. The first one consists in iterative adjustment of the prediction, the second one – in utilization of disturbance measurement. Though the methods can significantly improve control system operation, they modify the prediction in such a way that it is described by relatively simple analytical formulas. Thus, the prediction has such a form that the MPC algorithms using it are formulated as numerically efficient quadratic optimization problems. Efficiency of the MPC algorithms based on the prediction utilizing the proposed methods of improvement is demonstrated in the example control system of a nonlinear control plant with significant time delay.

Keywords: Fuzzy control · Fuzzy systems · Predictive control · Nonlinear control · Constrained control

1 Introduction

Model Predictive Control (MPC) algorithms are widely used in practical applications due to numerous advantages they offer. They use prediction of the control plant behavior during calculation of control signal [3,9,17,19]. Thanks to such an approach they can be successfully applied to processes with difficult dynamics (large time delays, inverse response), also constraints existing in the control system (put e.g. on manipulated and output variables) can be relatively easy taken into consideration in these algorithms. Moreover, all information available to a control system designer can be relatively easy used to improve prediction the MPC algorithm is based on and, as a result, to improve control performance offered by the MPC algorithm. This feature will be exploited in the paper.

In order to obtain prediction a model of the control plant is utilized. As different models can be used to obtain the prediction, different MPC algorithms were designed. In the standard MPC algorithms linear process models are used. In such a case however, if the control plant is nonlinear the MPC algorithm may generate inefficient results. Therefore, it is good to use nonlinear models during

© Springer-Verlag Berlin Heidelberg 2014
N.T. Nguyen (Ed.): TCCI XIV 2014, LNCS 8615, pp. 158–179, 2014.
DOI: 10.1007/978-3-662-44509-9_8

prediction generation. An interesting class of nonlinear models are Hammerstein models [7]. In these models the nonlinear static block precedes the linear dynamic block. Such structure of the model makes possible to do synthesis of the MPC algorithm relatively easy if the model is appropriately used.

Many MPC controllers based on Hammerstein models use the approach in which the inverse static model is used to compensate the nonlinearity of the control plant; see e.g. [1,8]. Unfortunately such an approach has disadvantages. Derivation of the inverse model may be difficult. Moreover, taking manipulated variable constraints into consideration in such algorithms is complicated, because after usage of the inverse static model, the constraints must be nonlinearly transformed [1].

The another approach consists in using the classical optimization–based MPC. In current research it is assumed that the dynamic part of the Hammerstein model has the form of the step response. It is also assumed that in the static block of the Hammerstein model the fuzzy Takagi–Sugeno (TS) model is used. Thanks to such an approach advantages offered by the fuzzy TS models [16,18], like e.g. relative easiness of model identification, relatively small number of rules needed to describe highly nonlinear functions or property that the fuzzy reasoning makes possible to obtain a linear approximation of the model relatively easy, can be utilized. The assumed form of the Hammerstein model makes possible to do synthesis of the MPC algorithm relatively easy if the model is appropriately used (see e.g. [12,14]). Moreover, in the case of analytical MPC algorithms, the structure of the controller may be simplified to the large extent; see [13].

Direct usage of a nonlinear process model in the MPC algorithm leads to its formulation as a nonlinear, nonquadratic, often nonconvex optimization problem, which must be solved in each iteration of the algorithm; see e.g. [6]. Despite improved versions of procedures solving the nonlinear optimization problems are designed (see e.g. [4] for modifications of particle swarm optimization and of genetic algorithms, taking into account properties of modern CPUs), nonlinear, nonconvex optimization has serious drawbacks. Time needed to find the solution of such an optimization problem is hard to predict. There is also problem of local minima. Moreover, in some cases numerical problems may occur. The drawbacks of the MPC algorithms formulated as nonlinear optimization problems caused that usually MPC algorithms formulated as the standard quadratic programming problems, and utilizing a linear approximation of the control plant model, obtained at each iteration, are used [10–12,14,15,19].

The methods of prediction improvement proposed in the paper can be divided into two groups. The first one consists in using sophisticated methods of prediction generation using the fuzzy Hammerstein model of the process, described in Sect. 4.2. Let remind that in [12] prediction is obtained using the original fuzzy Hammerstein model and its linear approximation. In [14] improvement of this method of prediction was proposed. It uses not only the original fuzzy Hammerstein model and its linear approximation but also values of the future control changes derived by the MPC algorithm in the previous iteration. In the paper it is described how to improve this method of prediction even more. It is possible because the prediction can be iteratively adjusted. As a result it is closer to the prediction obtained using the nonlinear process model only. However, still the prediction can be obtained relatively easy and the MPC algorithm using it can be formulated as the quadratic optimization problem. The second group of methods, described in Sect. 4.4, makes possible to take into consideration disturbance measurement during prediction generation. It will be demonstrated in the example control system that utilization of such mechanisms may radically improve control performance.

In the next section the general idea of the MPC algorithms is described. In Sect. 3 MPC algorithms based on linear models are described. In Sect. 4 the MPC algorithms based on the fuzzy Hammerstein models are reminded and extended with the proposed methods of prediction improvement. The efficacy of the MPC algorithms utilizing the proposed methods of prediction improvement is illustrated by the example results presented in Sect. 5. The last section contains summary of the paper.

2   General Idea of Model Predictive Control Algorithms

In the MPC algorithms a model of a control plant is used to predict future behavior of the plant many sampling instants ahead; number of these future sampling instants p is called the prediction horizon. It is assumed that many future values of the control signal (a trajectory of the control signal) are calculated; number of future changes of the control signal s is called the control horizon. Control horizon must be not greater than the prediction horizon ($s \leq p$); in practice it is assumed much smaller in order to simplify computations, without sacrificing control quality; see e.g. [19].

The future trajectory of the control signal is generated in such a way that the prediction of the control plant behavior fulfills assumed criteria. Usually it is demanded that future values of the output should be as close to the desired value as possible and, at the same time, the control signal should not change too much. Moreover, constraints existing in the control system should be fulfilled. The mentioned criteria are used to formulate the optimization problem, solved by the algorithm at each iteration. This optimization problem has usually the following form [3,9,17,19]:

$$\arg \min_{\Delta u} \left\{ J_{\mathrm{MPC}} = (\overline{y} - y)^T \cdot (\overline{y} - y) + \Delta u^T \cdot \Lambda \cdot \Delta u \right\} \qquad (1)$$

subject to:

$$\Delta u_{\min} \leq \Delta u \leq \Delta u_{\max}, \qquad (2)$$

$$u_{\min} \leq u \leq u_{\max}, \qquad (3)$$

$$y_{\min} \leq y \leq y_{\max}, \qquad (4)$$

where $\overline{y} = [\overline{y}_k, \ldots, \overline{y}_k]^T$ is the vector of length p, $\overline{y}_k$ is a set–point value, $y = [y_{k+1|k}, \ldots, y_{k+p|k}]^T$, $y_{k+i|k}$ is a value of the output for the $(k+i)^{\mathrm{th}}$ sampling instant, predicted at the kth sampling instant, $\Delta \boldsymbol{u} = \left[\Delta u_{k|k}, \ldots, \Delta u_{k+s-1|k} \right]^T$, $\Delta u_{k+i|k}$ are future changes in manipulated variable, $\boldsymbol{u} = \left[u_{k|k}, \ldots, u_{k+s-1|k} \right]^T$, $\boldsymbol{\Lambda} = \lambda \cdot \boldsymbol{I}$ is the $s \times s$ matrix, $\lambda \geq 0$ is a tuning parameter; $\Delta \boldsymbol{u}_{\min}$, $\Delta \boldsymbol{u}_{\max}$, $\boldsymbol{u}_{\min}$, $\boldsymbol{u}_{\max}$, $\boldsymbol{y}_{\min}$, $\boldsymbol{y}_{\max}$ are vectors of lower and upper limits of changes and values of the control signal and of the values of the output variable, respectively.

As a solution of the optimization problem (1–4) the vector of optimal changes of the control signal is obtained. It contains s elements, but only the first element $(\Delta u_{k|k})$ is applied in the control system. Then, the algorithm goes to the next iteration in which the optimization problem (1–4) is reformulated and solved.

The essential for the MPC algorithm is the way the predicted values of the output variable $y_{k+i|k}$ are derived. If prediction is obtained using a nonlinear model, and this model is used directly in the optimization problem (1–4), then in general, nonconvex, nonquadratic, nonlinear and hard to solve optimization problem is obtained; see e.g. [2,5]. It is, however, advisable to obtain such prediction that an MPC algorithm can be formulated as the standard quadratic programming problem. It is natural in the case of linear models (it will be reminded in the next section) and possible to obtain easy in the case when a Hammerstein model is used for prediction. In the latter case a linear approximation of the control plant model must be obtained at each iteration and utilized to obtain prediction; it is described in detail in Sect. 4.

3   DMC Algorithm as an Example of MPC Algorithms Based on Linear Models

The algorithms based on fuzzy Hammerstein models are related to the Dynamic Matrix Control (DMC) algorithm. Therefore it will be now described. Moreover, in the DMC algorithm incorporation of the mechanism of disturbance measurement utilization is relatively simple and can be adapted in the algorithms based on fuzzy Hammerstein models.

3.1   Model of the Process

In the DMC algorithm the process model in the form of the step response is used:

$$\widehat{y}_k = \sum_{i=1}^{p_d-1} a_i \cdot \Delta u_{k-i} + a_{p_d} \cdot u_{k-p_d} \tag{5}$$

where $\widehat{y}_k$ is the output of the control plant model at the kth sampling instant, Δu_k is a change of the manipulated variable at the kth sampling instant, a_i $(i = 1, \ldots, p_d)$ are step response coefficients of the control plant, p_d is equal to the number of sampling instants after which the coefficients of the step response can be assumed as settled, u_{k-p_d} is a value of the manipulated variable at the $(k - p_d)^{\text{th}}$ sampling instant.

3.2 Generation of the Prediction

The output prediction is calculated using the following formula:

$$y_{k+i|k} = \sum_{n=1}^{i} a_n \cdot \Delta u_{k-n+i} + \sum_{n=i+1}^{p_d-1} a_n \cdot \Delta u_{k-n+i} + a_{p_d} \cdot u_{k-p_d+i} + d_k \qquad (6)$$

where $d_k = y_k - \widehat{y}_{k-1}$ is assumed the same at each sampling instant in the prediction horizon (a DMC–type disturbance model), thus (6) can be transformed into the following form

$$y_{k+i|k} = y_k + \sum_{n=i+1}^{p_d-1} a_n \cdot \Delta u_{k-n+i} + a_{p_d} \cdot \sum_{n=p_d}^{p_d+i-1} \Delta u_{k-n+i} - \sum_{n=1}^{p_d-1} a_n \cdot \Delta u_{k-n}$$

$$+ \sum_{n=1}^{i} a_n \cdot \Delta u_{k-n+i|k} \qquad (7)$$

Thus, the vector of predicted output values y can be decomposed into the following components:

$$y = \widetilde{y} + A \cdot \Delta u, \qquad (8)$$

where $\widetilde{y} = \left[\widetilde{y}_{k+1|k}, \dots, \widetilde{y}_{k+p|k} \right]^T$ is a free response of the plant. It contains future values of the output variable calculated assuming that the control signal does not change in the prediction horizon, i.e. describes influence of the manipulated variable values from the past; $A \cdot \Delta u$ is the forced response which depends only on future changes of the control signal (decision variables); A is a matrix composed of the control plant step response coefficients and is called the dynamic matrix

$$A = \begin{bmatrix} a_1 & 0 & \dots & 0 & 0 \\ a_2 & a_1 & \dots & 0 & 0 \\ \vdots & \vdots & \ddots & \vdots & \vdots \\ a_p & a_{p-1} & \dots & a_{p-s+2} & a_{p-s+1} \end{bmatrix} \qquad (9)$$

In the DMC algorithm the free response is given by the following formula:

$$\widetilde{y} = y_k + \widetilde{A} \cdot \Delta u^p, \qquad (10)$$

where

$$\widetilde{A} = \begin{bmatrix} a_2 - a_1 & a_3 - a_2 & \dots & a_{p_d-1} - a_{p_d-2} & a_{p_d} - a_{p_d-1} \\ a_3 - a_1 & a_4 - a_2 & \dots & a_{p_d} - a_{p_d-2} & a_{p_d} - a_{p_d-1} \\ \vdots & \vdots & \ddots & \vdots & \vdots \\ a_{p+1} - a_1 & a_{p+2} - a_2 & \dots & a_{p_d} - a_{p_d-2} & a_{p_d} - a_{p_d-1} \end{bmatrix},$$

$y_k = [y_k, \dots, y_k]^T$ is a vector of length p, $\Delta u^p = [\Delta u_{k-1}, \dots, \Delta u_{k-p_d}]^T$ is a vector of past changes of the manipulated variable.

Remark 1. In any MPC algorithm based on a linear model the superposition principle can be applied and the prediction y is described by the formula (8) [3,9,17,19]. It can be also shown that the dynamic matrix A is present in all such algorithms [19]. However, formulas describing the free response will be different depending on the form of a linear model used to obtain the prediction.

3.3   Formulation of the Optimization Problem

After application of the prediction (8) to the performance function from the optimization problem (1) and to the output constraints (4) one obtains the following optimization problem:

$$\arg\min_{\Delta u} \left\{ J_{\mathrm{LMPC}} = (\overline{y} - \widetilde{y} - A \cdot \Delta u)^T \cdot (\overline{y} - \widetilde{y} - A \cdot \Delta u) + \Delta u^T \cdot \Lambda \cdot \Delta u \right\} \tag{11}$$

subject to:

$$\Delta u_{\min} \leq \Delta u \leq \Delta u_{\max}, \tag{12}$$

$$u_{\min} \leq u_{k-1} + J \cdot \Delta u \leq u_{\max}, \tag{13}$$

$$y_{\min} \leq \widetilde{y} + A \cdot \Delta u \leq y_{\max}, \tag{14}$$

where

$$J = \begin{bmatrix} 1 & 0 & \dots & 0 \\ 1 & 1 & \dots & 0 \\ \vdots & \vdots & \ddots & \vdots \\ 1 & 1 & \dots & 1 \end{bmatrix}.$$

Remark 2. Note that the performance function in (11) depends quadratically on decision variables Δu. Moreover, as the prediction (8) was applied in the constraints (4), all the constraints depend linearly on decision variables. As a result, the optimization problem (11–14) is a standard linear–quadratic optimization problem.

3.4   Mechanism of Disturbance Measurement Utilization

The utilization of the disturbance measurement in the DMC algorithm is relatively simple. It is because it is sufficient to expand the model of the control plant with components describing influence of the disturbance on the control plant and then generate the prediction using the expanded model; see e.g. [19]. In short the procedure is as follows. The expanded model in the form of the step response has now the following form:

$$\hat{y}_k = \sum_{i=1}^{p_d-1} a_i \cdot \Delta u_{k-i} + a_{p_d} \cdot u_{k-p_d} + \sum_{i=1}^{p_z-1} e_i \cdot \Delta v_{k-i} + e_{p_z} \cdot v_{k-p_z} \tag{15}$$

where Δv_k is a change of the disturbance variable at the kth sampling instant, e_i $(i = 1, \ldots, p_z)$ are coefficients of disturbance step response of the control plant, p_z is equal to the number of sampling instants after which the coefficients of the disturbance step response can be assumed as settled, v_{k-p_z} is a value of the disturbance variable at the $(k - p_z)^{\text{th}}$ sampling instant.

The output prediction is thus now calculated using the following formula:

$$y_{k+i|k} = \sum_{n=1}^{i} a_n \cdot \Delta u_{k-n+i} + \sum_{n=i+1}^{p_d-1} a_n \cdot \Delta u_{k-n+i} + a_{p_d} \cdot u_{k-p_d+i}$$

$$+ \sum_{n=1}^{i} e_n \cdot \Delta v_{k-n+i} + \sum_{n=i+1}^{p_z-1} e_n \cdot \Delta v_{k-n+i} + e_{p_z} \cdot v_{k-p_z+i} + d_k , \quad (16)$$

where $d_k = y_k - \widehat{y}_{k-1}$ is assumed the same at each sampling instant in the prediction horizon and describes the influence of disturbances which cannot be measured or estimated. Note that if an estimate of the disturbance v is available, then the components dependent on it in (16) are known. Therefore, after transformation, they will be present in the free response. As a result the free response will be given by:

$$\widetilde{y} = y_k + \widetilde{A} \cdot \Delta u^p + \widetilde{E} \cdot \Delta v^p , \quad (17)$$

where

$$\widetilde{E} = \begin{bmatrix} e_1 & e_2 - e_1 & e_3 - e_2 & \cdots & e_{p_z-1} - e_{p_z-2} & e_{p_z} - e_{p_z-1} \\ e_2 & e_3 - e_1 & e_4 - e_2 & \cdots & e_{p_z} - e_{p_z-2} & e_{p_z} - e_{p_z-1} \\ \vdots & \vdots & \vdots & \ddots & \vdots & \vdots \\ e_p & e_{p+1} - e_1 & e_{p+2} - e_2 & \cdots & e_{p_z} - e_{p_z-2} & e_{p_z} - e_{p_z-1} \end{bmatrix} ,$$

$\Delta v^p = [\Delta v_k, \Delta v_{k-1}, \ldots, \Delta v_{k-p_z}]^T$ is a vector of known changes of the disturbance variable v. Thus, in the prediction (8) only the free response component changes and the prediction linearly depends on decision variables. Thus, the optimization problem which must be solved at each iteration is the efficient linear–quadratic one.

4   MPC Algorithms Based on Fuzzy Hammerstein Models

4.1   Model of the Process

It is assumed that in the Hammerstein process model (Fig. 1) the static part has the form of a fuzzy Takagi–Sugeno model:

$$z_k = f(u_k) = \sum_{j=1}^{l} w_j(u_k) \cdot z_k^j = \sum_{j=1}^{l} w_j(u_k) \cdot (b_j \cdot u_k + c_j) , \quad (18)$$

where z_k is the output of the static block, $w_j(u_k)$ are weights obtained using fuzzy reasoning, z_k^j are outputs of local models in the fuzzy static model, l is the number of fuzzy rules in the model, b_j and c_j are parameters of the local models. Moreover, it is assumed that the dynamic part of the model has the form of the step response:

$$\widehat{y}_k = \sum_{n=1}^{p_d-1} a_n \cdot \Delta z_{k-n} + a_{p_d} \cdot z_{k-p_d} , \tag{19}$$

where $\widehat{y}_k$ is the output of the fuzzy Hammerstein model, a_i are coefficients of the step response, p_d is the horizon of the process dynamics.

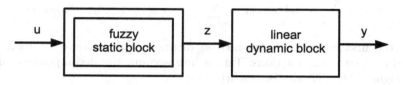

Fig. 1. Structure of the fuzzy Hammerstein model

Note, that form of the dynamic model is the same as of the model used for prediction in the DMC algorithm (Sect. 3). Thus, prediction can be obtained in a similar way as in the DMC algorithm.

Remark 3. If in a Hammerstein model the linear dynamic model is of different form than the step response, it can be always easily transformed to the form assumed here. Then the proposed approach can be applied.

4.2   Generation of the Prediction

In order to obtain the MPC algorithms in which the control signal is obtained using the linear–quadratic optimization problem, the prediction is obtained using a linear approximation of the fuzzy Hammerstein model. However, it is used only to obtain the dynamic matrix whereas the free response is obtained using the original nonlinear fuzzy model. Thanks to such an approach the algorithms offer very good control performance.

Generation of the Free Response. The free response can be obtained, like it was described in [12], using its definition, i.e. assuming that the control signal will not change on the whole control horizon. The prediction can be, however, improved thanks to utilization of future control increments derived by the MPC algorithm in the last sampling instant during calculation of the free response, like it was proposed in [14]. Now, the method of the free response generation will be improved comparing to [14] by adjusting the prediction iteratively.

In the first internal iteration assume that future control values can be decomposed into two parts:

$$u_{k+i|k}^{(1)} = \check{u}_{k+i|k}^{(1)} + u_{k+i|k-1} , \tag{20}$$

where $\breve{u}^{(1)}_{k+i|k}$ can be interpreted as the correction of the control signal $u_{k+i|k-1}$ obtained in the last $(k-1)^{\text{st}}$ iteration of the MPC algorithm; the upper index denotes the number of internal iteration of the prediction generation. Analogously, the future increments of the control signal will have the following form:

$$\Delta u^{(1)}_{k+i|k} = \Delta \breve{u}^{(1)}_{k+i|k} + \Delta u_{k+i|k-1} \, . \tag{21}$$

Note that the output of the model (19) in the ith sampling instant is described by:

$$\widehat{y}_{k+i} = \sum_{n=1}^{i} a_n \cdot \Delta z_{k-n+i} + \sum_{n=i+1}^{p_d-1} a_n \cdot \Delta z_{k-n+i} + a_{p_d} \cdot z_{k-p_d+i} \, , \tag{22}$$

where the first component depends on future action whereas the next ones depend on past control actions. Taking into account the decomposition of the input signal (20), (22) can be rewritten as:

$$\widehat{y}_{k+i} = \sum_{n=1}^{i} a_n \cdot \Delta \breve{z}^{(1)}_{k-n+i|k} + \sum_{n=1}^{i} a_n \cdot \Delta z_{k-n+i|k-1} + \sum_{n=i+1}^{p_d-1} a_n \cdot \Delta z_{k-n+i} + a_{p_d} \cdot z_{k-p_d+i} \, , \tag{23}$$

where $\Delta z_{k+i|k-1} = z_{k+i|k-1} - z_{k+i-1|k-1}$; $z_{k+i|k-1} = f(u_{k+i|k-1})$ and $\breve{z}^{(1)}_{k+i|k-1} = z^{(1)}_{k+i|k} - z_{k+i|k-1}$. In (23) the second component is known and can be included in the free response of the control plant. Therefore, the final formula describing the elements of the free response will have the following form:

$$\widetilde{y}_{k+i|k} = \sum_{n=1}^{i} a_n \cdot \Delta z_{k-n+i|k-1} + \sum_{n=i+1}^{p_d-1} a_n \cdot \Delta z_{k-n+i} + a_{p_d} \cdot z_{k-p_d+i} + d_k \, , \tag{24}$$

where $d_k = y_k - \widehat{y}_k$ is the DMC–type disturbance model containing influence of modeling errors, and of unmeasured disturbances.

In the next step, the free response together with the Dynamic Matrix obtained as described in the next part of Sect. 4.2 are used to formulate the optimization problem (Sect. 4.3) after solution of which a new control signal trajectory is obtained. Now, either the control signal is applied to the control plant or the prediction is improved in the next internal iteration of the algorithm. In the latter case the next internal iterations are as follows.

Now, as the next control signal trajectory is available, future control values can be decomposed as:

$$u^{(j)}_{k+i|k} = \breve{u}^{(j)}_{k+i|k} + u^{(j-1)}_{k+i|k} \, , \tag{25}$$

where the upper index denotes the number of internal iteration of the algorithm and $j = 2, 3, \dots$. The future increments of the control signal will now have the following form:

$$\Delta u^{(j)}_{k+i|k} = \Delta \breve{u}^{(j)}_{k+i|k} + \Delta u^{(j-1)}_{k+i|k} \, . \tag{26}$$

Then now (22) can be expressed as:

$$\widehat{y}_{k+i} = \sum_{n=1}^{i} a_n \cdot \Delta z_{k-n+i|k}^{(j)} + \sum_{n=1}^{i} a_n \cdot \Delta z_{k-n+i|k}^{(j-1)} + \sum_{n=i+1}^{p_d-1} a_n \cdot \Delta z_{k-n+i} + a_{p_d} \cdot z_{k-p_d+i} \cdot$$

(27)

As in the first internal iteration, in (27) the second component is known and can be included in the free response of the control plant. Therefore, the final formula describing the elements of the free response will now have the following form:

$$\widetilde{y}_{k+i|k} = \sum_{n=1}^{i} a_n \cdot \Delta z_{k-n+i|k}^{(j-1)} + \sum_{n=i+1}^{p_d-1} a_n \cdot \Delta z_{k-n+i} + a_{p_d} \cdot z_{k-p_d+i} + d_k \cdot \quad (28)$$

Remark 4. The smaller values of obtained corrections of the control trajectory are the better prediction is obtained. It is because then it will be closer to the prediction obtained using only the nonlinear fuzzy model.

Remark 5. Number of internal iterations of the algorithm can be chosen depending on what is the size of changes of the future control increments. If the corrections of the control signal trajectory become rather small, there is no use to do more internal iterations.

Remark 6. Note that the proposed method is a generalization of the method proposed in [14] as the latter one is obtained by assumption that only one internal iteration is made.

Generation of the Dynamic Matrix. Next, at each iteration of the algorithm the dynamic matrix can be easily derived using a linear approximation of the fuzzy Hammerstein model (19) [12]:

$$\widehat{y}_k = dz_k \cdot \left(\sum_{n=1}^{p_d-1} a_n \cdot \Delta u_{k-n} + a_{p_d} \cdot u_{k-p_d} \right), \quad (29)$$

where dz_k is a slope of the static characteristic near the z_k. It can be calculated either analytically (if possible) or numerically using the formula

$$dz_k = \frac{\sum_{j=1}^{l} \left(w_j(u_k + du) \cdot (b_j \cdot (u_k + du) + c_j) - w_j(u_k) \cdot (b_j \cdot u_k + c_j) \right)}{du},$$

(30)

where du is a small number. The dynamic matrix will be thus described by the following formula:

$$\boldsymbol{A}_k = dz_k \cdot \begin{bmatrix} a_1 & 0 & \cdots & 0 & 0 \\ a_2 & a_1 & \cdots & 0 & 0 \\ \vdots & \vdots & \ddots & \vdots & \vdots \\ a_p & a_{p-1} & \cdots & a_{p-s+2} & a_{p-s+1} \end{bmatrix}. \quad (31)$$

Finally, the prediction can be obtained using the free response (28) and the dynamic matrix (31):

$$y = \widetilde{y} + A_k \cdot \Delta \check{u}, \tag{32}$$

where $\Delta \check{u} = \left[\Delta \check{u}_{k|k}^{(j)}, \ldots, \Delta \check{u}_{k+s-1|k}^{(j)} \right]^T$.

4.3   Formulation of the Optimization Problem

After application of prediction (32) to the performance function from (1) and in constraints (4) one obtains:

$$\arg \min_{\Delta \check{u}} \left\{ J_{\text{FMPC}} = (\overline{y} - \widetilde{y} - A_k \cdot \Delta \check{u})^T \cdot (\overline{y} - \widetilde{y} - A_k \cdot \Delta \check{u}) + \Delta u^T \cdot \Lambda \cdot \Delta u \right\} \tag{33}$$

subject to:

$$\Delta u_{\min} \leq \Delta u \leq \Delta u_{\max}, \tag{34}$$

$$u_{\min} \leq u_{k-1} + J \cdot \Delta u \leq u_{\max}, \tag{35}$$

$$y_{\min} \leq \widetilde{y} + A_k \cdot \Delta \check{u} \leq y_{\max}, \tag{36}$$

where $\Delta u = \Delta \check{u} + \Delta u^p$, $\Delta u^p = \left[\Delta u_{k|k}^{(j-1)}, \ldots, \Delta u_{k+s-2|k}^{(j-1)}, \Delta u_{k+s-1|k}^{(j-1)} \right]^T$; compare with (26). Moreover, formulas (25) and (26) are used to modify the constraints (34) and (35) respectively. Then, the linear–quadratic optimization problem with the performance function (33), constraints (34)–(36) and the decision variables $\Delta \check{u}$ is solved at each iteration in order to derive the control signal.

Remark 7. It is also possible to use slightly modified performance function in which in the second component, only corrections of the control changes $\Delta \check{u}$ are penalized, i.e.

$$J_{\text{FMPC2}} = (\overline{y} - \widetilde{y} - A_k \cdot \Delta \check{u})^T \cdot (\overline{y} - \widetilde{y} - A_k \cdot \Delta \check{u}) + \Delta \check{u}^T \cdot \Lambda \cdot \Delta \check{u}. \tag{37}$$

Such a modification, however, causes that the meaning of the tuning parameter λ is different than in the classical performance function. As a consequence, the algorithm with the modified performance function generates faster responses. It will be demonstrated in the example control system.

4.4   Mechanisms of Disturbance Measurement Utilization

First Method of Disturbance Measurement Utilization consists in using the same approach as in the standard DMC algorithm. This method can be used e.g. when one wants to extend the existing algorithm with the disturbance measurement utilization mechanism. Then the process model should be extended like it is done in the standard DMC algorithm. Thus, the structure of the model will be as depicted in Fig. 2.

As a result the prediction changes. Precisely, to the free response obtained in Sect. 4.2 an appropriate term from (17) is simply added. As a result the following formula describing the prediction is obtained (compare with (32)):

$$y = \widetilde{y} + \widetilde{E} \cdot \Delta v^p + A_k \cdot \Delta \check{u}. \tag{38}$$

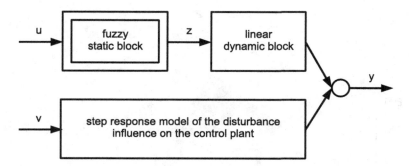

Fig. 2. Hammerstein model supplemented with step response model of influence of the disturbance on the control plant

Second Method of Disturbance Measurement Utilization is in fact easier to apply. It is because it consists in proper usage of knowledge about disturbance estimates and original Hammerstein model of the process during the free response generation. Assume that the model has structure shown in Fig. 3.

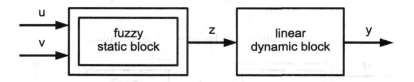

Fig. 3. Hammerstein model with static part dependent on the disturbance

Application of the method is straightforward it is because the fuzzy static model is given by the following formula:

$$z_k = f(u_k, v_k) = \sum_{j=1}^{l} w_j(u_k, v_k) \cdot z_k^j = \sum_{j=1}^{l} w_j(u_k) \cdot (b_j \cdot u_k + e_j \cdot v_k + c_j), \quad (39)$$

where v_k is the current disturbance estimate, $w_j(u_k, v_k)$ are weights obtained using fuzzy reasoning, e_j are parameters of the local models. Thus, the formulas describing the prediction in the FMPC algorithm given in Sect. 4.2 can be applied without changes.

5   Simulation Experiments

5.1   Control Plant

The control plant under consideration is an ethylene distillation column DA–303 from petrochemical plant in Plock. It is a highly nonlinear plant with a large

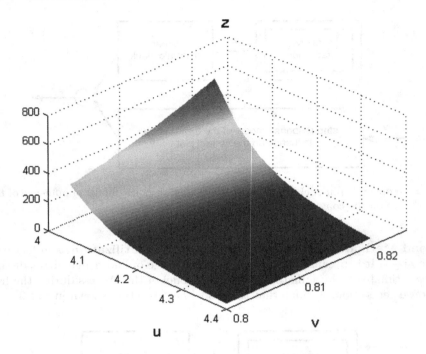

Fig. 4. Steady–state characteristic of the plant

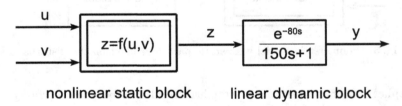

Fig. 5. Hammerstein model of the control plant

time delay. The steady–state characteristic of the plant is shown in Fig. 4. The Hammerstein model of the control plant has the structure shown in Fig. 5. The output of the plant y is the impurity of the product. The manipulated variable u is the reflux. The higher the reflux is the purer product is obtained. During experiments it was assumed that the reflux is constrained $4.05 \leq u \leq 4.4$. The measurable disturbance variable v is the composition of the raw substance.

In the Hammerstein model of the plant (Fig. 5) the static part was modeled using ANFIS from Matlab. In order to train the system two sets of data were used: one for training and the second one for validation. The number of membership functions (assumed the same for both inputs) and number of training epochs were set experimentally. During the experiments increase of both parameters brought decrease of the MSE for data used for training. However,

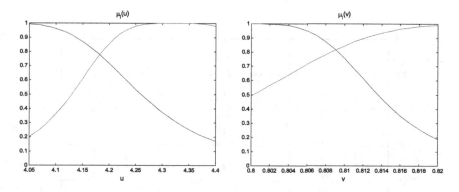

Fig. 6. Membership functions in the static part of the Hammerstein model

increase of the number of membership functions brought increase of the MSE obtained for validation data set. Therefore, two membership functions for both input variables were finally set. The number of epochs was assumed equal to 200. The system composed of 4 rules was finally obtained with the membership functions as shown in Fig. 6. The steady–state characteristic modeled by the ANFIS is almost the same as the one depicted in Fig. 4 (differences are negligible).

5.2   Results

A few MPC algorithms were designed:

- the NMPC one (with nonlinear optimization),
- the LMPC one (based on a linear model) and
- the FMPC ones (using the proposed method of prediction generation, based on the fuzzy Hammerstein model). Both versions of the algorithm were tested: the first one (FMPC1) with the classical performance function (33) and the second one (FMPC2) with the modified performance function (37). In both algorithms only one internal iteration was used.

The sampling period was assumed equal to $T_s = 20$ min, the prediction horizon $p = 44$ and the control horizon $s = 20$.

First, the experiments as in [14] were done because the control plant model used to design the FMPC and NMPC algorithms was changed (it was obtained using ANFIS instead of a heuristic approach). Example responses to the set–point changes, obtained for $\lambda = 10^7$ are shown in Fig. 7 and those obtained for $\lambda = 10^6$ — in Fig. 8.

The responses obtained with the LMPC algorithm to the set–point change to $\bar{y}_3 = 400$ ppm are unacceptable. The control system is very close to the boundary of stability in the case of $\lambda = 10^7$ and for $\lambda = 10^6$ it is unstable. Moreover, the overshoot in responses to the set–point change to $\bar{y}_2 = 300$ ppm are very big. On the contrary, both FMPC algorithms work well for all the set–point values and the responses have similar shape regardless the set–point value.

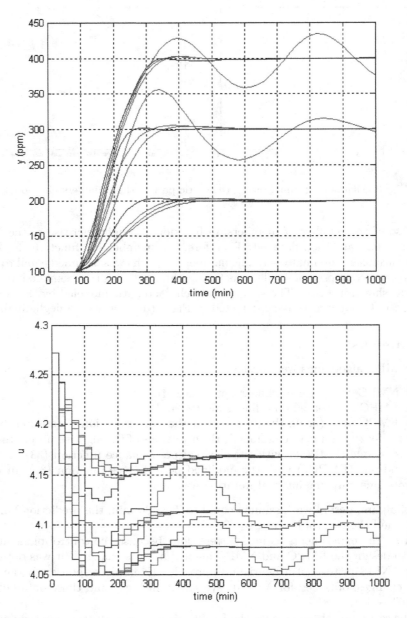

Fig. 7. Responses of the control systems to the changes of the set–point values to $\overline{y}_1 = 200\,\mathrm{ppm}$, $\overline{y}_2 = 300\,\mathrm{ppm}$ and $\overline{y}_3 = 400\,\mathrm{ppm}$, $\lambda = 10^7$; NMPC – red lines, FMPC1 – magenta lines, FMPC2 – blue lines, LMPC – green lines; above – output signal, below – control signal (Color figure online)

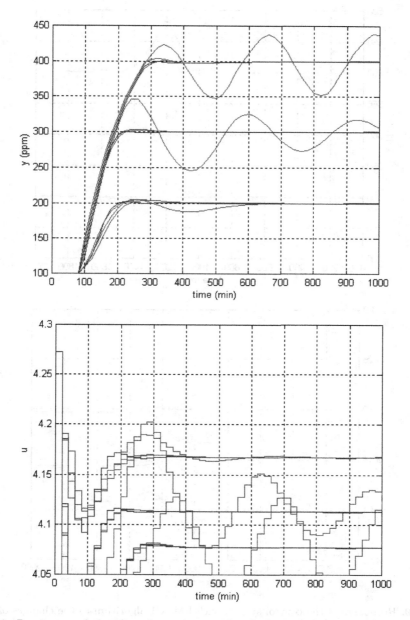

Fig. 8. Responses of the control systems to the changes of the set–point values to $\bar{y}_1 = 200\,\text{ppm}$, $\bar{y}_2 = 300\,\text{ppm}$ and $\bar{y}_3 = 400\,\text{ppm}$, $\lambda = 10^6$; NMPC – red lines, FMPC1 – magenta lines, FMPC2 – blue lines, LMPC – green lines; above – output signal, below – control signal (Color figure online)

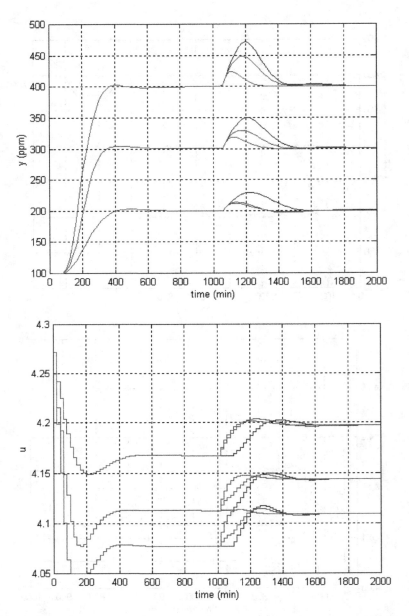

Fig. 9. Responses of the control system with FMPC1 algorithm to the changes of the set–point values to $\overline{y}_1 = 200\,\text{ppm}$, $\overline{y}_2 = 300\,\text{ppm}$ and $\overline{y}_3 = 400\,\text{ppm}$ at the beginning of experiment and changes of the disturbance v in the 1000th minute, $\lambda = 10^7$; disturbance measurement: not utilized – blue lines, utilized using the first method – magenta lines, utilized using the second method – red lines; above – output signal, below – control signal (Color figure online)

The responses obtained with the FMPC1 algorithm are very close to those obtained with the NPMC algorithm. However, it should be emphasized that the control signal is generated by the FMPC1 algorithm, after solving the numerically robust linear–quadratic optimization problem, much faster than in the case of the NMPC algorithm.

In the case of the NMPC algorithm numerical problems during calculation of the control signal may occur. It happened for $\lambda = 10^6$ in the case described in [14], when it utilized the fuzzy Hammerstein model in which the fuzzy static model was obtained heuristically. Fortunately, in the case considered now, the NMPC algorithm found the control signal at each iteration but it took much more time than in the case of the FMPC algorithms.

The fastest responses were obtained with the FMPC2 algorithm (blue lines in Figs. 7 and 8). They are better even than those obtained with the NMPC algorithm. It is however a result of assuming, in the optimization problem solved by the FMPC2 algorithm, a slightly different performance function than in other tested algorithms.

After decrease of the tuning parameter value to $\lambda = 10^6$, FMPC and NMPC algorithms work faster (Fig. 8) than in the case when $\lambda = 10^7$ (Fig. 7). The FMPC2 algorithm in response to the set–point change to $\bar{y}_1 = 200$ ppm works slightly faster even than the NMPC algorithm. In the case of set–point changes to $\bar{y}_2 = 300$ ppm and to $\bar{y}_3 = 400$ ppm the differences in operation between FMPC1, FMPC2 and NMPC algorithms are small. It is due to the fact that the control signal hits the constraint.

In the next experiments the mechanisms of disturbance measurement utilization were tested. In the case of both FMPC algorithms similar responses were obtained for different values of λ. The first method of disturbance measurement utilization (magenta lines in Figs. 9, 10 and 11) consisting in using the same approach as in the standard DMC algorithm, works surprisingly well especially near 200 ppm (there it is practically as good as the second method). It is because the model of disturbance influence on the control plant was obtained near this output value. However, for 300 ppm and 400 ppm the second method which uses appropriately prepared fuzzy Hammerstein model is the best (red lines). It can be also noticed that for $\lambda = 10^7$ the FMPC2 algorithm compensates the disturbance influence better than the FMPC1 algorithm. However, for $\lambda = 10^6$ the differences between algorithms were so small that only responses obtained in the control system with FMPC1 algorithm were presented (in Fig. 11). It can be also noticed that when λ was smaller (the algorithms were faster) the disturbance compensation was better.

6 Summary

The methods of prediction improvement in the MPC algorithms based on fuzzy Hammerstein models were described. The first method uses the future changes of the control signal, calculated in the last iteration by the MPC algorithm to derive the free response of the control plant. Such an approach causes that the

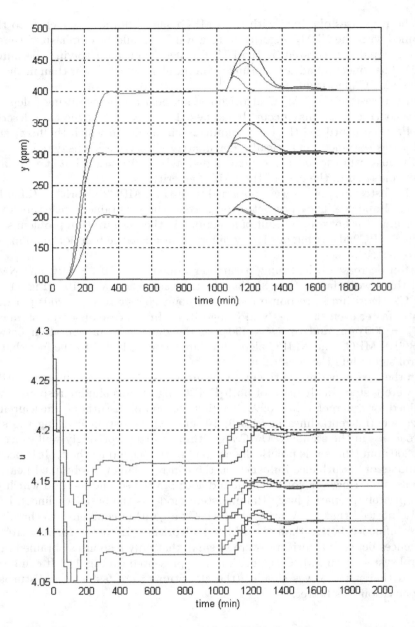

Fig. 10. Responses of the control system with FMPC2 algorithm to the changes of the set–point values to $\overline{y}_1 = 200$ ppm, $\overline{y}_2 = 300$ ppm and $\overline{y}_3 = 400$ ppm at the beginning of experiment and changes of the disturbance v in the 1000th minute, $\lambda = 10^7$; disturbance measurement: not utilized – blue lines, utilized using the first method – magenta lines, utilized using the second method – red lines; above – output signal, below – control signal (Color figure online)

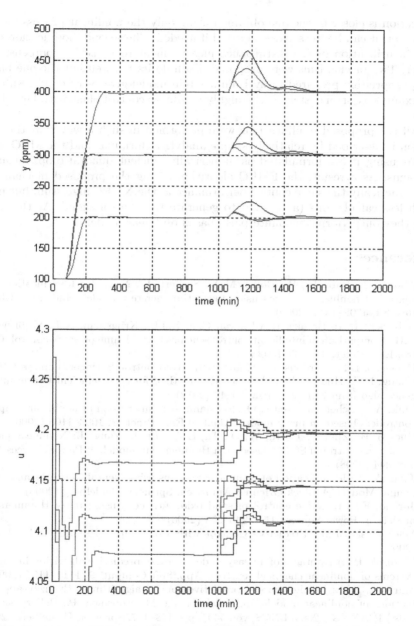

Fig. 11. Responses of the control system with FMPC1 algorithm to the changes of the set–point values to $\overline{y}_1 = 200$ ppm, $\overline{y}_2 = 300$ ppm and $\overline{y}_3 = 400$ ppm at the beginning of experiment and changes of the disturbance v in the 1000th minute, $\lambda = 10^6$; disturbance measurement: not utilized – blue lines, utilized using the first method – magenta lines, utilized using the second method – red lines; above – output signal, below – control signal (Color figure online)

prediction is closer to the one obtained using only the nonlinear process model. Moreover, it can be iteratively adjusted if needed. The second modification consists in utilization of the disturbance measurement to make its compensation better. Two mechanisms were proposed. Both do its job well but the one based on appropriately prepared fuzzy Hammerstein model gives very good results in the example control system of the highly nonlinear control plant with large time delay.

All the proposed modifications were performed in such a way that the prediction is described by relatively simple analytical formulas and the MPC algorithms using it are formulated as numerically efficient quadratic optimization problems. As a result, the FMPC algorithms using the proposed mechanisms offer practically the same control performance as the NMPC algorithm but need much less calculations (and time) to generate the control signal. At the same time they outperform its counterparts based on linear models.

References

1. Abonyi, J., Babuska, R., Botto, M.A., Szeifert, F., Nagy, L.: Identification and control of nonlinear systems using fuzzy Hammerstein models. Ind. Eng. Chem. Res. **39**, 4302–4314 (2000)
2. Babuska, R., te Braake, H.A.B., van Can, H.J.L., Krijgsman, A.J., Verbruggen, H.B.: Comparison of intelligent control schemes for real-time pressure control. Control Eng. Pract. **4**, 1585–1592 (1996)
3. Camacho, E.F., Bordons, C.: Model Predictive Control. Springer, London (1999)
4. Chang, F.C., Huang, H.C.: A refactoring method for cache-efficient swarm intelligence algorithms. Inf. Sci. **192**, 39–49 (2012)
5. Fink, A., Fischer, M., Nelles, O., Isermann, R.: Supervision of nonlinear adaptive controllers based on fuzzy models. Control Eng. Pract. **8**, 1093–1105 (2000)
6. Huo, H.-B., Zhu, X.-J., Hu, W.-Q., Tu, H.-Y., Li, J., Yang, J.: Nonlinear model predictive control of SOFC based on a Hammerstein model. J. Power Sources **185**, 338–344 (2008)
7. Janczak, A.: Identification of Nonlinear Systems using Neural Networks and Polynomial Models: A Block-Oriented Approach. Springer, Heidelberg (2005)
8. Jurado, F.: Predictive control of solid oxide fuel cells using fuzzy Hammerstein models. J. Power Sources **158**, 245–253 (2006)
9. Maciejowski, J.M.: Predictive Control with Constraints. Prentice Hall, Harlow (2002)
10. Marusak, P.: Advantages of an easy to design fuzzy predictive algorithm in control systems of nonlinear chemical reactors. App. Soft Comput. **9**, 1111–1125 (2009)
11. Marusak, P.M.: Efficient model predictive control algorithm with fuzzy approximations of nonlinear models. In: Kolehmainen, M., Toivanen, P., Beliczynski, B. (eds.) ICANNGA 2009. LNCS, vol. 5495, pp. 448–457. Springer, Heidelberg (2009)
12. Marusak, P.M.: On prediction generation in efficient MPC algorithms based on fuzzy Hammerstein models. In: Rutkowski, L., Scherer, R., Tadeusiewicz, R., Zadeh, L.A., Zurada, J.M. (eds.) ICAISC 2010, Part I. LNCS, vol. 6113, pp. 136–143. Springer, Heidelberg (2010)
13. Marusak, P.M.: Numerically efficient analytical MPC algorithm based on fuzzy Hammerstein models. In: Dobnikar, A., Lotrič, U., Šter, B. (eds.) ICANNGA 2011, Part II. LNCS, vol. 6594, pp. 177–185. Springer, Heidelberg (2011)

14. Marusak, P.M.: Advanced prediction method in efficient MPC algorithm based on fuzzy Hammerstein models. In: Jędrzejowicz, P., Nguyen, N.T., Hoang, K. (eds.) ICCCI 2011, Part I. LNCS, vol. 6922, pp. 193–202. Springer, Heidelberg (2011)
15. Morari, M., Lee, J.H.: Model predictive control: past, present and future. Comput. Chem. Eng. **23**, 667–682 (1999)
16. Piegat, A.: Fuzzy Modeling and Control. Physica-Verlag, Berlin (2001)
17. Rossiter, J.A.: Model-Based Predictive Control. CRC Press, Boca Raton (2003)
18. Takagi, T., Sugeno, M.: Fuzzy identification of systems and its application to modeling and control. IEEE Trans. Syst. Man Cybern. **15**, 116–132 (1985)
19. Tatjewski, P.: Advanced Control of Industrial Processes; Structures and Algorithms. Springer, London (2007)

Visualization of Semantic Data Based on Selected Predicates

Gábor Rácz, Gergő Gombos[(⊠)], and Attila Kiss

Eötvös Loránd University, Budapest, Hungary
{gabee33,ggombos,kiss}@inf.elte.hu

Abstract. Due to the spreading of semantic technologies, the volume of the datasets that are described in the Resource Description Framework (RDF) is dynamically growing. The RDF framework is suitable for integrating data from heterogeneous sources; however, the resulted datasets can be larger and extremely complex than before, new tools are needed to analyze them. In this paper, we present a method which aims to help to understand the structure of semantic datasets. It can reduce the size and the complexity of a dataset while preserves the selected parts of it. The method consists of a filtering and a compaction phases that are implemented according to the MapReduce distributed programing model to be able to handle large volume of data. The result of the method can be visualized as a labeled directed graph that is suitable to give an overview of the structure of the dataset. It may reveal hidden connections or different kinds of problems related to the completeness and correctness of the data.

Keywords: Semantic Web · Big data · Visualization · Hadoop · MapReduce

1   Introduction

Due to the evolution of technology, large volume of data are generated day by day. These can be scientific data from various fields, business reports, or user generated web contents. The integration of these data offers great opportunities to discover hidden correlations and complex structures among data coming form various sources, for example, if we connect biological and chemical datasets, we may get more detailed information about some compounds [7]. The paper [19] investigates whether the collective knowledge state is more proper than the knowledge states of the collective intelligence. However, due to the heterogeneity and the volume of data, both the integration and the processing of them pose serious challenges to the scientists. In this paper, we present a system that is based on the Semantic Web [4] technologies and the MapReduce [8] paradigm, and it aims to help understanding the inner structure of a dataset by visualize its important parts after a filtering and a compaction phase.

Tim Berners-Lee et al. introduced the Semantic Web [4] which is a collection of several technologies that aims to connect all the data and to organize them into

© Springer-Verlag Berlin Heidelberg 2014
N.T. Nguyen (Ed.): TCCI XIV 2014, LNCS 8615, pp. 180–195, 2014.
DOI: 10.1007/978-3-662-44509-9_9

the "web of data" in such format which is understandable for not only humans but machines as well. These technologies are built on the Resource Description Framework (RDF) [16] which is a general framework for information modeling or conceptual description based on making statements about resources identified by Internationalized Resource Identifiers (IRIs). The statements are called *triplets* and they are in from of subject-predicate-object or entity-attribute-value like natural language sentences. This representation method is flexible enough to integrate data from heterogeneous sources. In addition, the triplets can be seen as directed edges in a labeled graph, where an edge is going from the subject to the object of the statements and it is labeled by the predicate. This approach, to handle datasets as labeled directed graphs, is the basis of our method because a graph can be easily visualized and an illustrative figure can help to reveal the inner structure of the datasets. Namely, in a figure, the shape, the texture, the color, the size, or the position of the visual elements can express different kinds of information. However, because of the limitation of the display, it is not recommended to visualize too many elements at the same time as the elements easily overlap or cross each other making the figure unclear.

In this paper, we introduce a system which offers a novel technique to reduce the size and the complexity of semantic datasets. It is based on a filtering and a compaction phase. First, the user selects which predicates should be displayed from the ones that appear in the dataset. Some basic statistics are provided by the system to facilitate the decision, such as the cardinality, the domain, and the range of the predicates. Then, the selected predicates have to be marked as *chain* or *non-chain*. The *chain* means, that the structure of the objects connected by *chain* predicates needs to be preserved, while in case of *non-chain* predicates the concrete individuals that are connected to an object by *non-chain* predicates are not important, but their cardinality are. Next, the system filters out the statements whose predicates were not selected from the input dataset and the remaining statements are compacted based on the *chain* and *non-chain* properties. Our main contribution is the compaction technique that merges the nodes that are connected to the same nodes by the same predicates that are marked as *non-chain* together. The output of the process is a GraphML [6] file which contains the simplified dataset as a labeled directed graph. GraphML is an XML-based file format for describing graphs and it is suitable for various graph visualization tools. We used the yEd[1] tool in our experiments.

To handle large volume of data, our system is built on the top of an Apache Hadoop [23] cluster. Hadoop is an open-source implementation of the MapReduce [8] programming model which is wildly used for data-intensive distributed computations. A MapReduce program is composed of a Map and a Reduce phase. The Map performs filtering and sorting on the input and converts the data into key-value pairs. The Reduce collects and aggregates values that are sharing the same keys. In each phase multiple processes are working in parallel. Our solution is based on two MapReduce programs, where the first one is filtering the

---

[1] http://www.yworks.com/en/products_yed_about.htm

statements which contain selected predicates while the second one is performing the node compaction and creates the output file.

We tested our method on the DBpedia [2] and on the Freebase [5] datasets with various configurations (selecting *chain* and *non-chain* predicates). DBpedia contains information extracted from the Wikipedia as RDF triplets while Freebase is a large collaborative knowledge base managed by its own community. The experiments proved the usefulness of our technique because we discovered a lot of inaccuracies and deficiencies in the datasets, such as missing statements or wrong edges or node labels, ambiguous IRIs. In addition, our experiments suggest that the system can scale with the volume of input.

The paper is organized as follows. In Sect. 2, we give an overview of the related works. Section 3 describes some preliminaries and definitions. Our method and its evaluation are presented in Sects. 4 and 5 respectively. We summarize our results and describe our future plans in Sect. 6.

2   Related Work

As mentioned earlier, Semantic Web is a recent topic; the volume of semantic datasets described in RDF is dynamically growing. Accordingly, many approaches try to handle and keep understandable the datasets. SPARQL [13] is a standard query language for RDF databases. It is a declarative query language that allows for constructing queries which consist of triple patterns, optional patterns, filter expressions; the queries are based on triple pattern matching where the patterns can contain variables. However, in order to use this query language it is necessary to get familiar with the data. The main purpose of our system is to give an insight of the structure of the data to facilitate the understanding of it.

VoID [1] is an RDF Schema vocabulary that has the same purpose as our system but it has a different approach; it defines four kinds of metadata that can characterize a dataset

- general metadata such as title, description, or license,
- access metadata to describe the method of accessing (e.g. data dumps, SPARQL endpoints),
- structural metadata to give a high-level overview about the internal structure of the dataset, and
- description of links between datasets such as the number of resources that are used in other datasets as well.

The structural metadata, especially the ones that are providing numerical statistics about the contained classes and properties, can help to compose an input for our system as the frequent properties gives the structure of the dataset, therefore the *chain* and *non-chain properties* may be selected among them.

Our system processes the input dataset based on the predefined properties and it generates an output in GraphML format that is compatible with the yEd graph visualization tool. The visualization helps to reveal the structure of the dataset. There are several other systems that exploit the advantages of visualization and help to explore the data. Such systems are, for example, the PGV Explorer [9], LODmilla [17], or the VizBoard [22]. With the PGV Explorer, the RDF graphs became incrementally explorable which means starting from a small part of the original graph, the user can expand it with the relevant data and the irrelevant parts can be collapsed. A node is expendable along its neighbors, i.e. the neighbors became visible and they connect to the expanded node. Its reverse process is the collapse of an unrelated node when the connected neighbors of the node will be hidden. The technique presented in [10] is very similar to, however, in that system the nodes are composite objects which consist of not only the labels of the nodes, but each node contains the labels of its neighbors and the type of the connection as well. It gives a more detailed view of the nodes, but it results in a more complex figure, therefore only a small part of the graph can be displayed at the same time. LODmilla works in a similar way as well, however, it gives additional information of the node that is in focus, such as a description or an image. These systems are more suitable to examine small subgraphs in details in contrast to our approach that is giving an overall picture of the graph structure related to the selected properties.

The Vizboard system defines an information visualization workflow that enables users to visualize and analyze arbitrary semantic dataset without expert skills and programming knowledge. The workflow consists of five stages each one is supported by the system. The process starts at data uploading, and then some basic statistics are computed to help the human driven data preselection phase. After that, some clustering methods are applied to divide the datasets into subsets from which the user selects the interesting ones. Then, the system recommends visualization components that the user can configure. After the chosen components are integrated and configured, the visualization is completed and hidden knowledge may reveal. This workflow is very similar to our method which is also started with data upload followed by a pre-selection phase in which users can define the properties as *chain* or *non-chain* based on basic statistics about their cardinalities, domains and ranges. However, in case of our method, datasets are processed in a distributed system to be able to handle large volume of data, and the result is in a standard graph format (GraphML) in order to the replacement of the visualization tools can be easy.

As the volume of the datasets increase, processing of them are posing serious challenges to the scientists. The distributed computation models and distributed processing systems can be solutions for this problem. One of those models is the MapReduce that is used in our work. There are several experiments that try to take the advantages of this model in processing of semantic datasets. For example, in [15], Hussain et al. presented a system that can evaluate basic SPARQL queries with MapReduce. In [20], a data processing method was introduced which is based on the MapReduce paradigm as our method. However, that technique differs from ours because it uses an iterative algorithm to merge the similar nodes together which may consume much more time than the method presented in this paper.

3   Preliminaries

In this section, we give the formal definitions of the concepts that are used in our method including the RDF triplets, the semantic graph that can be built from the triplets, and a similarity relation among the vertexes of a semantic graph that is the basis of the compaction phase.

As we mentioned in the introduction, the Semantic Web is a collection of various technologies that aim to organize all the available information into the "web of data". The basis of these technologies is the Resource Description Framework [16] which is a general model for conceptual description. In this framework, the information are expressed as statements in form of subject-predicate-object or entity-attribute-value triplets.

```
@PREFIX dbpedia: <http://dbpedia.org/resource/> .
@PREFIX dbpedia-owl: <http://dbpedia.org/ontology/> .
@PREFIX rdf: <http://www.w3.org/1999/02/22-rdf-syntax-ns#> .
@PREFIX rdfs: <http://www.w3.org/2000/01/rdf-schema#> .

dbpedia:Eötvös_Loránd_University rdf:type dbpedia-owl:EducationalInstitution .
dbpedia:Eötvös_Loránd_University dbpedia-owl:city dbpedia:Budapest .
dbpedia-owl:EducationalInstitution rdfs:subClassOf dbpedia-owl:Organisation .
```

(a) Example of RDF triples

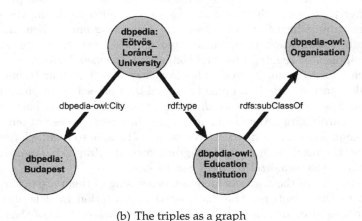

(b) The triples as a graph

Fig. 1. A small example for RDF triplets and their representations as a directed labeled graph

Figure 1(a) shows a short example with three statements connected to Eötvös Loránd University. Note, that the first four rows of the example only define abbreviations for the frequent IRI prefixes. The first row states that Eötvös Loránd University is an educational institute, the second row states that it is located in Budapest and the third one states that every educational institute is an organization as well. Based on [12], we define the RDF triple as follows.

Definition 1 *(RDF triple). Let I, B, and L (IRIs, Blank Nodes, Literals) be pairwise disjoint sets. An* RDF triple *is a* $(v_1, v_2, v_3) \in (I \cup B) \times I \times (I \cup B \cup L)$, *where* v_1 *is the subject,* v_2 *is the predicate and* v_3 *is the object.*

Note, that in the definition IRIs, Blank Nodes and Literals are distinguished where IRIs are used to identify objects, the Literals are the values in the entity-attribute-value like triples and the Blank Nodes are used to create compound data structures as pair, set or list. For example, a postal address consists of at least a city, a street and a postal code and these values belong together. In this case, all the values are assigned to a blank node whose name is unimportant, therefore it is not identified by an IRI, and it is used as a postal address. However, in our method all the three types of nodes are treated as the same. An RDF triple can be represented by a directed edge going from the subject to the object and labeled by the predicate. In Fig. 1(b), the example statements from Fig. 1(a) are represented by a semantic graph.

Definition 2 *(semantic graph). A semantic graph* $G = (V, E, label)$ *is a labeled directed graph consists of a set* $V = I \cup B \cup L$ *of nodes, a set* $E \subseteq V^2$ *of edges, and a labeling function* $label : E-> I$ *that assigns its predicate to each edge. An* $e = (s, o) \in E$ *edge of the graph where* $s, o \in V$ *are two nodes and* $label(e) = p$ *represents the (s,p,o) RDF triplet.*

In our method, users can select which predicates should appear in the output and by marking the selected predicates as *chain* or *non-chain* respectively whether the individual subjects of the statements (or the starting points of the corresponding edge) have to be preserved or only the cardinality of the similar subjects connected by the predicate has to be computed. In Definition 3, we introduce a similarity relation over the set of nodes that defines which nodes are similar. The definition is based on [14] where the authors introduced a similarity relation among nodes of labeled graphs.

Definition 3 *(simulation). A binary relation* $'\leq' \subseteq V^2$ *over the set of nodes is a simulation, if* $u \leq v$ *implies for all* $e = (u, w) \in E$ *that there is an* $e' = (v, w) \in E$ *edge such that* $label(e) = label(e')$. *The node* v *simulates the node* u *if there is a simulation* $\leq$ *such that* $u \leq v$. *The nodes* u *and* v *are similar, denoted as* $u \sim v$, *if* u *simulates* v *and* v *simulates* u.

Definition 4 *(mergeable nodes). Let* $u, w \in E$ *two nodes of a* $G = (V, E)$ *semantic graph.* u *and* v *is mergeable, if*

i. $u \sim v$ *and*
ii. all outgoing edges of u *are marked as* non-chain.

Our method has two main phases, the first one preforms the filtering of the statements with respect to the selected predicates while the second phase merges the mergeable nodes together. Two nodes are mergeable if they are similar and all their outgoing edges are labeled only with such predicates that are marked as *non-chain* as Definition 4 describes. Two nodes are merged into a single one which will be connected with the same nodes and an integer value will be assign to it that registers how many nodes has been merged already. The value is computed as follows; suppose that $u, v \in V$ nodes are merged into the new w node, then

$$value(w) := \begin{cases} 2, & \text{if } u \text{ and } v \text{ are not merged nodes} \\ value(u)+1, & \text{if } u \text{ is merged node, but } v \text{ is not} \\ value(v)+1, & \text{if } v \text{ is merged node, but } u \text{ is not} \\ value(u)+ \\ value(v), & \text{if } u \text{ and } v \text{ are both merged nodes} \end{cases} \quad (1)$$

Figure 2 shows a small example of how the node merging works. On the left-hand side of the figure there is the input graph with two kinds of edges. The dashed edges are marked as *non-chain* while the solid ones are marked as *chain* predicates. As can be seen on the right-hand side, the two nodes in the lower right have been merged into a new one with the value 2 as none of them were already merged.

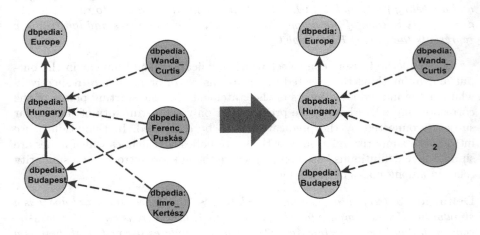

Fig. 2. Node merging example

It can be shown that iteratively applying the node merging technique on the input graph, the algorithm terminates if there are no other mergeable node pairs and the result is independent from the order of the merges.

4   Processing of Semantic Graphs

Nowadays, the number of semantic datasets increase as people start to discover the advantages of the RDF framework. Datasets can contain millions or even billions of triples which make it hard to process them. Therefore in this section, we investigate how the MapReduce paradigm can be applied to process these large datasets.

The MapReduce paradigm is a distributed programing model in which each program has two main phases the Map and the Reduce. Multiple processes work parallel during each phase. First, the Map reads in every line of the input files, and then computes a set of intermediate key/value pairs from them. Next, the Reduce combines the values that are sharing the same key in order to produce the result. Fortunately, the RDF framework has a line-based, plain text representation format, called N-Triples [3], that fits for the Map as input. We have designed and implemented a solution consisting of two MapReduce programs which perform filtering and compaction on the input graph in order to simplify that. The result of the process is a GraphML file that can be visualized with various tools which may offer additional features that help to understand the structure of the graph.

4.1 Filtering

Program 1 shows the pseudo code of the Filtering part of our method that prepares the data for the Compaction. The Map phase of the program reads in the input from N-Triples files, line by line. Each line is parsed into subject, predicate and object parts (line 2). If the predicate was selected, then a key/value pair is emitted to the Reduce phase whose key is the subject of the triple and whose value is the (predicate, object) pair (line 4). If the predicate was not a selected, then the triplet is filtered out. Next, the emitted pairs are processed in the Reduce phase which concatenates the (predicate, object) pairs, that are sharing the same key, and the pairs will be sorted based on their first elements (line 8) into a sequence. The form of the sequences is $(predicate_1\_object_1\_predicate_2\_object_2\_...\_predicate_n\_object_n)$. These sequences will be written into new files automatically by the system as an effect of the *emit* in line 9 which files will be the input of the second program.

4.2 Compaction

The second phase of our method, described in Program 2, is the Compaction that merges the similar nodes together. The Map of second programs reads back the sequences from the new files with the corresponding subjects (line 2) and emits them to the Reduce. It results, that the subjects which are similar to each other in term of Definition 3 will be identified by the same compound key, namely the ordered sequence of the (predicate, object) pairs that are derived from the connected edges by the first program. In the Reduce phase, for each compound key it is checked whether it contains any predicate that was marked as a *chain* predicate. If a key does not contain such predicate, it means that the subjects are mergeable nodes (see Definition 4) in the corresponding semantic graph. The merging of those nodes that belongs to the subjects results a single node which will be connected with the same nodes and its value will be the

Program 1. Filtering

1: **method** MAP(*line*)	▷ *line* is in *subject-predicate-object* format
2: $(s, p, o) = split(line)$	
3: **if** p is predefined **then**	
4: $emit(s, (p, o))$	
5: **end if**	
6: **end method**	

(* *key* is the subject, *values* is the list of emitted (predicate, object) pairs *)
7: **method** REDUCE(*key, values*)	
8: $sort(values)$	▷ sorts the (p, o) pairs based on the first elements
9: $emit(values, s)$	
10: **end method**	

number of the subjects. Therefore, a (count(values), predicate, object) triplet is emitted for each (predicate, object) pair in the key (line 9). However, if a key contains any predicate that was marked as *non-chain*, it means that the subjects are not mergeable, so the original triplet are emitted for each (predicate, object) pair (line 14).

4.3 Visualization

We have overridden the emit function of the Reduce phase of the second program to generate GraphML file as output of the process. GraphML is standard XML-based file format for describing graphs. It is supported by a lot of graph editors and visualization tools, for example, by the yEd. We chose this program because it provides additional features that facilitate the understanding of the data, such as various built-in layouts (hierarchical, organized, circle, etc.), the zooming or the searching capabilities. In addition, GraphML format is extended by the yEd with custom tags. These tags define the properties of the visual elements, the nodes and the edges. Figure 3 shows a fragment of a GraphML file with some custom tags, that describe a node by its shape, size, color and label, and describe an edge by its source and target and some additional properties like the color or the arrow type. We used these tags to distinguish the merged nodes whose colors differ from the non-merged ones and their size depend on their value. In addition, for each selected predicate users can define a unique color code for the corresponding edges.

5   Evaluation

We tested our method on two different datasets: on the DBpedia 3.8[2] and on the Freebase[3]. The DBpedia contains extracted data from the Wikipedia while the

---

[2] Available at http://wiki.dbpedia.org/Downloads38
[3] Available at http://download.freebaseapps.com

Program 2. Compaction

```
1: method MAP(line)
2:     (< (p, o), (p_2, o_2), ...(p_n, o_n) >, s) = split(line)
3:     emit(< (p, o), (p_2, o_2), ...(p_n, o_n) >, s)
4: end method

   (* key is a ordered list of (predicate, object) pairs, values is a list of subjects belong
   to the pairs*)
5: method REDUCE(key, values)
6:     p_list = getPredicatesFromKey(key)
7:     if p_list does not contain any predicate that was marked as chain then
8:         for all (p, o) ∈ key do
9:             emit(count(values), p, o)
10:        end for
11:    else
12:        for all s ∈ values do
13:            for all (p, o) ∈ key do
14:                emit(s, p, o)
15:            end for
16:        end for
17:    end if
18: end method
```

Freebase is a large collaborative knowledge base managed by its own community. Both datasets are available in N-Triples format which is a line-based, plain text representation format. The DBpedia contains approximately 40 millions triples and it requires 5.4 GB space on disk, the Freebase consists of approximately 1.9 billion triples and it requires 250 GB space on disk. We executed our method with various configurations which means that we have selected and marked the predicates in multiple combinations and we measured the runtime of the processes in each configuration. The analysis of the results revealed several problems related to the completeness and failures of the datasets such as missing statements or wrong identifiers.

5.1 Performance

To test the performance of our method, we have implemented the MapReduce programs from Sect. 4 and installed them into a Hadoop cluster. The cluster contains 13 nodes; each node has Intel Core i5-650 processor 2*3.2 GHz, 4 GB RAM and 150 GB disk. 1.6 TB disk space is available for the Hadoop Distributed File System on these nodes. We ran the programs six times for each configuration and computed the average of the runtime. Table 1 contains the results of the different executions with the datasets, the configurations, the average runtime and the number of the resulted statements after the filtering and compaction phases. Note that Hadoop has a basic cost of running a program because of the administration tasks; in our system it is approximately 30 s per programs.

```
<?xml version="1.0" encoding="UTF-8" standalone="no"?>
<graphml>
    ...
    <node id="72870">
        <data key="d6">
            <y:ShapeNode>
                <y:Geometry height="26.5" width="26.5" />
                <y:Shape type="ellipse"/>
                <y:Fill color="#00CC00"/>
                <y:NodeLabel>2</y:NodeLabel>
            </y:ShapeNode>
        </data>
    </node>
    <edge id="e6" source="72870" target="72871">
        <data key="d10">
            <y:PolyLineEdge>
                <y:Path sx="0.0" sy="0.0" tx="0.0" ty="0.0"/>
                <y:LineStyle color="#000099" type="line" width="3.0"/>
                <y:Arrows source="none" target="standard"/>
                <y:BendStyle smoothed="false"/>
            </y:PolyLineEdge>
        </data>
    </edge>
    ...
</graphml>
```

Fig. 3. GraphML fragment with custom yEd tags

First, a configuration was composed to compute the class hierarchy of the DBpedia with the number of instances belong to the classes. The rdfs:subClassOf predicate, that defines class-subclass relation between two classes, was selected and marked as *chain*. The rdf:type predicate, that represents an instance of relationship between an object and a class, was marked as *non-chain*. The next configuration was used to compute geographical containment between areas, therefore we selected only the dbpedia:locatedInArea predicate and marked as *chain*. In the third use case, we added the dbpedia:birthPlace predicate as *non-chain* to the previous configuration to compute how many people were born in a given area. From the Freebase, the hierarchy of the religions was extracted with a configuration in which the freebase:religion.religion.branched_from predicate is marked as *chain*, in addition the freebase:people.person.religion predicate, that states that a person follows a religion, is marked as *non-chain*.

As can be seen in Table 1, the runtime of the first use case is twice and a half as much as the third and four use case, however, all of them used the DBpedia dataset as input. It is because the rdf:type predicate is frequent in the dataset, therefore in the compaction phase more nodes had to be merged and that is a time consuming operation. Furthermore, the use case with the Freebase dataset suggests that the programs scale well with the size of the input as the difference

Table 1. Various configuration for the DBpedia and the Freebase dataset with the runtime of the MapReduce programs and the number of resulted statements

Dataset	Configuration	Runtime	# of results
DBpedia	rdfs:subClassOf (c) rdf:type (nc)	195 s	2, 212
	dbpo:locatedInArea (c)	80 s	32, 517
	dbpo:locatedInArea (c) dbpo:birthPlace (nc)	88 s	194, 806
Freebase	freebase:religion.religion.branched_from (c) freebase:people.person.religion (nc)	863 s	2, 382

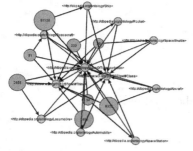
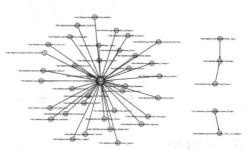

(a) Class hierarchy connected to the transportation with the number of instances

(b) Moon and its craters on the left-hand side, Ronda and Franklin Hills on right-hand side.

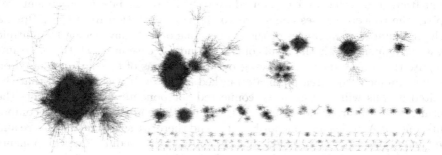

(c) Geographical containments of objects of DBpedia based on dbpedia:locatedInArea predicate

Fig. 4. Graph fragments extracted from the DBpedia dataset

between the runtime of the use cases with the DBpedia and the runtime of the use cases with the Freebase is less than the difference between the size of the datasets.

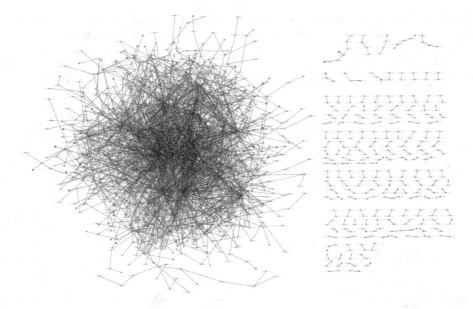

Fig. 5. Graph built from Freebase dataset

5.2   Graphs

After the programs were performed with the above mentioned configurations, the results was visualized by yEd graph visualization tool. Figure 4 shows fragments from graphs that were computed from the DBpedia dataset. Fragment 4(a) depicts the concept classes connected to the transportation from the DBpedia with the number of instances of the classes; one object may belong to multiple classes. Fragment 4(c) is the result of the second use case in which the programs compute the containments between geographical areas of the datasets based on the dbpedia:locatedInArea predicate marked as *chain*. It was expected that the resulted graphs will contain large connected components which represents the continents. However, as can be seen in the figure there are only two large components, one for America and one for Europe, and there are several medium size and many small ones. It was revealed that the most of the medium size components represent islands like Greenland and the Easter Island, but one of them belongs to the Moon and its craters for example. The existence of the small components is confusing; it suggests some kinds of error in the dataset because they should be contained by other areas. Therefore, we investigated the small components and we discovered that some of them belong to bridges or they are parts of different cities; in those cases, the IRIs are not conventional such as http://dbpedia.org/resource/Franklin_Hills,_Los_Angeles. The Fragment 4(b) shows the component that belongs to the Moon and two smaller components that belong to Ronda, a Spanish province, and Franklin Hill, a part of Los Angeles.

Figure 5 shows the result of our last use case in which the *freebase:branched_from* relationships were investigated among different religions and the number of their followers who appear in the Freebase dataset. The number of the different kinds of religions in the dataset is limited, however, there are many people who follow multiple religion at the same time, therefore they formed large component in the figure. Small components also appeared which belong to such religions that are not in *freebase:branched_from* relationship with any other religion, for example, the Thelema[4]. Moreover, among the small components we found interesting relationships that may refer to some failures. For example, according to the datasets James Zabiela's[5] religion is Jedi[6], however, Jedi is an artist, or Matthew Russell 's[7] religion is Production Designer[8], but it is a job.

6   Conclusion

Semantic Web aims to integrate all the available data into the "web of data" in a machine-understandable format to improve the searching capabilities and to reveal the hidden connections among data coming from various sources. The most of technologies connected with the Semantic Web are based on the Resource Description Framework which provides a descriptive language for integrating data from heterogeneous sources. In this paper we presented a method which can process large semantic datasets described in this framework to help to understand the structures of the datasets.

Our method consists of two main phases a filtering and a compaction phase. The former one performs a filtering on the input data based on user defined configurations that determine what predicates should be kept and transformed. Then, in the compaction phase the similar nodes with respect to the configuration, the *chain* and *non-chain* predicates, will be merged to reduce the complexity of the graphs. The result of the method is a GraphML file that is a standard format for describing graphs and that can be visualized by various tools. Both two phases are implemented according to the MapReduce distributed programming model to be able to handle large datasets as the volume of semantic datasets increases day by day.

We tested the method on two different datasets, on the DBpedia which contains RDF triplets extracted from the Wikipedia and on the Freebase which is a collaborative knowledge base. Our experiments show how the visualization helps to understand the inner structure of a dataset and how it can help to reveal different kinds of problems related to the completeness and the correctness of a dataset. For example, when visualizing the statements that contain the dbpedia:locatedInArea predicate we have got lots of components that consist of only

---

[4] See www.freebase.com/m/07grj
[5] See www.freebase.com/m/01rh56d
[6] See www.freebase.com/m/01wtsmx
[7] See www.freebase.com/m/0plk41m
[8] See http://www.freebase.com/m/02pjxr

a few geographical areas that are not contained by any other area according to the dataset, which shows the incompleteness of the dataset.

We are currently investigating how our method can be applied in the field of entity resolution and ontology integration. Namely, if we select and mark the appropriate predicate carefully, than the mergeable nodes can be the bases of an entity resolution method such as [18]. Moreover, the values of the merged nodes can give the number of common instances of two ontology classes that helps to match ontology classes [11]. For example, in the DBpedia dataset, the most of the objects are assigned to a class of the YAGO [21] ontology beside the class of its own ontology.

Acknowledgments. This work was partially supported by the European Union and the European Social Fund through project FuturICT.hu (grant no.: TAMOP-4.2.2.C-11/1/KONV-2012-0013) and the Hungarian and Vietnamese TET (grant no.: TT_10-1-2011-0645) project.

References

1. Alexander, K., Hausenblas, M.: Describing linked datasets-on the design and usage of void, the vocabulary of interlinked datasets. In: Linked Data on the Web Workshop (LDOW 09), in conjunction with 18th International World Wide Web Conference (WWW 09) (2009)
2. Auer, S., Bizer, C., Kobilarov, G., Lehmann, J., Cyganiak, R., Ives, Z.: DBpedia: a nucleus for a web of open data. In: Aberer, K., et al. (eds.) SWC/ASWC 2007. LNCS, vol. 4825, pp. 722–735. Springer, Heidelberg (2007)
3. Beckett, D., Barstow, A.: N-triples (2001)
4. Berners-Lee, T., Hendler, J., Lassila, O., et al.: The semantic web. Sci. Am. **284**(5), 28–37 (2001)
5. Bollacker, K., Evans, C., Paritosh, P., Sturge, T., Taylor, J.: Freebase: a collaboratively created graph database for structuring human knowledge. In: Proceedings of the 2008 ACM SIGMOD International Conference on Management of Data, pp. 1247–1250. ACM (2008)
6. Brandes, U., Eiglsperger, M., Lerner, J., Pich, C.: Graph markup language (GraphML). Bibliothek der Universität Konstanz (2010)
7. Chen, B., Ding, Y. Wang, H. Wild, D.J., Dong, X., Sun, Y., Zhu, Q., Sankaranarayanan, M.: Chem2bio2rdf: a linked open data portal for systems chemical biology. In: 2010 IEEE/WIC/ACM International Conference on Web Intelligence and Intelligent Agent Technology (WI-IAT), vol. 1, pp. 232–239. IEEE (2010)
8. Dean, J., Ghemawat, S.: MapReduce: simplified data processing on large clusters. Commun. ACM **51**(1), 107–113 (2008)
9. Deligiannidis, L., Kochut, K.J., Sheth, A.P.: RDF data exploration and visualization. In: Proceedings of the ACM First Workshop on CyberInfrastructure: Information Management in eScience, pp. 39–46. ACM (2007)
10. Dokulil, J., Katreniaková, J.: Visual exploration of RDF data. In: Geffert, V., Karhumäki, J., Bertoni, A., Preneel, B., Návrat, P., Bieliková, M. (eds.) SOFSEM 2008. LNCS, vol. 4910, pp. 672–683. Springer, Heidelberg (2008)
11. Duong, T.H., Jo, G., Jung, J.J., Nguyen, N.T.: Complexity analysis of ontology integration methodologies: a comparative study. J. UCS **15**(4), 877–897 (2009)

12. Gutierrez, C., Hurtado, C., Mendelzon, A.O.: Foundations of semantic web databases. In Proceedings of the Twenty-Third ACM SIGMOD-SIGACT-SIGART Symposium on Principles of Database Systems, pp. 95–106. ACM (2004)

13. Harris, S., Seaborne, A.: Sparql 1.1 query language. Technical report, W3C (2010)

14. Henzinger, M.R., Henzinger, T.A., Kopke, P.W.: Computing simulations on finite and infinite graphs. In: Proceedings of 36th Annual Symposium on Foundations of Computer Science, 1995, pp. 453–462. IEEE (1995)

15. Husain, M., Khan, L., Kantarcioglu, M., Thuraisingham, B.: Data intensive query processing for large RDF graphs using cloud computing tools. In: 2010 IEEE 3rd International Conference on Cloud Computing (CLOUD), pp. 1–10. IEEE (2010)

16. Lassila, O., Swick, R.R., et al.: Resource description framework (RDF) model and syntax specification (1998)

17. Micsik, A., Turbucz, S., Tóth, Z.: Browsing and traversing linked data with lodmilla. ERCIM News **2014**(96), 35–36 (2014)

18. Molnár, A.J., Benczúr, A.A., Sidló, C.I.: Flexible and efficient distributed resolution of large entities. In: Lukasiewicz, T., Sali, A. (eds.) FoIKS 2012. LNCS, vol. 7153, pp. 244–263. Springer, Heidelberg (2012)

19. Nguyen, N.T.: Inconsistency of knowledge and collective intelligence. Cybern. Syst. Int. J. **39**(6), 542–562 (2008)

20. Schätzle, A., Neu, A., Lausen, G., Przyjaciel-Zablocki, M.: Large-scale bisimulation of RDF graphs. In: Proceedings of the Fifth Workshop on Semantic Web Information Management, p. 1. ACM (2013)

21. Suchanek, F.M., Kasneci, G., Weikum, G.: Yago: a core of semantic knowledge. In: Proceedings of the 16th International Conference on World Wide Web, pp. 697–706. ACM (2007)

22. Voigt, M., Pietschmann, S., Meißner, K.: Towards a semantics-based, end-user-centered information visualization process. In Proceedings of the 3rd International Workshop on Semantic Models for Adaptive Interactive Systems (SEMAIS 2012) (2012)

23. White, T.: Hadoop: The Definitive Guide. O'Reilly Media Inc, Sebastopol (2012)

Author Index

Ceglarek, Dariusz   20

Dudek-Dyduch, Ewa   136

Godfrey, W. Wilfred   49
Gombos, Gergő   180
Granmo, Ole-Christoffer   1

Haugland, Vegard   1

Jha, Shashi Shekhar   49

Kiss, Attila   180
Kjølleberg, Marius   1
Kucharska, Edyta   136

Larsen, Svein-Erik   1

Marusak, Piotr M.   158

Nair, Shivashankar B.   49

Omran, Masoud T.   71
Oommen, B. John   71

Rácz, Gábor   180
Resconi, Germano   120

Sakhravi, Rokhsareh   71
Skorupa, Grzegorz   100

Printed in the United States
By Bookmasters